Corporate Governance and Banking in China

As China began its economic reforms in the late 1970s and made a transition from planned to a market economy, corporate governance of the banking sector became an increasingly pressing issue. Further, in the aftermath of the Asian Financial Crisis in the late 1990s, Chinese authorities became acutely aware of the importance of corporate governance to ensure that their banking system would not suffer similar fates to those of other Asian countries.

This book examines corporate governance in City Commercial Banks, which are the main source of loans to the dynamic small and medium enterprises that are crucial to the development of China's economy. By the end of 2008, there were 136 City Commercial Banks in China, 13 of which had foreign partners, and this book clearly demonstrates the positive effect of these foreign partnerships on corporate governance practices, in addition to financial performance. With evidence from extensive interviews with ten City Commercial Banks in China, Michael N.T. Tan explores the different models of corporate governance, and in turn, asks which model is most suitable to China, how are Chinese authorities overcoming problems with corporate governance, and how do these problems compare with those in other transition economies?

Whilst the primary focus of this study is on China's City Commercial Banks, there are lessons that apply much more broadly to the industry and it therefore will be invaluable to foreign banking institutions wishing to invest in China. This book will also be of great appeal to students and scholars of Chinese business and economics, corporate governance and banking.

Michael N.T. Tan was awarded his PhD by the University of New South Wales in 2011 and currently works as a Financial Planning Specialist for Michael N.T. Tan & Associates in Australia.

Routledge contemporary China series

1 **Nationalism, Democracy and National Integration in China**
Leong Liew and Wang Shaoguang

2 **Hong Kong's Tortuous Democratization**
A comparative analysis
Ming Sing

3 **China's Business Reforms**
Institutional challenges in a globalised economy
Edited by Russell Smyth and Cherrie Zhu

4 **Challenges for China's Development**
An enterprise perspective
Edited by David H. Brown and Alasdair MacBean

5 **New Crime in China**
Public order and human rights
Ron Keith and Zhiqiu Lin

6 **Non-Governmental Organizations in Contemporary China**
Paving the way to civil society?
Qiusha Ma

7 **Globalization and the Chinese City**
Fulong Wu

8 **The Politics of China's Accession to the World Trade Organization**
The dragon goes global
Hui Feng

9 **Narrating China**
Jia Pingwa and his fictional world
Yiyan Wang

10 **Sex, Science and Morality in China**
Joanne McMillan

11 **Politics in China Since 1949**
Legitimizing authoritarian rule
Robert Weatherley

12 **International Human Resource Management in Chinese Multinationals**
Jie Shen and Vincent Edwards

13 **Unemployment in China**
Economy, human resources and labour markets
Edited by Grace Lee and Malcolm Warner

14 **China and Africa**
Engagement and compromise
Ian Taylor

15 **Gender and Education in China**
Gender discourses and women's schooling in the early twentieth century
Paul J. Bailey

16 **SARS**
Reception and interpretation in three Chinese cities
Edited by Deborah Davis and Helen Siu

17 **Human Security and the Chinese State**
Historical transformations and the modern quest for sovereignty
Robert E. Bedeski

18 **Gender and Work in Urban China**
Women workers of the unlucky generation
Liu Jieyu

19 **China's State Enterprise Reform**
From Marx to the market
John Hassard, Jackie Sheehan, Meixiang Zhou, Jane Terpstra-Tong and Jonathan Morris

20 **Cultural Heritage Management in China**
Preserving the cities of the Pearl River Delta
Edited by Hilary du Cros and Yok-shiu F. Lee

21 **Paying for Progress**
Public finance, human welfare and inequality in China
Edited by Vivienne Shue and Christine Wong

22 **China's Foreign Trade Policy**
The new constituencies
Edited by Ka Zeng

23 **Hong Kong, China**
Learning to belong to a nation
Gordon Mathews, Tai-lok Lui, and Eric Kit-wai Ma

24 **China Turns to Multilateralism**
Foreign policy and regional security
Edited by Guoguang Wu and Helen Lansdowne

25 **Tourism and Tibetan Culture in Transition**
A place called Shangrila
Åshild Kolås

26 **China's Emerging Cities**
The making of new urbanism
Edited by Fulong Wu

27 **China-US Relations Transformed**
Perceptions and strategic interactions
Edited by Suisheng Zhao

28 **The Chinese Party-State in the 21st Century**
Adaptation and the reinvention of legitimacy
Edited by André Laliberté and Marc Lanteigne

29 **Political Change in Macao**
Sonny Shiu-Hing Lo

30 **China's Energy Geopolitics**
The Shanghai cooperation organization and Central Asia
Thrassy N. Marketos

31 **Regime Legitimacy in Contemporary China**
Institutional change and stability
Edited by Thomas Heberer and Gunter Schubert

32 **U.S.-China Relations**
China policy on Capitol Hill
Tao Xie

33 **Chinese Kinship**
Contemporary anthropological perspectives
Edited by Susanne Brandtstädter and Gonçalo D. Santos

34 **Politics and Government in Hong Kong**
Crisis under Chinese sovereignty
Edited by Ming Sing

35 **Rethinking Chinese Popular Culture**
Cannibalizations of the Canon
Edited by Carlos Rojas and Eileen Cheng-yin Chow

36 **Institutional Balancing in the Asia Pacific**
Economic interdependence and China's rise
Kai He

37 **Rent Seeking in China**
Edited by Tak-Wing Ngo and Yongping Wu

38 **China, Xinjiang and Central Asia**
History, transition and crossborder interaction into the 21st century
Edited by Colin Mackerras and Michael Clarke

39 **Intellectual Property Rights in China**
Politics of piracy, trade and protection
Gordon Cheung

40 **Developing China**
Land, politics and social conditions
George C.S. Lin

41 **State and Society Responses to Social Welfare Needs in China**
Serving the people
Edited by Jonathan Schwartz and Shawn Shieh

42 **Gay and Lesbian Subculture in Urban China**
Loretta Wing Wah Ho

43 **The Politics of Heritage Tourism in China**
A view from Lijiang
Xiaobo Su and Peggy Teo

44 **Suicide and Justice**
A Chinese perspective
Wu Fei

45 **Management Training and Development in China**
Educating managers in a globalized economy
Edited by Malcolm Warner and Keith Goodall

46 **Patron-Client Politics and Elections in Hong Kong**
Bruce Kam-kwan Kwong

47 **Chinese Family Business and the Equal Inheritance System**
Unravelling the myth
Victor Zheng

48 **Reconciling State, Market and Civil Society in China**
The long march towards prosperity
Paolo Urio

49 **Innovation in China**
The Chinese software industry
Shang-Ling Jui

50 **Mobility, Migration and the Chinese Scientific Research System**
Koen Jonkers

51 **Chinese Film Stars**
Edited by Mary Farquhar and Yingjin Zhang

52 **Chinese Male Homosexualities**
Memba, Tongzhi and Golden Boy
Travis S.K. Kong

53 **Industrialisation and Rural Livelihoods in China**
Agricultural processing in Sichuan
Susanne Lingohr-Wolf

54 **Law, Policy and Practice on China's Periphery**
Selective adaptation and institutional capacity
Pitman B. Potter

55 **China-Africa Development Relations**
Edited by Christopher M. Dent

56 **Neoliberalism and Culture in China and Hong Kong**
The countdown of time
Hai Ren

57 **China's Higher Education Reform and Internationalisation**
Edited by Janette Ryan

58 **Law, Wealth and Power in China**
Commercial law reforms in context
Edited by John Garrick

59 **Religion in Contemporary China**
Revitalization and innovation
Edited by Adam Yuet Chau

60 **Consumer-Citizens of China**
The role of foreign brands in the imagined future china
Kelly Tian and Lily Dong

61 **The Chinese Communist Party and China's Capitalist Revolution**
The political impact of the market
Lance L.P. Gore

62 **China's Homeless Generation**
Voices from the veterans of the Chinese civil war, 1940s–1990s
Joshua Fan

63 **In Search of China's Development Model**
Beyond the Beijing consensus
Edited by S. Philip Hsu, Suisheng Zhao and Yu-Shan Wu

64 **Xinjiang and China's Rise in Central Asia, 1949–2009**
A history
Michael E. Clarke

65 **Trade Unions in China**
The challenge of labour unrest
Tim Pringle

66 **China's Changing Workplace**
Dynamism, diversity and disparity
Edited by Peter Sheldon, Sunghoon Kim, Yiqiong Li and Malcolm Warner

67 **Leisure and Power in Urban China**
Everyday life in a medium-sized Chinese city
Unn Målfrid H. Rolandsen

68 **China, Oil and Global Politics**
Philip Andrews-Speed and Roland Dannreuther

69 **Education Reform in China**
Edited by Janette Ryan

70 **Social Policy and Migration in China**
Lida Fan

71 **China's One Child Policy and Multiple Caregiving**
Raising little Suns in Xiamen
Esther C.L. Goh

72 **Politics and Markets in Rural China**
Edited by Björn Alpermann

73 **China's New Underclass**
Paid domestic labour
Xinying Hu

74 **Poverty and Development in China**
Alternative approaches to poverty assessment
Lu Caizhen

75 **International Governance and Regimes**
A Chinese perspective
Peter Kien-Hong YU

76 **HIV/AIDS in China – The Economic and Social Determinants**
Dylan Sutherland and Jennifer Y.J. Hsu

77 **Looking for Work in Post-Socialist China**
Governance, active job seekers and the new Chinese labour market
Feng Xu

78 **Sino-Latin American Relations**
Edited by K.C. Fung and Alicia Garcia-Herrero

79 **Mao's China and the Sino-Soviet Split**
Ideological dilemma
Mingjiang Li

80 **Law and Policy for China's Market Socialism**
Edited by John Garrick

81 **China-Taiwan Relations in a Global Context**
Taiwan's foreign policy and relations
Edited by C.X. George Wei

82 **The Chinese Transformation of Corporate Culture**
Colin S.C. Hawes

83 **Mapping Media in China**
Region, province, locality
Edited by Wanning Sun and Jenny Chio

84 **China, the West and the Myth of New Public Management**
Neoliberalism and its discontents
Paolo Urio

85 **The Lahu Minority in Southwest China**
A response to ethnic marginalization on the frontier
Jianxiong Ma

86 **Social Capital and Institutional Constraints**
A comparative analysis of China, Taiwan and the US
Joonmo Son

87 **Southern China**
Industry, development and industrial policy
Marco R. Di Tommaso, Lauretta Rubini and Elisa Barbieri

88 **State-Market Interactions in China's Reform Era**
Local state competition and global market building in the tobacco industry
Junmin Wang

89 **The Reception and Rendition of Freud in China**
China's Freudian slip
Edited by Tao Jiang and Philip J. Ivanhoe

90 **Sinologism**
An alternative to orientalism and postcolonialism
Ming Dong Gu

91 **The Middle Class in Neoliberal China**
Governing risk, life-building, and themed spaces
Hai Ren

92 **The Chinese Corporatist State**
Adaption, survival and resistance
Edited by Jennifer Y.J. Hsu and Reza Hasmath

93 **Law and Fair Work in China**
Sean Cooney, Sarah Biddulph and Ying Zhu

94 **Guangdong and Chinese Diaspora**
The changing landscape of qiaoxiang
Yow Cheun Hoe

95 **The Shanghai Alleyway House**
A vanishing urban vernacular
Gregory Bracken

96 **Chinese Globalization**
A profile of people-based global connections in China
Jiaming Sun and Scott Lancaster

97 **Disruptive Innovation in Chinese and Indian Businesses**
The strategic implications for local entrepreneurs and global incumbents
Peter Ping Li

98 **Corporate Governance and Banking in China**
Michael N.T. Tan

99 **Gender, Modernity and Male Migrant Workers in China**
Becoming a 'modern' man
Xiaodong Lin

Corporate Governance and Banking in China

Michael N.T. Tan

Routledge
Taylor & Francis Group
LONDON AND NEW YORK

First published 2013
by Routledge
2 Park Square, Milton Park, Abingdon, Oxon OX14 4RN

Simultaneously published in the USA and Canada
by Routledge
711 Third Avenue, New York, NY 10017

Routledge is an imprint of the Taylor & Francis Group, an informa business

British Library Cataloguing in Publication Data
A catalogue record for this book is available from the British Library

Library of Congress Cataloging in Publication Data
Tan, Michael, 1945–
Corporate governance and banking in China/Michael N.T. Tan.
p. cm. – (Routledge contemporary China series; 98)
Includes bibliographical references and index.
1. Banks and banking–China. 2. Banks and banking–Government policy–China. 3. Corporate governance–China. I. Title.
HG3334.T46 2013
332.10951–dc23 2012037433

ISBN: 978-0-415-65591-0 (hbk)
ISBN: 978-0-203-07836-5 (ebk)

Typeset in Times New Roman
by Wearset Ltd, Boldon, Tyne and Wear

Contents

Tables

Foreword

It gives me much pleasure to pen this foreword for this book based on a PhD thesis. At an age when most are retired, the author commenced his doctorate at the University of New South Wales in Sydney, Australia, and successfully completed a few years later. His love and concern for China led him to study the role of corporate governance in the reform of City Commercial Banks.

China's economic dynamics and 'miracle' in the reform era lie mainly in the rapid development of the small and medium enterprises in the private sector. The emergence of a competent banking system in supporting the small and medium enterprises is vital in this process. After three decades of reform, the banking sector in China has evolved from the communist mono-banking system with the single People's Bank of China serving as the Central Bank and providing all of the other banking services at the same time, to the current modern banking system consisting of the Central Bank, Policy Banks, State-Owned Commercial Banks, Joint-Stock Commercial Banks, City Commercial Banks, Rural Commercial Banks, Rural Cooperative Banks and Foreign Banks. This profound transformation is of great interest to the academic community and the public in general.

The book provides a convincing account and analysis on the progress of corporate governance in the banking sector and its contribution to the overall economic development in China. I am particularly impressed by the case studies on the ten Chinese City Commercial Banks with foreign partners. At the end of 1970s and the beginning of the 1980s when China was put on the path of transition from the command economy to a market economy, the country's commercial banks suffered from complete lack of experience and corporate governance structure under the wider institutional context of the inadequate conditions in the rule of law and government accountability. One shortcut for Chinese commercial banks to make giant strides is to learn from the commercial banks in the developed economies and this is exactly the case of the Chinese City Commercial Banks chosen as targets for investigation in the book. These targeted banks were turned into partnership with foreign banks, which have introduced international standards to China through involvement in day-to-day operation. Making use of comprehensive statistics and data generated through survey and interviews, the author has shown how the foreign partners of those Chinese City Commercial Banks transformed the banking management by improving corporate governance.

His research broke new ground and investigated ten City Commercial Banks in China, which, with the assistance of foreign strategic partners not only vastly improved their standards of corporate governance but also helped them to achieve superior financial performance when compared to other City Commercial Banks.

This book makes an important contribution to our understanding of the reform of Chinese banking system and economic development in China since the 1980s. It is essential reading for university students, academics and all those interested in understanding corporate governance and banking in China. Although the research was based on the City Commercial Banks, its findings in fact can be applied to the whole banking system in China.

Chongyi Feng
Associate Professor in China Studies, University of Technology, Sydney, Australia
Adjunct Professor of History, Nankai University, China

Preface

This text is an adaptation of my PhD thesis 'The Role of Corporate Governance in the Reform of Foreign Partnered City Commercial Banks in China' for which the University of New South Wales in Sydney, Australia conferred on me the degree of Doctor of Philosophy in August 2011. This text has been prepared not only with scholars and academicians in mind, but also businessmen and executives with an interest in the corporate and financial landscape in China. China is in the throes of rapid change and it is necessary to understand the background and the changeover from a planned to a market economy. Why is corporate governance such an important issue in China today and in particular why should it concern the foreign investor so much? These are issues that the text deals with in a detailed and logical manner. For those wishing to invest in or understand China's banking sector, this book is essential reading.

Michael N.T. Tan

Acknowledgements

I would like to first of all express my thanks and gratitude to Dr Yu Yanjing from Kunming, China, who encouraged me to embark on my PhD course in Sydney, Australia. My deep appreciation is also due to Professor Peter Collins, Associate Professor Stephen Fortescue, Associate Professor Jon Von Kowallis, Associate Professor You Ji, Dr Seong-Chul Shin, Dr Kayako Evon and Mary Stringer, all from the University of New South Wales; Associate Professor Niv Horesh from the University of Western Sydney, Professor Chongyi Feng from the University of Technology, Sydney, and Professor Hans Hendrischke from Sydney University.

My thanks are also due to Mr Chung Chi-Wah, Assistant General Manager at the Bank of China in Sydney and Jane Jing Li, also from the Bank of China, both of whom helped me in gathering valuable data. I would also like to thank Alex Thursby, Managing Director of ANZ Bank, Asia Pacific for granting me an interview, the China Banking Regularity Commission, the China Securities Regularity Commission and KPMG who provided essential statistics used in the text, and, last but not least, my dear wife Sandy who gave unstinting support in this endeavour.

The views, findings and conclusions expressed in this book are all mine and any mistakes, errors and omissions are strictly my responsibility.

Michael N.T. Tan

Acronyms and abbreviations

ADB	Asian Development Bank
AMC	Asset Management Company
ANZ	Australia & New Zealand Banking Group
ASBE	Accounting Standards for Business Enterprises
BCG	Boston Consulting Group
BOB	Bank of Beijing
BOS	Bank of Shanghai
BNP	Bank National de Paris
CAR	Capital Adequacy Ratio
CBA	Commonwealth Bank of Australia
CBRC	China Banking Regulatory Commission
CCB	City Commercial Bank
CCCB	Chengdu City Commercial Bank
CCP	Chinese Communist Party
CEEFSU	Central and Eastern Europe and the Former Soviet Union
CSRC	China Securities Regulatory Commission
DEG	Deutsche Investitions und Entwicklungsgesellschaft mbH
FIE	Foreign Invested Enterprise
GFC	Global Financial Crisis
HCCB	Hangzhou City Commercial Bank
HLBG	Hong Leong Banking Group
HSBC	Hongkong Shanghai Banking Corporation
IAS	International Accounting Standards
IFAC	International Federation of Accountants Code
IFC	International Finance Corporation
IFRS	International Financial Reporting Standards
ING	Internationale Nederlandse Groep
JCCB	Jinan City Commercial Bank
JSCBs	Joint Stock Commercial Banks
KGB	Komitet Gosudarstvennoy Bezopasnosti
KPMG	Klynveld Peat Marwick Goerdeler
NcCCB	Nanchong City Commercial Bank
NgCCB	Ningbo City Commercial Bank

NjCCB	Nanjing City Commercial Bank
NDRC	National Development & Reform Commission
NGO	Non-Government Organization
NPLs	Non-Performing Loans
NYSE	New York Stock Exchange
OCBC	Overseas Chinese Banking Corporation
PBOC	People's Bank of China
PwC	Pricewaterhouse Coopers
PPP	Purchasing Power Parity
QFII	Qualified Foreign Institutional Investor
RCCs	Rural Credit Cooperatives
SASAC	State Assets Supervision & Administration Commission
SEC	Securities Exchange Commission
S&P	Standard & Poor's
SMEs	Small and Medium Enterprises
SOCBs	State-Owned Commercial Banks
SOEs	State-Owned Enterprises
SRCB	Shanghai Rural Commercial Bank
TCCB	Tianjin City Commercial Bank
TVEs	Town & Village Enterprises
UCCs	Urban Credit Cooperatives
WTO	World Trade Organisation

1 Introduction

1 Preamble

This book concerns the role of corporate governance in the reform of China's City Commercial Banks and especially the role of foreign investors in these reforms. It starts off with an examination of the various models of corporate governance and contextualizes them within the Chinese perspective. Chapter 2 examines the various models of corporate governance. In liberal democracies, there are basically two models of corporate governance: the 'Shareholder Value' model as practised in the United States and UK and the 'Stakeholder' model as practised in France, Germany and Japan. The features of each model are examined for their applicability to China. The model chosen for China is the 'Shareholder Value' model. Why was it considered inappropriate? Which model is more suitable for China if we analyse and consider issues from a historical point of view?

Many former centrally planned economies are in transition to market economies and in Chapter 3 we look at corporate governance in transitional economies. We compare the experience of China with Russia and the transitional economic models adopted. What are the corporate governance problems of transitional economies and how different are China's problems compared to other transitional economies; what did the Chinese authorities do to improve corporate governance? How did all this impact on economic growth? Research indicated that China's rapid economic progress was due to the confluence of many factors including corporate governance improvements, the population exodus from villages to the cities and a series of gradual, incremental changes implemented by the state. These issues are all dealt with in later chapters.

In Chapter 4 we look at corporate governance from a Chinese perspective and examine it from a historical perspective. Basically it can be divided into four sections:

1 pre-reform stage (1949–1978);
2 economic reform stage (1979–1991);
3 transitional stage (1992–2002);
4 convergence stage (post-2002).

Chapter 5 looks at corporate governance problems in China from both a macro and micro level while Chapter 6 studies the external determinants of corporate governance.

Chapter 7 examines the relationship between economic growth and financial systems while Chapter 8 studies the historical antecedents of City Commercial Banks (CCBs). In studying the theoretical foundations of these banks we examine the role played by banks on economic development and look at how financial systems impact on economic growth. We also investigate what causes long-term economic growth. The economist Schumpeter theorized that economic development resulted from advances in banking and finance, but Goldsmith studied the financial data on 35 countries over 103 years from 1860 to 1963 and came to the conclusion that financial and economic development occurred simultaneously. Goldsmith's views on finance and economic development were confirmed by Berger *et al.* (2004) who studied the impact of community banks on economic growth using data from 1993 to 2000 in 49 countries. Be that as it may, the reform of the CCBs is a necessary corollary to the reform of the banking system in China. China's CCBs have had a relatively short history: they were all formed from the amalgamation of various Urban Credit Cooperatives (UCCs) in cities from the mid 1990s onwards. And the process continues to this day. Most of the problems faced relate to corporate governance and symptomatic of these problems was the high ratio of Non Performing Loans (NPLs) which swamped the banking system in China from the mid 1990s onwards. The high NPLs were due to the lack of a strong credit culture in the banks and details of this problem will be considered in later chapters. Literature on the reform of China's banking sector was spearheaded by Lardy (1998) and Naughton (1998) who wrote on the need to control the NPLs or risk the systemic collapse of the banking system. These problems have been overcome as evidenced in subsequent research by Brandt and Rawski (2008) and Brandt and Zhu (2007).

Authorities initially attempted to resolve these problems via a two-pronged approach: the establishment of the China Banking Regulatory Commission (CBRC) [中国银行业监督管理委员会] in 2003 to specifically regulate the banking industry and the encouragement of the CCBs to seek foreign shareholders. Government policies impacting on CCBs are also considered, especially policies aimed at narrowing the rich–poor divide; with the result that CCBs were encouraged to extend loans to Small and Medium Enterprises (SMEs).

How did CCBs begin in China? Their antecedents are traced to the Urban Credit Cooperatives (UCCs) which were established in the late 1980s and early 1990s to cope with the need for financial services from the Town and Village Enterprises (TVEs) which sprang up with the economic reforms. These UCCs were subsequently reorganized into CCBs to bring them under the purview of the CBRC. This subject is discussed in Chapter 8 and Chapter 9 looks at government policies which impact on these CCBs in China.

Chapters 10 and 11 focus on research conducted by the author on corporate governance reforms in those CCBs with foreign shareholder partners. The author's research showed that these banks have remarkably improved their corporate governance standards. Most of the foreign partners took equity stakes of between 10 and 20 per cent; appointed one or more directors to the board and participated actively in the management of the bank they invested in. The active participation of the foreign shareholder is the favoured approach of the foreign investors and is confirmation of the empirical results of Garcia-Herrero and Santabarbara (2008) that foreign investors brought benefits to the Chinese banking system through active management participation. Garcia-Herrero and Santabarbara also wrote that improvements in corporate governance are important too and this is substantiated by the author's investigations into those CCBs with foreign partners. Such CCBs showed superior financial performances when compared to financial statistics for the whole City Commercial Banking sector. These improvements are reflected in growth of bank assets, reduction of NPLs and increases of Capital Adequacy Ratios (CARs). Understandably some CCBs have improved more than others: this is attributable to the quality of the partnership and partly due to the degree of time, effort and energy invested by the foreign partner.

The Basel Committee on Banking Supervision is an international committee of central bankers of leading nations who meet regularly to discuss banking standards and practices to safeguard banks worldwide. In studying corporate governance in China's CCBs, reference is made to the Basel Committee on Banking Supervision who published a Consultative Document, 'Enhancing Corporate Governance for Banking Organisations', in July 2005. To what extent have the CCBs with foreign shareholders implemented the guidelines? The survey results showed a positive response. The principles enunciated in this document have been incorporated into the questionnaire used in our survey (see Appendix 7).

2 Overview of banking system

China's economic reforms started in 1979 when the mono banking system was abolished. At that time, the People's Bank of China (PBOC) was the only financial institution serving as the Central Bank and at the same time providing banking services all over the country. The People's Bank of China's (PBOC) specialist banking functions were subsequently devolved to three State-Owned Commercial Banks (SOCBs): namely the Agricultural Bank of China (ABC) in charge of agriculture, the China Construction Bank in charge of loans for construction and fixed asset long-term loans and the Bank of China (BOC) for handling foreign exchange business. The functions of the PBOC were further reorganized in 1984 when the PBOC became the effective Central Bank and all of its branches were transferred to the Industrial Commercial Bank of China (ICBC) which became the fourth main SOCB.

China's banking sector may now be conveniently divided into three sectors (see Appendix 1): the top tier comprising the big five SOCBs, the second tier comprising the Joint Stock Commercial Banks (JSCBs) and the third tier comprising the City Commercial Banks (CCBs). There are also three policy banks:

the China Development Bank, the Export Import Bank of China and the Agricultural Development of China which handles politically sensitive loans, overseas aid projects and other national infrastructure projects which the commercial banks do not wish to finance and following the recent restructurings of the SOCBs there are now four Asset Management Companies (AMCs).[1] Occupying a niche space in the banking system are the rural banks and finally of course the foreign banks occupy a small but highly important position. It was always recognized by Chinese authorities and scholars, however, that the reorganization of the banking and the financial system would be a difficult part of the reform process and they were not wrong. China's banking sector was in the beginning plagued by the NPLs which resulted from the ongoing collusion between State-Owned Enterprises (SOEs) and the state-owned banking sector as these SOCBs used the soft budget constraint to prop up ailing SOEs. These large SOCBs have chosen an internationalization strategy to divest themselves of NPLs and at the same time to improve their corporate governance by listing on overseas stock exchanges and inviting overseas shareholders. This is in line with standard convergence strategies under globalization.

The CBRC has also encouraged the third tier i.e. the CCBs to seek foreign partners. This is being done not only to resolve the NPL problems faced by the smaller banks but, more importantly, to help these banks attain higher standards of banking service and expertise all round. This banking sector has grown through local government initiatives who arranged for the amalgamation of UCCs into CCBs in each city. Like the state-run banking sector, it tends to be controlled by government, in this case at the provincial level, and was initially burdened by NPLs. In tandem with the NPL position in major commercial banks, the scenario in the CCBs has changed dramatically over the last few years. Different from the large state-owned banks, these local banks are more closely tied to their economic and commercial environment and are under increasing pressure to finance local industries. This requires a new set of skills and procedures on the part of the local banks, but equally, an increasing separation from local government influence.

It would be simplistic to assume that the introduction of formal corporate governance structures will be an answer to all these structural problems, as is often claimed in published articles and official policy statements. This issue is studied by placing corporate governance into an institutional context, specifically by asking what role corporate governance can play in an environment that is still characterized by administrative interference and where organizational reform might not resolve underlying issues.

3 Research objectives

The book looks into several broad areas and attempts to provide answers to the following questions:

1 What were the corporate governance problems faced by the City Commercial Banks and how were they resolved?

2 What role did corporate governance play in the reform of the City Commercial Banks?
3 What role did foreign partners play in the City Commercial Banks they invested in?
4 What were the results of foreign investor participation?

Later chapters answer the above questions. The book confirms that corporate governance did play a very important role in the reform of foreign partnered CCBs in China and Chapter 11 expands on the reforms made. Research was only done into those CCBs with foreign shareholders and results show that foreign shareholders contributed substantially to corporate governance reforms. This book does not research those CCBs without foreign shareholders, and this may be an area for future investigations. This is especially true as only about 10 per cent of the total number of CCBs had foreign strategic shareholders as of the end of 2008.

Critics may allude to the fact that CCBs form only the third tier of China's banking sector, so how important are they? It is important because the CCBs in China comprise an extremely dynamic segment of the banking system. As of the end of 2008 there were 136 CCBs dispersed all over China and the growth rate of the CCBs has always exceeded the growth rate of the whole banking industry. Between 2005 and 2008, assets of the whole banking industry grew by 66.5 per cent whereas the assets of the CCBs increased by 102.8 per cent (see Appendix 2). CCBs also increased their share of total banking assets from 5.28 per cent in 2003 to 6.62 per cent of total banking assets by the end of 2008 (CBRC Annual Report 2008). It is also important to remember that CCBs lend most of their loans to SMEs, which constitute one of the most dynamic sectors of the Chinese economy. The book addresses banking reform in China's CCBs as one of the last remaining issues in the transition from a planned economy to a market economy and queries the degree to which changes in corporate governance are able to bring about the development of regional banks, particularly in the new category of CCBs. This book adds a local and institutional perspective to the literature on banking reform.

4 The reform of China's banking sector

Reforms of China's banking sector centred around the following – establishment of the CBRC, a push to list the SOCBs and JSCBs on both local and overseas stock exchanges; a programme of cash injections in exchange for NPLs and encouragement to the CCBs to seek out foreign partners.

The reform of China's banking sector was initially slow and piecemeal. The Asian Financial Crisis of 1997/1998, however, was a wake-up call as critics proclaimed that the Chinese banking system was awash with NPLs. DeCosta and Foo (2002) and Leung *et al.* (2002) wrote that the NPLs were at 40 per cent; Tenev and Zhang wrote that China's NPLs stood at between 25 per cent and 40 per cent (2002). These scholars were all pessimistic about the very high ratios of

NPLs in the Chinese banks. However, as China's trade surplus grew and the strategy of listing the big SOCBs eventuated, the reform process was initiated (Ma 2007) whereby cash was injected into these banks and NPLs transferred out.

What role did foreign banking shareholders play in the reform of China's banks? Garcia-Herrero and Santabarbara found that the Chinese banking system benefited from the entry of foreign investors through higher profitability and increased efficiency (2008). This finding was corroborated by Bonin *et al.* who found that strategic foreign bank ownership improves cost efficiency (2004) while Leigh and Podpiera (2006) conclude that China appears well positioned to benefit from further opening of the banking sector to foreign investors. This book further studies the role of foreign partners in the CCBs as part of the ongoing reform process.

5 Conceptual tools to analyse corporate governance

In order to ascertain the role of corporate governance in the reform of China's CCBs, it is necessary to first determine what constitutes good corporate governance. This is done by reference to the Consultative Document published by the Basel Committee on Banking Supervision entitled 'Enhancing Corporate Governance for Banking Organisations' (Bank for International Settlements 2005). To what extent have the CCBs with foreign shareholders implemented the guidelines? According to Consultative Document there are various practices that should be implemented to ensure sound corporate governance.

The first step towards enhancing corporate governance calls for the establishment of strategic objectives and corporate values. Ideally a bank's corporate statement should mention corporate governance as one of the bank's corporate values or objectives, but if this is not the case, then the corporate values should allude to profitability, progress, modernity and growth. These are all objectives which are directly affected by corporate governance mechanisms and structures and hence enhance its implementation.

The second practice that should be established relates to setting and enforcing clear lines of responsibility and accountability throughout the banking organization. This is important as every bank should have clear lines of authority for approval of loans, for approval of investments, and for capital expenditure. Limits must be demarcated for senior/junior managers so that there is a paper trail and proper accountability for every decision made. The practice should start from the top, at board level, and permeate down to management and staff so that every staff member knows what is expected of them.

The third practice to be established relates to the board. It is vital to ensure that all board members are qualified for their positions. This does not necessarily mean board directors have to be university professors or professionals, but that they should at least have requisite experience for what they are called upon to perform. They should not be political appointees with no idea of banking practices, organizations or finance.

The fourth practice requires a sound corporate governance system to ensure there is appropriate oversight by senior management and this is necessary to prevent mistakes, errors, misdemeanours and fraudulent activity. Senior management themselves have to report to the board and at the board level all decisions made must be carefully recorded so that there is proper accountability.

The fifth step relates to auditors. Auditors perform a very important function in any organization and a bank should have both internal and external auditors who report directly to the board. This ensures a certain degree of independence and one of the main duties of auditors is to examine the internal control functions of a bank to ensure that controls in place are adequate to prevent fraud and malfeasance. External auditors perform audits on their banking clients only once a year and, not being *in situ* all year round, have to depend on internal auditors to complement their own work.

The sixth practice relates to compensation policies and staff promotions. The bank should promote staff and management on merit and compensation policies must reflect current market practice and be adequate.

The seventh and last step is to ensure an environment supportive of sound corporate governance. This can be achieved in several ways: by constantly reminding staff of corporate governance precepts during training sessions, handing out awards to staff who have contributed to the bank's corporate governance objectives and by implementing a policy of rewarding 'whistle-blowers' who detect corporate governance transgressions.

6 Summary

Corporate governance as a study became relevant in China in the aftermath of the Asian Financial Crisis in 1997/1998 when Chinese authorities realized how important it was that their banking system be placed on a proper footing or suffer the same fate as the banks in Thailand, Indonesia, Philippines, Malaysia and South Korea.

The banking system in China may be conveniently categorized as having three tiers. The first tier comprises the large SOCBs, the second tier is the JSCBs which have branches nationwide and the third tier comprises the CCBs which are mainly local in character. For the purposes of our study, we have narrowed the definition of the local banking sector to denote the CCBs.

The twin topics of corporate governance and banking reform in China are areas of research that scholars have written extensively on. However, the subject of corporate governance in the CCBs of China is a new area that has attracted little attention and my research focuses on those CCBs with foreign partners. My investigations indicated that those CCBs with foreign shareholders showed substantial improvements in their governance standards. The Basel Committee on Banking Supervision Standards entitled 'Enhancing Corporate Governance for Banking Organisations' was used as a guide for preparing the questionnaire used to analyse corporate governance in the CCBs.

The CCBs form the third tier of China's banking sector but it is a very important sector. It is important because the CCBs in China comprise an extremely dynamic segment of the banking system and the majority of their loans are extended to SMEs. As of the end of 2008 there were 136 CCBs dispersed all over China; however, only 13 of them have foreign equity partners. Most of them held between 10 and 20 per cent of the total shareholding equity and the foreign partners took an active role in the management of the banks they invested in. In the early stages, the CCBs had average or below average standards of corporate governance but after partnering with foreign shareholders, their corporate governance standards lifted substantially. This was reflected in their improved financial performances which were markedly superior to that attained by the CCB sector as a whole.

2 Models of corporate governance

1 Introduction

This chapter studies the various models of corporate governance and places them in the China context. It considers the different models – agency, shareholder value, stakeholder, stewardship, transitional and the convergence approach. The form and theory of each model of corporate governance is considered and evaluated. As each model is evaluated, its relevance and applicability to China is also considered so that readers may understand which model is best suited to China.

The OECD defines corporate governance as: 'the set of relationships between a company's management, its board, its shareholders and other stakeholders. It provides the structure through which the company's objectives are set, and the means of attaining these objectives and monitoring mechanisms are determined' (OECD 2004b). There is another more generalized view of corporate governance from Lord Cadbury (who headed the Cadbury Code of Conduct of Corporate Governance adopted by the London Stock Exchange in 1994), who opined that 'the purpose of corporate governance of a corporation is to align as nearly as possible the interests of individuals, corporations and society'.

The scope of corporate governance is therefore wide and studies differ in approach, methodology and emphasis. Sometimes these conclusions are contentious, sometimes not. Corporate entities are governed differently in different countries because of differing emphasis on the relationships between the various parties that comprise the corporation, because of different legal frameworks; because they evolved from different economic and political systems and sometimes because the economic environments they operate in are in a state of transition.

2 Models of corporate governance

How should a corporation be managed? Should it be managed solely in the interests of the shareholders or is there a broader agenda? If so, how broad should the agenda be? What is the role of management? How should they be rewarded? Should the interests of employees, customers and creditors be considered? What about other interest groups? What about the society in which it operates? With the growth of globalization, is there convergence towards an internationally accepted code of good corporate governance? These are all relevant questions and the answers determine the tools and mechanisms employed in the corporate governance structures of corporations.

An additional question would be – who should be the arbiters and supervisors of good corporate governance? Today, in response to changed economic circumstances, financial institutions like pension funds (CALPERS 2005), sovereign funds, insurance companies and mutual funds are the largest shareholders of many of the large listed corporations. By way of example, pension funds held 24 per cent of US corporate stock in 1997 compared to 0.3 per cent in 1945 (Lazonick and O'Sullivan 2004: 301). As a result these institutions are now the arbiters and supervisors of good corporate governance, a role that they play very well. The various types of models of corporate governance are discussed below.

2.1 Agency model

The separation of ownership and control is inevitable in modern business corporations as these entities necessitate huge capital outlays resulting in equally large numbers of shareholder owners. This has resulted in the creation of a class of professional managers and the relationship between the shareholders and managers is a topic of study (Berle and Means 1932). The rise of professional managers in large corporations has led to the separation of decision and risk bearing functions (Fama and Jensen 1983a) and the manager/shareholder relationship is the most important relationship in any corporate entity. This model is the Agency theory, where the shareholders are the principal and the management is their agent. This theory does not take into account competing interests of other groups and merely defines corporate governance as being 'how to ensure that shareholders returns are maximized' and simultaneously 'how do suppliers of finance (shareholders) control managers' (Schleifer and Vishny 1997).

But how do shareholders ensure that management acts in the best interests of the principals? According to economic theory, both shareholders and managers would want to maximize their own individual utility (Jensen and Meckling 2004); the shareholders wanting to maximize profits and the managers wanting to maximize their own personal interests resulting in a dichotomy of interests. How do shareholders ensure a similar alignment of interests between principal and agent?

There are various ways for the shareholders to ensure a congruence of interests. A 'carrot and stick' approach is usually employed. First there must be sufficient controls in place to monitor and control the actions of managers to ensure that they do not make corporate decisions in their own selfish interests which are detrimental to the shareholders. These are monitoring costs and would comprise, in addition to the supervisory role of the board, the formation of audit, remuneration and investment committees to supervise managerial decisions. Second, incentives can be established to reward managers when the company's objectives, primarily profits, are met. These incentives would be usually financial and may comprise either stock options or remuneration, or a combination of both. However, there is also the performance/cost element to be considered and, where the managerial performance is obviously incompetent, the shareholders have the right to change the Chief Executive Officer (CEO). This is usually done at the company's Annual General Meeting (AGM) where the incompetent CEO is replaced. This is a standard mechanism used in corporate governance to ensure that corporate objectives are met and to prevent entrenchment of ineffective management.

The protection of shareholders is an important theme in corporate governance research and La Porta *et al.* found that countries like the United States and the UK have much larger capital markets than countries like France, Germany and Japan because shareholders in those two countries are well protected by law from expropriation by managers and controlling shareholders of a firm (La Porta *et al.* 1997, 2000a). A paper from the Harvard Business School also indicated that stronger shareholder rights result in higher firm value, higher profits and higher sales growth (Gompers and Ishii 2003).

Various questions, however, arise vis-à-vis the nature of the relationship: is this a typical commercial agency relationship where the shareholder as principal is accorded all the normal rights of ownership associated, say, with the ownership of a piece of private property? Or are the ownership rights somewhat diluted? Berle and Means (1932) argued that shareholders of modern corporations should not be accorded the same ownership rights as they had effectively assigned their control rights to the managers and had therefore only retained for themselves the role of recipients of wages of passive capital.

The UK/US approach to corporate governance over the last century has been that the corporation should be managed exclusively in the interests of the shareholders and this model has worked well. Nevertheless, there were abuses of corporate governance practices in the late 1980s and the early years of the twenty-first century. How did this happen? A historical journey into the American corporate landscape is necessary.

From the 1960s until the early 1980s, during a period of long and sustained economic growth, the American corporations expanded – they all wanted to be conglomerates and mergers and acquisitions were common. The credo of the corporate manager was to 'retain and re-invest'; in other words, they retained corporate earnings and re-invested in the existing business or acquisitions of competitors. However, from the late 1980s onwards, these same corporations suddenly found themselves under attack from corporate raiders who used 'junk bonds'[1] to take over these huge, bumbling conglomerates. In order to thwart corporate raiders, corporate managers quickly changed their motto from 'retain and re-invest' to 'downsize and distribute' (Lazonick and O'Sullivan 2004) and a return to core values of maximization of shareholder value. By distributing a large percentage of profits, instead of re-investing them, corporate managers were able to substantially increase the values of listed companies they managed and thus thwart corporate raiders. An example of how much the trend had taken root in American corporate culture can be found in the fact that by the 1990s, even solid lifelong career culture companies like IBM had significantly downsized their blue- and white-collar workers.

During the 1980s and 1990s, US corporations not only downsized, but also distributed an even larger portion of their earnings when compared to the 1960s and 1970s. This was done by increasing dividend payouts and by implementing substantial stock repurchase programmes. In the United States, the corporate payout ratio which expresses the corporate dividends paid as a percentage of corporate profits earned increased from 42.3 per cent during the period 1970–1978 to 49.6 per cent in the period 1990–1998. To this figure must be added the stock repurchase programme which increased from 5 per cent of corporate profits in 1978–1982 to 20 per cent during the period 1992–1996 (Lazonick and O'Sullivan 2004). Thus, in the late 1990s, US corporations were spending close to 70 per cent of their profits on dividend payouts and stock repurchases (49.6 per cent + 20 per cent).

Similarly, in the UK, Stephen Dorrell, former financial secretary to the Treasury, stated in 1994 that he felt that the dividend payout policy pursued by UK listed companies was too high and too inflexible. In October 2002, Michael McLintock, CEO of M&G which is part of the Prudential Group, one of the largest financial institutional investors, sent a letter to major UK companies emphasizing the importance of maintaining dividends even in the face of falling profits (Da Silva *et al.* 2004). The result of all this was a swift return to maximizing Shareholder Value.

2.2 Shareholder Value model

An offshoot of the Agency model of corporate governance is the Shareholder Value model, which basically seeks to maximize returns to the shareholder. (Lazonick and O'Sullivan 2004) A corollary to the shareholder maximization value model was the need to incentivize the corporate manager. CEOs' pay scales rocketed with the increased incentives paid to senior managers. Statistics show that in 1965 average CEO pay packages were 44 times greater those of factory workers, but by 1998, the multiple had gone up by 419 times (*Business Week*, 20 April 1998). In such a situation the question may be rightly asked – is this morally justified?

Stock options too became increasingly popular. As stock options became an ever more important part of corporate managers' rewards, they became obsessed with the need to keep the listed share price as high as possible in the short term; so that they could either cash out or prevent their corporation from becoming a target of corporate raiders. This resulted in financial irregularities and creative accounting, sometimes with the connivance of partners of the Big Five international accounting firms. The disasters of the corporate giants in the United States in 2001–2012 prove the failure of the doctrine of maximization of Shareholder Value when carried to extremes. Coffee (2004) attributes these corporate collapses to the failure of gatekeepers like auditors to perform their duty.

In China, the corporate landscape over the last three decades has been one of constant change and transition. Where once there were unprofitable and unwieldy SOEs dependent on the soft budget constraint for survival, these were corporatized and listed on local stock exchanges. Almost overnight they had to operate according to commercial principles and meet hard budget constraints. The Shareholder Value model was placed before management as a desirable goal but the reality was of course different. Management usually comprised of seconded public servants or bureaucrats who were more subservient to their political masters than to shareholders. There were also few financial incentives for the Chinese corporate managers to maximize profits, unlike their Western counterparts, and the Chinese system has not evolved to the UK/US standards.

The Shareholder Value model of corporate governance is the model practised in the United States and UK. It works there because both countries have strong financial institutions, free market mechanisms, efficient markets and strong rule of law. Strong rule of law refers to a judiciary which is corruption free, independent of the executive and legislative organs of government. Shareholdings in UK and US companies are also highly dispersed, and mergers and acquisitions are indicative of the strong free market forces that exist to force managers to govern corporations optimally. In China, the shareholdings of listed SOEs are largely concentrated in the hands of the state or SOEs and corporate mergers and takeovers cannot occur without the approval of the state. In addition, China's judiciary is not truly independent as it operates as an extension of the executive. China, therefore does not possess all those free market forces and institutions of the UK and United States and those that exist, exist in limited forms only. Another way of describing the differences would be to describe China as a developing economy whose institutions are in varying stages of development and to define the UK/US economies as mature economies with strong institutions. Hence the Shareholder Value model is not the most appropriate model for China.

2.3 Stakeholder model

It is perhaps appropriate to paraphrase the OECD's view on stakeholders, which is that 'the corporate governance framework should recognize the rights of stakeholders established by law or through mutual agreements and encourage active co-operation between corporation and stakeholders in creating wealth, jobs, and the sustainability of financially sound enterprises' (OECD 2004b).

The stakeholder theory of corporate governance is attributed to Freeman and Reed (1983) who wrote that 'the emergence of numerous stakeholder groups require a re-thinking of the traditional picture of the firm'. According to the stakeholder approach, corporations should be governed for the benefit of all stakeholders, stakeholders being defined by the Stanford Research Institute as 'those groups without whose support the corporation would cease to exist'. This theory broadly takes cognizance of the fact that the success of any corporation is due to teamwork and contributions from a large number of resource providers including employees, creditors, bankers, suppliers and not just shareholders, directors and senior management. In addition, in an imperfect market, the

Stakeholder model of corporate governance may be more appropriate than the Shareholder Value model.

The theoretical basis for this approach is that the corporation is a bundle of relationships; some formal and others informal. Formal relationships would be those between the firm and the shareholders, the managers, the employees, the creditors and external professionals (auditors, bankers, lawyers, etc.). Informal relationships would be those between the firm and the media, consumers, various associations, political parties, government departments, schools of higher learning, etc. The economic well-being of the society which the corporation operates in is also a relationship that must be considered. The tools of governance in this model take into account various stakeholders in the corporate governance processes; it means that their voices must be heard and perhaps even representation given them. This can be done by having representation on both the board of directors and to a lesser extent the board of supervisors. In the capitalist countries, independent directors constitute the board majority of corporations and they often voice the concerns of both formal and informal stakeholders.

France, Germany and Japan are countries that have adopted the Stakeholder model as a means of corporate governance (Guillen 2004). It is said that this has been responsible for their industrial success and social stability. The reason is because this model allows the board of directors to govern for the long term, unlike the Shareholder Value model which tends to concentrate on short-term results. Another tool of corporate governance is the payment of dividends and research has shown that dividend payments in Stakeholder economies like Germany show greater consistency over time and that a lower proportion of net profits is paid out as dividends compared to the United States and UK.

It would appear that the Stakeholder model of corporate governance may be more suitable for China given that the country has adopted socialist principles and concepts in its forward planning since 1949. A model of corporate governance that is inclusive of all those interest groups without which the modern corporation would be unable to function optimally is, to my mind, a more suitable model than a model that caters exclusively to the myopic interests of the shareholder as encased in the Shareholder Value model. In China's case the stakeholders would include not only shareholders, but also directors, managers, staff, bankers and consumers.

2.4 Differences between Shareholder Value and Stakeholder model

The main difference between the Shareholder Value and the Stakeholder model of corporate governance relates to the degree of legal protection against expropriation enjoyed by shareholders under both systems (La Porta *et al.* 1997). Shareholders under the Shareholder Value model enjoy substantially more legal rights and protection than those under the Stakeholder model because the legal system in the United States and UK places strong emphasis on common law, while in the European countries, statute law is predominant. The legal system in the United States and UK can trace its origins to common law which originated in the UK and has evolved in such a way that more protection is given to the rights of shareholders than in the European countries. This is not to say that there is no abuse of minority shareholders in the United States and UK – there is as one often reads about such instances in the media.

Countries like the United States and UK follow the Shareholder Value model and as a result have much bigger equity markets than countries like Germany, France and Japan. Another result is that the majority of finance raised for corporations in the United States and UK comes from the stock markets whereas in the European countries and Japan, most of new finance comes from banks. Hence, the stock markets in New York and London are far larger than Paris, Bonn and Tokyo.

Research has also indicated that dividends paid out tend to be higher in the Shareholder Value model than under the Stakeholder model of corporate governance (La Porta *et al.* 2000b). This is understandable, as under the Stakeholder model, the shareholder is but one stakeholder to be considered whereas under the Shareholder Value model, only the shareholder's interests are considered and managers in pursuit of maximization of Shareholder Value would tend to pay out more in dividends than their counterparts operating under the Stakeholder model.

2.5 Stewardship model

Stewardship theory merely states that managers find satisfaction when acting as stewards of corporations. As stewards, they identify completely with the corporation and subsume their personal interests into the company's goals. For stewardship theory to be fully implemented, stewards would want sweeping powers, believing that all decisions they make will be in the best interests of the corporation (and by inference the shareholders). Davis *et al.* (1997) argue that Stewardship theory demands that structures be put in place empowering the CEO and not restrict him.

Under the Stewardship model of governance, the CEOs who are stewards would also chair the board of directors. However, in reality this does not happen because of the risk factor: the possibility that manager stewards may wittingly or unwittingly make corporate decisions detrimental to the interests of the shareholders. Monitoring and internal control measures will therefore always be present as a safeguard measure for the shareholders.

The search for steward managers may lead to the employment of senior managers with credible reputations and proven track records of excellence. In such a scenario, monitoring costs are alleviated while financial incentives would naturally be higher. Reputation of managers is a form of self-governance that shareholders and the marketplace should pay attention to. The Stewardship theory has not found acceptance as it is generally accepted that there needs to be a system of checks and balances to ensure that managers act in the best interests of the company and should not be allowed free rein to manage the company as the theory would appear to suggest.

In China situations existed in the past where powerful CEOs were also chairmen of the board of directors but this is becoming less frequent as concepts of modern corporate governance have come into practice. In addition, the case for the Stewardship theory is less compelling as currently many of the corporate managers of the Chinese SOEs and listed entities are bureaucrats and officials who do not necessarily make for good stewards. And given the performance record of the listed SOEs, there is definitely a need for the close monitoring of the CEOs by the board of directors and shareholders. So we can rule out the Stewardship theory as a model for China to follow.

2.6 Transitional model

Since the 1980s, there have been various centrally planned economies making the transition to market economies. How have they attempted to solve the problems of corporate governance? What tools and mechanisms have they used and how successful have they been? Studies of corporate governance in transitional economies focus on two areas: Eastern Europe, including Russia, and China. The former may be said to have adopted the instantaneous Big Bang approach whilst the latter has taken the Gradualist approach – an approach which has been described as 'walking on two legs' or 'growing out of the plan' (Naughton 1995).

In most of these economies, it has been a steep learning curve. Along the way they have encountered numerous problems as many of the basic financial and legal infrastructure present in Western democracies were absent in China, Russia and the Eastern European countries. Ownership and private property rights are also weak. The legal framework in these countries is also fragile and subject to manipulation and enforcement is often feeble. The judiciary often functions as an extension of the executive and is subject to corrupt practices. Transparency and information disclosure is often weak and related party transactions are often the norm – not the exception.

The Russians paid a heavy price in the transition to a market economy. Their economic framework was simply not ready and Russian organized crime emerged as a significant force in the economic environment (Finckenauer and Voronin 2001; Yun 2003).

China was the first socialist economy to make market-based reforms in 1979 but there was no theoretical basis or historical precedents to facilitate the process. Thus the authorities took the gradualist path to effect change and scholars today consider the process successful. Nevertheless numerous problems remain as listed entities – former SOEs – grapple with the demands of corporate governance in a modern corporate environment. The transition from being an 'iron rice bowl' (where lifelong employment is guaranteed) outfit in a planned economy to a profit-oriented corporation with hard budget constraints in a market economy has not been complete. Many of the listed companies have the state as the largest shareholder – conflicts of interest often arise and such ambiguity leads to opportunities for fraud.

Qian (2002) writes about China's reform and how it has managed to grow so rapidly despite the absence of many conventional institutions such as strong rule of law and secure private property rights. To understand how reform works in a transitional economy that has great growth potential, Qian postulates that it is not enough to study the conventional best-practice institutions as a desirable goal. One should also study how feasible, imperfect institutions have evolved to complement the initial conditions and to function as stepping stones in the transition towards the goal. Underlying China's reform is a series of institutional changes concerning the market, firms and the government in the novel form of transitional institutions. These institutions succeed when they achieve two objectives: to improve economic efficiency by unleashing the standard forces of incentives and competition on the one hand, and to make the reform process a win-win game on the other.

Transitional models of corporate governance reflect the degree and rate of change embraced by the relevant authorities in those economies. Obviously some are progressing faster than others, but they all exhibit the same problems of corporate governance. Chapter 3 deals with the subject of corporate governance in transitional economies.

2.7 Convergence model

The Convergence theory of corporate governance simply states that with increasing globalization and the rapid growth of multinational corporations over the last few decades, international boundaries and borders are becoming irrelevant as these corporations seek new markets and invest in developing countries. These multinational companies are also a homogenizing force (Guillen 2004). Their capital movements are huge; as an example China attracted foreign direct investment of US$62.39 billion in 2000 (Lai 2002) and, as a result of these massive investments, there is a theory that this will lead to a convergence of systems and the adoption of an international model of corporate governance. This is true to a certain extent with the proliferation of international accounting firms and their models of corporate practices.

London and New York are the two biggest financial centres in the world where the most finance is raised. As a result, corporations wishing to list on these two markets have to abide by their corporate governance practices. Thus Daimler Benz, the first German company to list on the New York Stock Exchange (NYSE) in the mid 1990s, had to change its accounting standards to comply with the NYSE rules. Several Mainland Chinese firms have also listed on the NYSE and adopted the American model of corporate governance, thus setting the standard for other Chinese corporations. In Russia, the standards of corporate governance are patterned on the United States too and, as in the Chinese experience, several companies have listed on the NYSE.

The Convergence theory postulates convergence towards a model of corporate governance that is universally accepted. There is widespread acknowledgement that the agency theory with its emphasis on shareholder value is most practical for how else can the interests of shareholders who are scattered all over the world be protected as global corporations invest in the economies of the developing world. The emphasis on shareholder value, however, received a setback with the recent Global Financial Crisis (GFC) and the American theories of corporate governance were perceived to be not robust and somewhat lacking. There is widespread disillusionment with the corporate United States and a realization that the GFC was caused by the greed and excesses on Wall Street which happened because of the lack of regulation and oversight by the Securities Exchange Commission (SEC) and relevant banking authorities in the United States.

There is now greater interest in the Stakeholder theory of corporate governance as the preferred international model given that the Stakeholder model seems less likely to display the excesses exhibited by the Shareholder Value approach.

3 Conclusion

There is no 'one size fits all' model of corporate governance. Different countries have different economies at different stages of socio-economic development which are manifested in their laws and legal processes. These economies have different socio-economic needs and hence may adopt different models of governance. Again their needs will be influenced by culture and traditions, by the political and legal systems practised in that country.

As mentioned earlier, the business corporation has many key players apart from the shareholders and the managers. Each would prefer to have its own corporate governance model. From the viewpoint of the investor, the Shareholder Value model is ideal because it calls for the maximization of shareholder value. From the point of view of the CEO, the Stewardship model would be ideal as the CEO would be endowed with more powers. For the bankers, creditors and employees, the Stakeholder model would protect their interests better.

Which model of corporate governance is most appropriate for China? Is it the Shareholder Value model, the Stakeholder model or some other? From our analysis and observations in the above sections, it appears that the most suitable model for China is the Stakeholder model. This model appears better equipped to meet the needs of a socialist economy in transition to a market economy and takes into account the interests of various parties necessary for the well-being of a corporation: the directors, managers, staff, bankers, creditors, consumers, associations, society at large, etc. The Shareholder Value model with its emphasis on returns to shareholders has been somewhat tarnished because it is the model practised in the United States, which was responsible for the recent GFC.

3 Corporate governance in transitional economies

1 An overview of transitional economies

In this chapter, we study transitional economies, centrally planned economies in transition to market economies. This chapter helps in understanding the corporate governance problems China faced as it transited from planned to market economy and compares them with other transitional economies. There were both similarities and differences: similarities in the corporate governance problems faced and differences in the approaches to the transition.

After the Second World War, the world was divided into two competing blocs, the socialist bloc countries led by Russia and China and the capitalist countries led by the United States. The socialist bloc included the Central and Eastern European countries while the US-led countries included Western Europe and Japan. The socialist bloc countries had centrally planned economies while the West had market economies and both competed for influence on the world stage. By the late 1970s, it was obvious that the market economies were winning in the economic arena.

China was the first centrally planned economy to experiment with free market mechanisms. Economic reforms began in 1979 with privately rented farming plots being allowed to co-exist with state-owned lands. SOEs and factories were allocated certain production targets with the excess production over targets being sold on the free market. Profits earned were shared between the management and workers of the business enterprises. The result was dramatic. After a decade of economic dislocation and stagnation caused by the Cultural Revolution (1966–1976), the economy picked up and showed sustained and substantial growth over the next two decades. According to China's National Bureau of Statistics, Gross Domestic Product (GDP) growth for the period 1979–2004 averaged 9.6 per cent per annum.

The Soviet Union, after the debacle in Afghanistan and with a new leader, Gorbachev, watched the initial economic reforms in China with interest. Gorbachev implemented 'Glasnost' and the 'Perestroika' movement in 1987 (a series of political and economic reforms) which ultimately led to the fall of the Berlin Wall in 1989 and signalled the collapse of communism in Central and Eastern Europe and the Former Soviet Union (CEEFSU). Authorities in the

CEEFSU economies had no doubt that they wanted to transit to free market economies, but the big question was how to manage the transition? Should it be done gradually as in China or should a rapid Big Bang approach be adopted?

This chapter studies the two models of economic transition: the Gradualist model of China and the Big Bang approach as adopted by CEEFSU. Why did the countries adopt different models? What was corporate governance like before and after the transition? Our study finds that there are broad similarities in the corporate governance problems. We study these problems and examine how these corporate governance problems are being resolved.

2 The Big Bang approach versus the Gradualist approach

When economic reforms started in the CEEFSU, most economists in the West favoured a Big Bang approach which recommended introducing free market mechanisms as quickly as possible (Blanchard *et al.* 1993; Lipton *et al.* 1990). Economists from the United States, delighted with the fall of the Berlin Wall in 1989 and the collapse of communism soon after, were only too happy to advise Russia and the former Soviet bloc countries on the economic transition. This was the Washington Consensus (Williamson 1993) and basically called for an instantaneous approach with the adoption of free market discipline, the introduction of strong property rights, privatization of SOEs, liberalization of the economy and the establishment of free market institutions. The model of corporate governance recommended was based on that of the United States, i.e. the Shareholder Value model. The result was that most of the countries in CEEFSU adopted this approach.

When China began its road to economic reform, there were no economic theories to model itself on and no blueprints to follow. The reform process was therefore gradual, piecemeal, incremental, experimental and without large scale privatization of the SOEs (Lin *et al.* 1996b). China chose instead to corporatize the SOEs (CEEFSU in contrast privatized the SOEs) and this process started in the late 1980s and accelerated in the 1990s when the two stock exchanges in Shanghai and Shenzhen were established in 1990/1991.

China's reform process was gradual and incremental because it was the first centrally planned economy to attempt the transition to a market economy. By comparison, when the CEEFSU countries began their economic reforms, the Western economists had formulated a roadmap for them to follow. The Big Bang economic theory made sense and appeared perfectly feasible. The fact that the CEEFSU countries were ethnically, culturally and geographically close to the Western democracies made it easier for them to follow what the Western economists recommended. Western economists explained that the Big Bang theory of economic transition would have a 'J curve' effect, i.e. the GDP of the country would fall initially but would within a short period of time experience strong recovery. Unfortunately, the strong recovery did not happen and most of the CEEFSU economies experienced continued declines of GDP with high inflation rates and high unemployment. In fact, during the period 1990–1999 Russian

GDP fell by almost 60 per cent (Leng 2009). Brada and King (1992), based on their study of what happened in Poland, Hungary and the Czech Republic, wrote that there was no such J curve and attributed the steep declines in those three countries to incorrect macro policies. China in comparison not only did not suffer GDP declines but continued to attain strong economic growth.

3 Reasons for the different economic results

Economists are at a loss to explain the success of China's Gradualist model of transition as it is not supported by any economic theory (Nolan 1993, 1994). Why would a bottom-up incremental approach prove superior to a comprehensive, top-down model sanctioned by authorities? It has been argued that China's success is due to its unique conditions: the large agrarian sector of the economy, low percentage of industry in the economy, low financial subsidies to the population and a rich diaspora of overseas Chinese (Sachs and Woo 1994, 1997; Qian and Xu 1993) – that these were special conditions which other economies of CEEFSU could not emulate. Another explanation which is more plausible as to why China succeeded is that correct macro policies were implemented; fostering rural markets, encouraging private enterprises, reform of state enterprises, price reform, decontrol of consumer goods, an open-door investment policy and changes in the role of government planning (Chow, 1993).

The Big Bang transition model attempts to replace inefficient economic systems with a more efficient one based on free market forces which was to be implemented instantaneously. Unfortunately the privatization of SOEs in CEEFSU was slow and took much longer than expected (Muriel and Wang 1993) with the result that it was effectively a Gradualist approach. However, the heavy costs of the shock treatment and dislocation to the CEEFSU economies outweighed subsequent gains; these were problems China avoided because of its Gradualist approach. China's Gradualist model was regarded by several economists as being superior to the Big Bang model (McMillan and Naughton 1992; Murrell 1993; Jefferson *et al.* 1992) but unfortunately the CEEFSU countries chose not to follow it.

4 Corporate governance in Russia

The Russian corporate environment is today characterized by high ownership concentration: especially in the hands of insiders (Table 3.1), weak legal institutions, underdeveloped capital markets, a segmented labour market and significant involvement of the state in businesses (Lazareva *et al.* 2008).

What went wrong? Many Russians today see the bold moves in the early 1990s to privatize the state property and end price control as unmitigated disasters for their country (Djatej *et al.* 2008). Proponents of the Big Bang approach had hoped that the profit incentive unleashed by the privatization of the SOEs would soon revive faltering centrally planned economies. That revival did not happen in Russia and there are explanations. First, mass privatization led to massive self dealing by managers and controlling shareholders, and second, profit incentives to restructure privatized enterprises were swamped by high taxes, corrupt officialdom, organized crime and an unfriendly bureaucracy (Black *et al.* 2000).

The capital market in Russia today remains relatively underdeveloped. Statistics in 2005 show that the stock market capitalization relative to GDP stood at 44 per cent while comparable figures was 72 per cent for France, 81 per cent in Japan and 135 per cent in the United States. The volume of private sector credit as a share of GDP was 21 per cent in Russia compared to 90 per cent for France and 75 per cent for Japan (Lazareva *et al.* 2008). Most Russian firms therefore have to rely on internally generated funds for expansion.

Russia, like most transitional economies, has weak legal institutions and this has discouraged investors and negatively affected its ability to raise external finance (Pistor *et al.* 2000). There have been plenty of laws enacted; the Law on Joint Stock Companies, Law on Securities Markets, Law on Investor Protection, Bankruptcy Law and Tax Law. However, their enforcement is weak because of corruption, official interference and the tendency to resort to unofficial means. Nevertheless, progress in corporate governance has been made (Puffer and McCarthy 2003a), as Russia's intention to join the WTO (achieved in 2012) and the desire to attract foreign direct investments have been prime levers in raising corporate governance standards (Puffer and McCarthy 2003b).

4.1 Corporate governance problems in Russia

Corporate governance problems in Russia arise mainly between controlling shareholders and minority shareholders. The ownership structure is thus very important and is studied in Table 3.1. These problems arose because weak legal institutions and underdeveloped capital markets encourage controlling shareholders to behave opportunistically towards minority shareholders. These actions have included transfer pricing, asset stripping, share dilution and outright theft (Lazareva *et al.* 2008).

Another problem relates to the conflict between the state as a shareholder and the controlling shareholders. During the early 1990s, the Russian government, under advice from American economists, instituted the 'voucher-for-shares' and the 'loan-for-shares' schemes and these have come to be viewed as state-sponsored theft of state property. According to Guriev and Rachinsky (2005) and Shekshnia *et al.* (2004) about 40 per cent of total Russian industry belong to 22 large business groups controlled by oligarchs. The Russian government is now aggressively pursuing a policy of re-nationalization of these industries with the Yukos case being the most famous example (Yukos used to be the largest oil producing company in Russia). This is due to the nationalistic view in Russia today that corporate governance should serve the objectives of the state rather than those of individual shareholders (Djatej *et al.* 2008).

4.2 Ownership and corporate governance in Russia

Table 3.1 shows the ownership structure of Russian industry. Insiders comprising managers and workers own over 50 per cent of the shareholdings. Such high concentrations arose because of the mass privatizations of state-owned assets to the workers and managers, the 'voucher-for-shares' issue to workers/managers and the state-sponsored loans for the purchase of shares throughout the mid to late 1990s (Sprenger 2002).

Although the managers do not have majority control, their influence is overwhelming as workers tend to vote with management. Together, the workers and managers have effective control of the company and they often make decisions that infringe on the rights and economic benefits of the state and outsiders. This happens because of weak legal institutions and corrupt bureaucracies. Hence the importance of building market supporting institutions in the transition to market economies and this applies equally to both Russia and China (Leng 2009). The foreign investment holding companies do not play an active role in promoting sound corporate governance at all. This is because they hold small stakes (on average less than 5 per cent, see Table 3.1) and do not participate in the management of the firms they invest in. Foreign investors use the international media to highlight gross abuses when it affects them (Dyck *et al.* 2007).

One of the results of insider control is the frequency of asset stripping, where the company's prime assets are transferred or sold at below market prices to an entity controlled by insiders. Another example of asset stripping is through the practice of transfer pricing, where goods/products are sold by the company to

Table 3.1 Ownership structure in Russian industry from different surveys

Survey data	*Bureau of economic analysis 2000 (%)*	*Russian economic barometer 1999 (%)*	*Biasi 1996 (%)*	*Nottingham sample 1995/1996 (%)*	*World Bank sample 1994 (%)*
Insiders	**62.3**	**46.2**	**58**	**59.6**	**66.1**
Managers	17.7	14.7	18	14.0	19.6
Workers	34.5	31.5	40	45.6	46.2
State	**5.7**	**7.1**	**9**	**9.3**	**15.0**
Outsiders	**32.0**	**42.4**	**32.1**	**31.3**	**18.9**
Individuals	0	18.5	6	6.5	5.9
Non-Finance	0	13.5	15.3	10.3	6.7
Firms	0	1.0	1.6	1.5	1.0
Banks	0	3.9	5	4.6	4.6
Investment firms	0	2.0	1.6	1.0	0.4
Foreigners	0				
Investment	0	3.5	2.6	5.4	0.0
Companies	0	4.3	0.9	1.7	0.0
Sample size	364	139	357	314	235

Source: adapted from Sprenger (2002).

another entity controlled by insiders at below market prices which are then sold on to the marketplace for handsome profits. Both are common occurrences in Russia (Fox and Heller 1999). Yet another method is share dilution, where preferential shares or convertible bonds were issued to insiders or insider-controlled companies which resulted in outside minority shareholders being disadvantaged. Share dividends were also delayed and non-transparent investment projects proposed instead of dividend payments. Minority shareholders depend on the company for information disclosure and transparency to be advised on the company's activities and dealings. These were often blocked or not performed at all. There was restricted access to annual shareholder meetings, barring outside investors from taking seats on the board of directors, voting irregularities and violations of laws relating to share issues (Sprenger 2002).

4.3 What role do directors, managers and employees play?

Russian companies show a heavy concentration of shareholdings and the controlling shareholders are the insiders who, together with management, exercise control over the board of directors. Independent directors do not play a significant role in Russia and much board time is devoted to investment strategies, warding off state encroachment and abusing outside minority shareholders. Worker employees are fairly significant shareholders in the company, but they are not represented on the board of directors (Blasi and Schleifer 1996). Also, as they are part of the insider group that controls the company, they vote along the lines directed by the board.

There is a market for takeovers and acquisitions in post-Soviet Russia but the players have different rules which are often unethical. Weak institutions like inefficient legal courts, weak property rights, corrupt bureaucracies and lack of free market forces result in bribery, coercion and mafia tactics to achieve predatory takeovers. These targets are often firms with bad corporate governance, but a successful takeover is no guarantee of future success. Often the takeover is motivated by the takeover benefits of personal control rather than the desire for efficiency. International media sometimes play a role in changing corporate governance when corporate governance violations arise (Dyck *et al.* 2007). Overall the net effect of takeovers and acquisitions on corporate governance is unclear.

4.4 Transparency and disclosure levels in Russia

Traditionally, Russians have distrusted transparency because of their long years of Soviet-dominated surveillance by the KGB (Russian secret police), when information was hidden and secrecy abounded. Company officials have also learned, early on, the value and reality of secrecy, opacity and obfuscation (Dean 2004). In a survey of Russian companies in 2007, Standard & Poor's found that the Russian companies had an average corporate governance score of 5.7 out of a maximum of 10. Scores of 7–10 indicate strong global standards of corporate governance, scores of 4–6 indicate basic corporate governance standards are in

Table 3.2 Russian companies' corporate governance scores: 2007

	Ownership structure and external influence	*Shareholder rights and stakeholder relations*	*Transparency, disclosure and audit*	*Board structure and effectiveness*
Average	5.6	6.7	5.7	5.3

Source: adapted from Standard & Poor's (2007a).

Note:
Maximum score of ten per category.

place but shortcomings exist and scores of 1–3 indicate that there are serious and fundamental weaknesses in corporate governance practices. Table 3.2 thus shows that Russian companies have basic corporate governance structures and mechanisms in place but that shortcomings still exist.

Transparency and disclosure levels in Russian companies have been improving although government corruption in Russia remains high (Standard & Poor's 2007a). Another survey of the transparency index for Russia's 30 largest banks indicated that the level of transparency was 36 per cent compared with 85 per cent for international banks (Standard & Poor's 2005).

5 Corporate governance in Central and Eastern European countries

Central and Eastern European countries underwent the same experiences as Russia, as most of them also adopted the Big Bang approach or a variation thereof for the transition to a market economy. Therefore their problems of corporate governance are similar to those of Russia. We will examine the corporate governance of several of those countries. Tables 3.3 to 3.6 contain data extracted from seven leading countries in Central and Eastern Europe who are more advanced in the corporate governance arena. We have omitted the smaller countries like Armenia, Azerbaijan, Croatia, Georgia, Latvia, Macedonia and Slovenia.

Table 3.3 Eastern Europe: protection of shareholder rights

Country	*Observed*	*Mostly observed*	*Partly observed*	*Mostly not observed*	*Not observed*
Bulgaria		X			
Czech Republic		X			
Hungary			X		
Poland	X				
Romania			X		
Slovakia			X		
Ukraine			X		

Source: adapted from McGee (2008).

5.1 Shareholder rights

Poland has the best corporate governance practices among the former Soviet dominated countries. It was the first country where radical market reforms were instituted and where strong economic performances were achieved (Belka *et al.* 1999). Table 3.3 shows that of the seven countries selected, only Poland has largely implemented the protection of shareholder rights. Bulgaria and Czech Republic mostly observe shareholder rights protection while Hungary, Romania, Slovakia and the Ukraine only partly observe such rights.

5.2 Board functions

Board of directors' duties and responsibilities and their fulfilment are crucial for the exercise of good corporate governance. This is an area that is grossly lacking in Eastern Europe. Poland and the Czech Republic are better off than the others but then fulfilment of board functions is only partially observed. The other five countries in the list mostly do not observe board functions.

5.3 Timely and accurate disclosure

Timely and accurate disclosure of all material matters is crucial to the establishment of sound corporate governance models. Table 3.5 shows that in Eastern Europe, only Hungary and Poland mostly observe this requirement. Bulgaria, the Czech Republic and Romania partly observe while Slovakia and the Ukraine mostly do not observe it at all.

The timely and accurate disclosure of information refers to two main areas: the preparation of financial accounts for management and the lodgement of annual reports to the relevant stock exchanges. For accounts to be useful to management, they must be accurate, frequent and timely. Hence, company accounts must be prepared on a monthly basis and they must be made available to management a few days after the month's end, not one or two months later. Similarly annual reports including annual accounts of the corporation must be lodged with

Table 3.4 Eastern Europe: fulfilment of board functions

Country	*Observed*	*Mostly observed*	*Partly observed*	*Mostly not observed*	*Not observed*
Bulgaria				X	
Czech Republic			X		
Hungary				X	
Poland			X		
Romania				X	
Slovakia				X	
Ukraine				X	

Source: adapted from McGee (2008).

Table 3.5 Eastern Europe: timely and accurate disclosure of all material matters

Country	*Observed*	*Mostly observed*	*Partly observed*	*Mostly not observed*	*Not observed*
Bulgaria			X		
Czech Republic			X		
Hungary		X			
Poland		X			
Romania			X		
Slovakia				X	
Ukraine				X	

Source: adapted from McGee (2008).

the stock exchange within a short time frame of the end of the financial year, not one year later. For all this to happen, the company needs a high degree of computerization and fairly high-tech management information systems. Not many of the companies in the Eastern European countries have such up-to-date systems.

5.4 Independent auditors

The concept of independent auditors is integral to good corporate governance in market economies and we find that, in Eastern Europe, the only country that practices this concept is Poland. The Czech Republic mostly observes it but Bulgaria, Hungary, Slovakia and the Ukraine only partly observe it while Romania mostly does not observe it at all. However Kosmala and Sucher (2006) have raised doubts as to the practicality of independent auditors as practised in the Anglo-American context being applied to Central and Eastern Europe. This is because many of these Eastern European countries lack the free market mechanisms of the West and the concept and practice of independent auditors is completely new to these economies. Nevertheless, it is noted that Poland and the

Table 3.6 Eastern Europe: independent audits

Country	*Observed*	*Mostly observed*	*Partly observed*	*Mostly not observed*	*Not observed*
Bulgaria			X		
Czech Republic		X			
Hungary			X		
Poland	X				
Romania				X	
Slovakia			X		
Ukraine			X		

Source: adapted from McGee (2008).

Czech Republic have implemented the recommendations of the International Federation of Accountants Code (IFAC) in regards to independent auditors.

5.5 Corruption index

Transparency International, a Non-Government Organization (NGO) devoted to measuring transparency and corruption in major world countries, conducted a survey in 2007 and found on a scale of 1–10 with 10 being the most transparent and least corrupt, that the Central and Eastern European countries had indices ranging from 2.6 for Ukraine to 5.2 for both the Czech Republic and Hungary. The survey shows that Ukraine is the most corrupt and least transparent of the seven countries measured and is far behind the Czech Republic and Hungary. These two countries may be considered to be fairly transparent and fairly free from corruption.

5.6 Summary of corporate governance in Central and Eastern Europe

The conclusion to be drawn from Sections 5.1 to 5.5 is that corporate governance in Central and Eastern Europe still has some way to go. While it has improved and is improving, it is not at a fast pace. The tables above indicate that after some two decades of economic transition, major indicators of good corporate governance show that most of these governance practices are either only 'partly observed or mostly not observed'. The above data are from the more advanced economies of Central and Eastern Europe and other smaller states are even more backward in their governance structures. Poland is the most advanced country in terms of its governance practices because it was the first Eastern European country to pursue radical economic reforms. The Czech Republic and Hungary are also more advanced than the other countries surveyed.

6 Comparison of corporate governance in Russia and China

Russia and China are both large continental countries and former centrally planned economies in transition to market economies. There are both similarities and differences: similarities because of their socialist background and differences because of the different model each adopted for the transition. China in the

Table 3.7 Corruption indicators

Country	*Bulgaria*	*Czech Republic*	*Hungary*	*Romania*	*Slovakia*	*Ukraine*	*Poland*
Corruption Index	4.0	5.2	5.2	3.6	4.8	2.6	4.2

Source: adapted from Lambstaff (2007).

1950s copied in large measure Russia's economic model, embracing centralized planning with an emphasis on heavy industries but China opted for the Gradualist approach to a market economy. It has proven successful. Russia, in comparison, adopted the Big Bang approach with disastrous consequences. A strong prevailing view in Russia today is that the United States and the West shamelessly and deceitfully exploited the Russian people and the nation during the 1990s when there was goodwill and trust in them (Djatej *et al.* 2008).

Standard & Poor's compiled a report, 'How Does Corporate Governance in Russia Stack up Against the BRIC Countries?' (2008). The report used four parameters to measure corporate governance in the BRIC countries and while it is not comprehensive it is indicative. We only use the information for Russia and China to make this comparison.

6.1 Market infrastructure

This is an indication of the extent of the development of institutions which are normally associated with free market economies and would include stock and commodity exchanges, securities markets, the sophistication of the banking system, foreign exchange markets, etc. China is ahead of Russia in this category because China started its economic reforms earlier than Russia and China has had relatively fewer problems in its transition to free market status than Russia.

Both Russia and China, however, are similar in that they suffer from high concentrations of ownership. Standard & Poor's own disclosure research (2007c) indicated that three-quarters of Russia's largest 80 public companies had controlling shareholders, some of which were government agencies. In China about 70 per cent of public listed companies are controlled by the state.

6.2 Legal infrastructure

Standard & Poor's believes Russia maintains a relatively effective legal infrastructure for corporate governance with well defined minority shareholder rights, low holding thresholds required to nominate directors, annual board elections and universal cumulative voting for directors. China's legal infrastructure is notable for guaranteeing equality of voting rights at shareholder meetings. It also

Table 3.8 Comparison of stock markets in Russia and China (June 2008)

	Russia	*China*
Number of companies on domestic exchanges	320	1,507
Daily turnover January 2008 (US$ billions)	4.49	40.38
Stock market capitalization (US$ billions)	1,298.8	5,424.4
Stock market capitalization (% of GDP)	106.7	167
Number of companies with USA listing	7	73
Number of companies with UK listing	51	73

Source: adapted from Standard & Poor's Report (2008).

offers minority shareholders pre-emptive rights on new shares. On the whole China's legal infrastructure is adequate with a variety of laws and regulations to supervise corporate governance.

A critique of the legal infrastructure is however the fact that legal enforcement in both countries is weak with the Russian legal enforcement being compromised by a corrupt judiciary (Zhuplev and Shein 2004) and in China's case by a judiciary which tends to make judgments in favour of local parties.

6.3 Regulatory infrastructure

Russia's regulatory infrastructure is not well developed. The Corporate Governance Code is voluntary for all public companies and touches only 22 out of a total of 320 public companies (Standard & Poor's 2008). Because it is voluntary and limited, corporate governance improvements have been slow. Other regulatory weaknesses include the independent directors who are not really independent at all. Many directors in SOEs are also executives in other SOEs; yet they meet the criteria for the definition of independent directors. There are also other irregularities which exist in determining the rules of the independence of share registrars and also rules regarding the independence of internal auditors. Another result of Russia's lack of regulatory infrastructure is that NPLs tend to be on the high side. According to a senior central banking official, the share of NPLs in Russian banks may reach 12 per cent by the end of 2009.

China has two important pieces of legislation relating to corporate governance – they are Rules Governing Listing of Stocks & Shares and the Code of Corporate Governance, both of which are compulsory for listed companies. The Code of Corporate Governance is based on the Anglo-Saxon model of corporate governance while the Shanghai Stock Exchange's Rules Governing the Listing of Stocks is based on the Hong Kong Stock Exchange. Apart from the above legislations, the Company Law and the Securities Law also impinge on corporate governance.

Unlike Russia, China has a strong and adequate regulatory infrastructure in place. However enforcement is lacking as the judiciary is weak and the regulatory bodies lack sufficient resources.

6.4 Information infrastructure

Transparency and information disclosure are extremely important to investors and in Russia minority investors are especially concerned about this because of widespread abuses perpetrated by insiders. Unfortunately Russian corporate governance is sorely lacking on information infrastructure. In terms of accounting standards, Russian standards are not useful for investors and Russian companies do not need to consolidate accounts. Russian accounting standards differ from Internationally Financial Reporting Standards (IFRS) in several key areas which make Russian company accounts difficult to interpret. Russian corporate accounts are also prepared to minimize revenue and profits so that less tax is paid to the government. This results in skewed and inaccurate accounts. Only a small number (22) of Russian companies prepare their accounts according to US Generally Accepted Accounting Standards.

China, by comparison, has made tremendous progress in transparency and information disclosure over the past decade. This is due to the strong regulatory regime and the desire by all parties involved in the corporate governance process to achieve better corporate governance. In 2007, China adopted new accounting standards which are close to IFRS (Standard & Poor's 2008), and this has certainly helped in the inflow of foreign investments into Chinese stock markets.

Transparency International, an NGO devoted to measuring transparency and corruption in major world countries, conducted a survey (Lambstaff 2007) and found, on a scale of 1–10 with 10 being the most transparent and least corrupt, that Russia had an index of 2.5 while China had an index of 3.5. Both indices are not good but Russia is lumped at the bottom end with Indonesia and Angola, both of which are notoriously corrupt countries while China is gauged to have similar standards as Brazil and India.

7 Conclusion

The conclusion to be drawn about corporate governance in transition economies is that many problems still exist. The last three decades have been tumultuous, as first China and then CEEFSU made the transition from planned to market economies. China adopted the Gradualist model while CEEFSU mostly adopted the Big Bang approach. Today, all of them have large portions of their economy functioning as market economies. These economies either privatized or corporatized their SOEs using their own chosen model of economic transition.

An interesting observation is that, in the main, the problems of corporate governance are similar regardless of which model of economic transition was chosen. Both Russia and China have corporate governance problems relating to insider dealing, controlling shareholders, abuse of minority shareholders, fraud and misappropriation. There are also NPLs, lack of transparency, lack of information disclosure and regulatory shortcomings which each has yet to overcome. The Central and Eastern European countries underwent the same experiences as Russia and manifest to a greater or lesser degree similar problems. The problems may vary slightly because of peculiar situational circumstances and because of differences in cultural legacies.

We can make the assertion that China's Gradualist model of change to a market economy has been a success whereas the Big Bang transition to a market economy chosen by CEEFSU has been less successful. To call it a failure would be incorrect because those countries have functioning market economies today; they just paid a heavy price for that privilege.

We can conclude that in Central and Eastern Europe, Poland is the most advanced country in terms of corporate governance practices. Similarly when comparing the corporate landscape in Russia with China, China can be considered to be ahead of Russia. Nevertheless much remains to be done in all these countries.

4 The Chinese perspective on corporate governance

1 Introduction

Chapter 2 studied the various models of corporate governance and came to the conclusion that a more suitable model of corporate governance for China is the Stakeholder model. It is considered more suitable because it is an all-inclusive model of governance which embraces the interests of various stakeholders including shareholders, directors, managers, employees, creditors, bankers and customers. It is more appropriate than the Shareholder Value model in the Chinese context, as the Shareholder Value model calls for the maximization of returns to the shareholder only.

The Chinese authorities, in drafting the Company Law and other legal statutes in the early 1990s, have chosen a model of corporate governance closer to the United States and UK Shareholder Value model than the European Stakeholder model. However, in my opinion the Chinese model contains elements of both and can be better described as a hybrid model of governance. An example of why I call it hybrid is the provision for the establishment of both a board of directors and a supervisory board to supervise the company's activities in the Chinese Company Law promulgated in 1994. (The supervisory board is characteristic of the German Stakeholder model of corporate governance.) Further, there was also provision for the establishment of a branch of the Chinese Communist Party (CCP) within the company. For these reasons I have described the model of corporate governance chosen by the Chinese authorities as being a 'hybrid' model.

Why did the Chinese authorities not adopt a corporate governance model based wholly and entirely on the Stakeholder model? The reasons may have as much to do with politics as they have to do with economics. What I mean by this statement is that, in the aftermath of the Tiananmen crackdown in 1989, economic activity and foreign direct investments remained slow. Foreign Direct Investment (FDI) amounted to US$3.5 billion in 1990, US$4.4 billion in 1991; US$11 billion in 1992 (Ministry of Commerce, PRC, www.mofcom.gov.cn). To counter the slowdown, Chinese authorities aggressively promoted economic reform and economic growth, establishing the Shanghai and Shenzhen Stock Exchanges in 1990/1991, the China Securities Regulatory Commission (CSRC) in 1992 and the Company Law in 1994. The Company Law was written with the objective of luring foreign investors and FDI into China and hence the US and UK model was chosen. One result was that FDI increased by 241 per cent between 1992 and 1995 from US$11 billion to US$37.5 billion. In Chapter 2 we mentioned that the UK and US model is best suited to mature economies with strong free market mechanisms, well established financial institutions, stable banking systems and an independent judiciary free of corruption. These are attributes that China did not have then.

There are arguments for China choosing to align its model of corporate governance closer to the UK and US model of corporate governance. History may provide some answers. In the early 1990s, the Berlin Wall had fallen, communism had collapsed in Eastern Europe and Russia and China were in economic limbo. Socialism and its central planning concepts were seen to be inferior to the free market forces and the corporate governance models of the United States and UK appeared superior to other models. That was why China chose a model of corporate governance that bore semblance to that of the United States and UK.

Scholars have written about models of corporate governance for China (Tam 2000a, 2000b; Hawes and Chiu 2006) and have questioned the applicability of the Shareholder Value model (Tam 2000b; Paredes 2005). In addition, Western-style corporate governance reforms may be unsuited in the Chinese context. These concerns appear vindicated as Chinese leaders have begun to stress that the right model of corporate governance for China was one 'with Chinese characteristics'. Zhou Xiaochuan, governor of the PBOC, in an address in 2005 stated clearly that China will not 'copy the international practices in corporate governance – as governance is closely related to a nation's culture. China should look towards a model of corporate governance with Chinese characteristics' (Zhou 2005). This view merely confirms my belief that the model of corporate governance that China has adopted may be best described as hybrid.

2 The history of corporate governance in China

Rudimentary Chinese corporate governance concepts and practices can be traced back to the late nineteenth century when joint stock banks were first established in Shanghai. However, when considering the history of corporate governance in China, 1949 is a convenient starting point for its analysis. Scholars broadly agree with the timelines discussed in Sections 2.1 to 2.4 below (Hu and Hu 2004; Schipani and Liu 2002).

2.1 The pre-reform stage (1949 to 1978)

In 1949, when the present government came into power, it inherited an economy in ruins, torn by decades of civil war and compounded by the Japanese invasion and occupation. With the help of the Soviets, it implemented the basic framework of a planned economy where the state was the owner of all factors of production and the state predetermined factory output. Commercial principles did not enter the economic equation and profit was certainly not a prescribed objective. Banks were 100 per cent owned by the state and acted merely as repository savings conduits for the population at large whose savings were channelled to the SOEs as disbursements to meet their production commitments. These cash disbursements by banks to the SOEs at that stage did not have to be repaid: they were just another factor of production and were not considered as loans.

There were no laws relating to the regulation of economic activities as existed in the capitalist countries. There was no Contract Law, Commercial Law and Securities Law. The fact is that there was no need. The state decided on what the production plans were for each business enterprise. Production inputs including labour, raw materials and bank credits were supplied by the state at state-controlled prices and products manufactured were sold at state-determined prices. The free market forces of supply and demand did not exist at all in China. The profits or losses arising from the economic transactions were absorbed by the state – there were no profit incentives for either managers or employees. It was the socialist maxim of 'from each his best, to each his needs'.

During this era there was basically no need for corporate governance. There was no private ownership and there were no business corporations. Yes, there were SOEs but they operated as an extension of the state. They were 100 per cent owned and controlled by the state. The state and the CCP were indivisible. In fact the local party secretary often wore two hats and served as the SOE chief.

2.2 The economic reform stage (1979–1992)

Deng Xiaoping is credited with the words 'it does not matter whether the cat is black or white so long as it catches mice'. With that adage he set China on the economic reform path in 1979. China wanted economic progress and development and it was obvious that the socialist model with its planned economy had been inferior to the capitalistic model. All over the world, countries that had adopted the planned economic models showed slower economic progress than those countries who had inherited or adopted market economies. The economic development of Japan and the East Asian tiger countries was also obvious and impressive.

The era of economic reform ushered in a period when the command economy and the beginnings of a market economy co-existed. It was a period of many innovations and experimentations whereby some of the tools of the free market were applied to prise open the strictures of the planned economy. Economists have described this period as 'walking on two legs' (one leg being socialist and the other being capitalist) and 'growing out of the Plan' (Naughton 1995).

The economic reform stage may be considered to have started in 1979 and extended to 1992. This was when China's reforms began in earnest with various strategies implemented including the contract system where business enterprises and peasant farmers were under contract to produce fixed quantities for the state and any excess produced by the enterprise or farmers would be shared amongst the workers. This was also the period when some SOEs were corporatized and others were listed on the stock exchanges which were established in 1990/1991.

During this period corporate governance was in its infancy as managers attempted to grapple with the demands of managing business enterprises free of the command economy and more attuned to the needs of a market economy. At this stage, however, the separation of ownership and control was not clear nor was any attention paid to the various theories of corporate governance and their applicability to China. During the reform stage, control of the business enterprises still rested mainly with the government. SOEs were initially registered according to the Enterprise Law which did not allow for boards of directors; the SOEs had general managers who were appointed by the government and they reported to the government. However this resulted in confusion, contradictions and corruption and the Chinese authorities realized that there had to be a separation of ownership and control. This led to the next stage of corporate governance with the large SOEs being gradually listed on the local stock exchanges. This was the beginning of corporate governance structures in that SOEs listed on the stock exchanges under the Company Law allowed for clear separation of ownership and control.

2.3 The transitional stage (1993–2002)

The decade from 1992–2002 was one of great change. The Company Law was promulgated in 1994 and it ushered in a new era of corporate governance. First of all, the government officially proclaimed its intention to develop China into a market economy (China's Company Law, Chapter 1, Clause 1) and that the SOEs were to be transformed into modern corporate enterprises.

The importance of corporate governance was underscored by the Asian Financial Crisis which reverberated around Asia in 1997/1998 when freely convertible currency countries with badly managed banks saddled with a high percentage of NPLs had their currencies savagely attacked by international speculators. According to the International Monetary Fund (IMF), the Asian financial crisis of 1997/1998 was caused by 'weaknesses in financial systems and, to a lesser extent, governance exacerbated by a combination of inadequate financial sector supervision, poor assessment and management of financial risk' (IMF Fact Sheet January 1999). The financial crisis that erupted in Asia in 1997/1998 led to sharp declines in the currencies, stock markets and other asset prices of a number of Asian countries including Thailand, Indonesia, Philippines, South Korea and Malaysia.

Under the Company Law passed in 1994 and amended in 2005, the rights, duties and responsibilities of shareholders, managers and directors were clearly laid out. Responsibility was transferred from the state to the directors and shareholders who were to be responsible for profits and losses and the operations of the company. However the Company Law had a proviso to allow the local committee of the CCP to have input into the management of the corporate entity and this provision appears to have retained vestigial influence for the CCP.

Under the transitional stage, control was thus clearly placed in the hands of the directors, who had to report to the shareholders during their shareholders' meetings. The model of corporate governance adhered to the Company Act which itself was based on the UK and US laws on companies. The financial accounting standards were also in the process of change with the Certified Accountants Law promulgated in 1993 and the Audit Law promulgated in 1994. The significance of these changes indicated the gradual transition away from the Enterprise Accounting Standards as practised in socialist China and the gradual adoption of International Accounting Standards (IAS). The Audit Law also provided for the audit of public companies and their role is extremely important. Auditors have to conduct interim and end of financial year audits where they investigate the company's finances. They also have to audit the financial accounts prepared by the company accountants and express an opinion on whether the financial accounts are 'true and fair' and whether proper accounting records have been kept and internal controls are adequate.

All these meant that auditors play a crucial role in ensuring that there is good corporate governance. They are in fact the first bulwark against fraud, corporate malfeasance and misappropriation. Thus the transitional stage was one where major reforms were made and steps undertaken to improve corporate governance in the corporate world.

2.4 The convergence stage (post-2002)

A historical perspective of the immediate post-2002 period showed much promise for positive change on the Chinese landscape. The economy had weathered the Asian Financial Crisis relatively well, although it was due to the fact that the Chinese currency and banking system was cordoned off from the rest of the world. The country had been granted admission to the WTO, although it had been on more onerous terms than other developing countries and foreign investors were beginning to invest in the Chinese economy again. This was evidenced by the strong inflows of FDI throughout the period (2002 US$55 billion, 2003 US$53.5 billion, 2004 US$60.6 billion, 2005 US$60.3 billion, 2006 US$70.4 billion (source: Ministry of Commerce PRC)). There had also been a smooth handover of power from Jiang Zemin to Hu Jintao in 2002 and this boded well for the economy.

Chinese scholars (Hu and Hu 2002) see the post-2002 period as the convergence stage where the Chinese model of governance is converging towards the international model of corporate governance and the model of corporate governance that it is trying to emulate is the Shareholder Value model (Lu 2004; Wang 2005; Hu 2005b). The Chinese government pronounced that 'large and medium state-owned enterprises must continue their reform to convert themselves into standard companies in compliance with the requirements of the modern enterprise system and improve their corporate governance' (Jiang 2002). This was the first time a senior government pronouncement had paid such explicit importance to corporate governance which added urgency to the matter.

The convergence period also saw many active steps taken to improve corporate governance. Round-table conferences were held in both Shanghai and

Beijing to discuss progress, implications and implementation of corporate governance in China. The CBRC was established in 2003 with a mandate to regulate all banks and to bring them closer to international best practices (Liu 2003). During this period, the CSRC, in response to critics that it was not doing enough to curb malfeasance and corporate mismanagement, promulgated the Code of Corporate Governance for Listed Companies in 2002. This is a very detailed document and it attempts to redress many weaknesses not covered in the Company Law of 1994 which was itself revised in 2005.

3 Chinese scholarship on corporate governance

This section looks at the Chinese perspective on corporate governance through the writings of several Chinese academics and scholars. This is necessary to get an understanding of how Chinese scholars view corporate governance. We need to understand why, after the economic reforms of the 1970s and the emergence of stock markets in the early 1990s, the Chinese corporate entities are still dogged by problems of corporate governance. First of all there is broad agreement that China's model of corporate governance, like the economy itself, is in transition. Like the economy which is in transition from planned to a market economy, the model of corporate governance practised is in transition: from a situation in the 1970s when there were no corporations and hence no corporate governance to the ideal model of corporate governance based on the United States and UK. Remembering that there are basically two models of governance practised in the Western democracies, the Shareholder Value model practised in the United States and UK and the Stakeholder model practised by France, Germany and Japan, which is the more appropriate model for China? Is the Stakeholder model not more appropriate? Hu and Hu (2004) agree that the Stakeholder model is indeed worthy of more study and that Chinese firms should not rush into copying the United States and UK model. It is interesting that Hu and Hu (2004) make the observation that corporate governance is about the control of corporations and that control (of a corporation) is determined not only by the internal power structure but by external forces as well. They proffer the view that China, being an economy in transition, practises a model of corporate governance which they call the evolution model – a model which, according to them, is evolving towards the Shareholder Value model practised by the United States and UK.

3.1 A Chinese perspective: evolution theory of corporate governance

Lu (2004) agrees with Hu and Hu (2004) that China is an economy in transition, and she suggests also that China is in transition to the UK and US model of corporate governance. My criticism of her view is that she does not mention what makes the Shareholder Value model successful in the United States and UK nor does she analyse whether similar conditions exist in China.

Both Hu and Hu and Lu consider that the evolution or transitional model of corporate governance is extant in China. Their writings identify major problems of corporate governance to revolve around the fact that the concentration of shareholding power results in insider control, abuse of minority shareholders and the appointment of incompetent directors. Further problems relate to the shortcomings of the legal system and brazen interference by government agencies.

Although Lu, Hu and Hu are leading academics on corporate governance in China, they do not come out explicitly with radical suggestions on how to overcome problems of corporate governance in China. Why are there shortcomings in the legal system and why is there misappropriation by controlling shareholders? Why are the directives from the CSRC not being followed? Is the answer more bureaucracy, more power to the bureaucrats? Should not there be calls for sweeping changes, for fundamental changes? It is possible that there is a degree of self-restraint in their writings, knowing what is possible and what is permissible.

Hu and Hu propose a bureaucratic response in terms of strengthening the supervisory and legal infrastructure. This is not new and, while recognizing the problem of conflict of interest between the state as a shareholder and the state as a stakeholder representing social interest, it does not suggest a solution. The issue of protecting the interests of minority shareholders is only addressed in the form of proclaiming positive intent to do so, but not in any meaningful way that could make a difference or lead to real change.

3.2 A Chinese perspective: corporate governance problems

Hu, director of the research department at the Shanghai Stock Exchange, has co-authored several articles on corporate governance in China (Opper *et al.* 2002; Wong *et al.* 2004) and is well aware of its problems. Like Hu and Hu and Lu in Section 3.1, he identifies the current problems of corporate governance in China's listed SOEs as revolving round the separation of ownership and control. We read earlier from Berle and Means (1932) that a feature of the modern corporation was the separation of ownership and control and this development has both advocates and detractors. This separation of ownership and control unfortunately has not quite happened in China and this omission has resulted in all kinds of governance problems. One of the more serious problems concerns the key person model: a favourite structure employed by the state to ensure influence and control. Other attendant problems relate to lack of information disclosure, low accountability, poor minority shareholder protection and a non-comprehensive legal framework.

In a paper on the corporate governance of China's listed SOEs, Hu (2005) enumerates the steps taken by the CSRC to improve corporate governance. The first was the enactment of the Code of Corporate Governance promulgated in 2002 applicable to all listed companies. The second was the tightening up of rules for information disclosure by listed entities requiring them to submit not only yearly reports but also half yearly and quarterly reports as well, with stronger penalties for non-compliance. The role of independent directors was also strengthened with at least one-third of the board to comprise independent directors; diversified share ownership was encouraged and rules for corporate control were more clearly laid out. The revised Company Law also provided for shareholders to sue directors and management where their interests have been damaged by directors or managers (Article 153 of the Revised Company Law 2005).

Although Hu was able to identify problems and state steps taken by the CSRC to combat them, he does not ask why they have not been successful. Could it be because the CSRC is under-resourced? Could it be because the CSRC bureaucracy is burdened with duties and responsibilities which it is unable to execute? Do the courts and the judiciary have some responsibility for the state of affairs in China? These are questions that Chinese academicians have not posed.

3.3 A Chinese perspective: the role of directors in China

In the Western free market economies, directors play a very important role in the corporate governance models. The majority of the board comprises independent directors and there are very strict criteria for selecting such directors. China however has widely different rules and norms for the selection of directors. Currently most of the directors are appointed by the state, which is the majority shareholder in most cases. Although it is required by the CSRC that one-third of their board members should be independent by December 2002, the fact remains that many have not complied and those that have are not generally perceived to be genuinely independent directors. There are simply not enough professionals and senior executives with expertise and experience to merit such descriptions, as many of the independent directors are ex-management who have connections to the listed company or who have business dealings with the listed entity.

Wang (2005) examines independent directors and the role they play in China. He traces the history and development of corporate governance in China and identifies problems that arise with majority ownership: major shareholders embezzle the assets of listed corporations. Major shareholders conduct non-arm's-length transactions detrimental to minority shareholders by selling valuable assets at below market prices or buying assets at inflated values. In order to better protect the rights of minority shareholders, the CSRC issued the 'Guide for Appointing Independent Directors in Listed Companies' in August 2001. This edict provided that as from December 2002 at least one-third of the board must be independent directors. Unfortunately the independent directors are often not really independent at all and are often mainly recruited by the listed companies themselves. They also tend to be former advisers to the companies and are usually elected because of their reputation and expertise.

By comparison the US National Association of Corporate Directors stipulates very strict conditions for independent directors. They must not have been employed by or affiliated with the company for the last five years; they must not be affiliated with a company that is an adviser in the last five years; they must not be affiliated with a significant customer or supplier to the company; they must not have personal services contracts with the company or the senior management of the company; they must not be affiliated with a company that receives significant contributions from the company; they must not have had any business relationship with the company in the last five years other than as a director; they must not be employed by a public company for which an executive officer of the company serves as director; they must not have had any of the relationships described above with an affiliate of the company and finally they must not be a member of the immediate family of any of the persons described above.

Wang examines how the role of independent directors evolved in the United States and UK and finds the concept of shareholder sovereignty to be the compelling difference between China and the United States and UK. In the United States and UK the shareholder sovereignty concept is paramount but over time it has evolved to embrace the Stakeholder theory where the company is still the shareholders' company but the interests of other stakeholders are also considered.

Wang points out that the theory and practice of independent directors arose from this school of thought as outside competing interests had to be considered. He investigates the record of directors and independent directors in China and comes to the conclusion that independent directors will not cure all the ills and problems associated with corporate governance in China. He suggests a closer look at the board of supervisors and to strengthen its powers and functions so that it actually supervises the board of directors as it was originally meant to do. He also suggests that the board of supervisors be strengthened so that decisions of the board of directors should be ratified by the board of supervisors before implementation.

Wang basically subscribes to the Shareholder Value model of corporate governance which places emphasis on the shareholders and their quest for values. While it is true that independent directors can and should play a more prominent role in the corporate governance of corporate enterprises in China, he does not explain why it has not happened and his suggestion that decisions of the board of directors be ratified by the board of supervisors is contentious.

4 Conclusion

This perspective of corporate governance has chosen the period from 1949 onwards when the PRC was founded. Since that date Chinese corporate governance developments may be conveniently divided into four sections:

1 pre-reform stage (1949–1978);
2 economic reform stage (1979–1991);
3 transitional stage (1992–2002);
4 convergence stage (post-2002).

We follow the changes in the corporate landscape as the economic model evolved from planned to market economy with its attendant panoply of laws, financial institutions and corporate governance models. In the pre-reform stage there was no need for corporate governance as there were no business corporations and there were no listed entities but as the economic system changed from planned to market economy, a basic framework gradually developed to meet the needs of the shareholders, managers and other stakeholders.

Corporate governance in China emerged as a key research area during the late 1990s as the listed entities on the Shanghai and Shenzhen stock exchanges began to show severe symptoms of corporate misgovernance. Former SOEs which had been weaned and listed on the stock exchanges continued with their old practices showing little regard for the principles of corporate governance that govern listed entities in world financial markets. The result was that the Chinese stock exchanges became speculative and volatile. Statistics indicate that the majority of shares are bought and sold within a year, indicating the short-term nature of investors.[1] Lack of transparency, information disclosure, insider trading, non-arm's-length transactions, oppression of minority shareholders were corporate governance problems faced. Corporate governance measures and directives were enacted as Chinese authorities realized that robust corporate governance was essential to a modern enterprise system.

China's Company Law is based on that of the United States and UK. China has also adopted a model of corporate governance based more on the Shareholder Value than the Stakeholder model. This is understandable given the dominance of the American economy in the 1990s compared to the European countries. My view is that China's model of corporate governance contains elements of both the UK and US model and the European model of governance and may be described as a hybrid model. However, it is now the responsibility of the Chinese government bodies like the CSRC and the CBRC to make it work. This means that there will be more changes, probably along the evolutionary path as stated by Hu and Lu. The reform of Chinese corporate governance will follow the gradualist path that Naughton outlined in his earlier writings by focusing on practical measures rather than on theoretical breakthroughs.

5 Chinese corporate governance problems encountered

1 Misconceptions about corporate governance

In Chapter 4, we traced the history of corporate governance as it gradually evolved from a situation where there was no necessity for governance to one where there was a growing need and the basic framework of corporate governance was developed to meet the framework of the market economy. Problems of corporate governance arose because of the rapidly changing economic environment. China throughout the reform period was in a state of flux, of constant and rapid change. What was applicable yesterday was no longer applicable tomorrow; what was the exception yesterday became the norm tomorrow and what were grey areas yesterday became prohibited areas tomorrow. Thus there was much confusion about what to do and what not to do, and directors and managers of listed corporations had to contend with new laws and new regulations which were being promulgated on a regular basis.

And yet there was a need for corporate governance because there was fraud, corruption and malfeasance. Such losses in the banking industry amounted to tens of millions of dollars. It is understandable if losses were due to inadvertent mistakes by management but these were blatantly corrupt acts by senior managers who seized the opportunities afforded by a lack of corporate governance mechanisms to defraud the banks towards whom they had a fiduciary duty.

The transition from planned to market economy resulted in a plethora of new regulations. Under the planned economy, the business enterprise and the state are one and the same entity. Factors of production and bank credits were freely transferred from one business enterprise to another. However during the transition stage to a market economy everything (except the management of the business entities) changed. The business enterprise became corporatized, some were even listed on the stock exchanges and managers and directors had to learn a whole new set of rules. Transfers of assets and transfers of factors of production between related entities at non-commercial values which once were the norm became prohibited. And yet it continued because old habits die hard and the soft budget constraint (Kornai 1986, 1998; Kornai *et al.* 2002) continued to be in force.

Misconceptions also existed about the practice of corporate governance. The term corporate governance is written in Chinese as 公司 治理, which literally translates as 'Company Control'. Hence to the Chinese managers the initial perception was that corporate governance was all about the control of companies. Another misinterpretation was that it was about management styles – whether the CEO was a 'Key Person' manager (a dynamic leader who pounds the table during board meetings) or a 'Team Player' (someone who believes in teamwork and consults colleagues). This is entirely wrong of course and we read in Chapter 2 the OECD definition that corporate governance is 'the set of relationships between a company's management, its board, its shareholders and other stakeholders, providing the structure through which the company's objectives are set, the means of attaining these objectives and monitoring mechanisms are determined'. It took time for CEOs to realize and understand the correct perspective of corporate governance. This was helped by the regulatory bodies like the CSRC and the CBRC which expanded their supervision over the years; the media which highlighted the governance issues; and the judicial courts which became increasingly involved in corporate governance litigations pertaining to shareholder rights (Lin *et al.* 2009).

2 Problems of governance at the micro level

Corporate governance problems encountered in China may have their origins traced to two sources: at the micro level and at the macro level. At the micro level, corporate governance problems arise from the interplay of rights, duties and responsibilities between individuals and entities acting in their capacity as shareholders, CEOs, directors, managers and employees. The following section studies the micro-level governance problems.

2.1 Shareholding structure: ownership and control

The shareholding structure in any corporation impacts upon its management style and modus operandi. Where the ownership largely comprises diversified small shareholders, it allows for the entry of professional managers who will manage the corporation according to the Shareholder Value or the Stakeholder model of corporate governance. There is thus separation of ownership and control and this feature is an essential structure of large Western corporations; but this has not happened in China.

The state, directly or indirectly, owns the majority shareholdings of SOEs including the CCBs. They are the controlling shareholders and as controlling shareholders they execute actions either through the directors and/or the management which are often detrimental to minority shareholders. The prevalent view is that in China controlling shareholders wield too much power (Kenyon 2005; Yang 2007). One consequence is that misappropriation of funds by the controlling shareholders is a common occurrence in China and this extends to both bank and non-bank entities and amongst both listed and unlisted entities. In China the CBRC found that speculation in share dealings typically account for a substantial portion of the misappropriation that beset the banking sector.

It has been suggested that limits be placed on state ownership of CCBs. This process of divestment of state ownership has already started and in those CCBs with foreign strategic partners, the state shareholding in some cases is less than 30 per cent. An example is the Bank of Ningbo where the state shareholding as at 31 December 2008 was 17.96 per cent (see Table 10.11) and the Bank of Nanjing where the state shareholding as at 31 December 2008 was 24.2 per cent (see Table 10.9).

Boards of directors in free market economies normally have the majority of the board as independent directors – independent in every sense of the term with no connections to the ownership of the corporate entity. In China the majority shareholdings of listed entities are owned by the state or SOEs and because of this shareholding power, they appoint most of the directors (Tenev and Zhang 2002). This holds true for most of the banks as well as those CCBs with foreign strategic shareholders. The foreign strategic banking partners would normally only appoint one or at most two board members. Thus at the board level we have the board composition being an issue that is responsible for many corporate governance problems. Under the code of corporate governance promulgated in 2002 for listed entities, one-third of the board was to comprise independent directors and, while this is a good start, many of these directors appointed are not really independent at all and do have some connections to state ownership or to the bank chairman or CEO. Although research has not found a strong relationship between the presence of independent directors and corporate performance (Clarke 2006), the CSRC issued a directive on the Role of the Independent Director in Listed Companies (2001).

The board is the most important structure governing the corporation and hence all matters pertaining to the activities of the board must be correctly handled. This means that all board meetings must be properly recorded, minutes circulated and signed off, and proper notifications sent out. This is important so that a proper audit trail can be established confirming how important decisions are made bearing in mind that such decisions can be costly. When we keep in mind that CCBs were originally Urban Credit Cooperatives, we can understand if the procedural matters at the board level of the CCBs were initially skimpy at best and totally lacking at worst. In the majority of cases, procedures were extremely lacking by Western standards. There were no planned quarterly board meetings – these were usually called on an ad hoc basis with 24–48 hours' notice being given. Board papers and minutes were not circulated in advance and the board minutes merely comprised details of resolutions passed with no details being recorded of the discussions that preceded the resolution being voted on. These failings resulted in directors being unable to discharge their duties properly.

2.2 Abuse of minority shareholders

The Company Law of 1994 was initially designed to facilitate the business enterprises of the state and thus did not contain sufficient safeguards for the minority shareholders (Tang 2008). Initially, minority shareholders were undoubtedly abused as controlling shareholders condoned non-arm's-length transactions described by some as 'tunneling' (Johnson *et al.* 2000). However, with the explosion in stock ownership in the early years of the twenty-first century and the constant abuse of minority shareholders, Chinese authorities recognized the need to redress the situation and this was remedied under Article 2 of the Code of Corporate Governance (2002) which stated that minority shareholders are to enjoy equal rights as other shareholders and Article 4 gives them the right to protect their interests through legal action. Previously, aggrieved individual shareholders were slow to take legal action against errant listed companies as it is a prolonged and costly process with uncertain outcomes. However, these legal changes have resulted in minority investors being more willing to initiate legal action because of (1) the higher degree of commonality among interested parties and (2) immediately measurable and tangible damages (Chen 2003). These two characteristics not only allow investors to identify with each other more easily, but also create a basis for more debate in the media, which in turn promotes the development of a legal culture.

However in China's revised Company Law (2005), there is no regulation on indemnity for the plaintiff shareholders. Nevertheless, some local courts have recognized the necessity of such indemnity and have allowed it. For instance, the High People's Court of Jiangsu Province provides three alternatives for the reimbursement of expenses:

1 prevailing shareholders should be reimbursed by the company for reasonable litigation fees such as lawyers' fees and travel costs;
2 if the court does not support the legal claims, the litigation costs should be paid by the plaintiff shareholders;
3 if the court partly support the claims, the plaintiff shareholder and the company should bear the cost pro rata.

The Shanghai High People's Court also promulgates guidelines where it can decide that the benefiting company should pay a reasonable indemnity to the plaintiff shareholder (X. Huang 2009).

An example of legal action taken was when defrauded shareholders took action against Guangdong Kelon Electrical Appliance Co. Ltd (a local listed company) and Deloitte Touche Tohmatsu (an international firm of accountants) which gave an unreserved opinion on its financial reports. The company had been submitting false accounting reports for the period 2000–2002 and had been fined by the CSRC for grossly overstating profits. The Guangzhou court found both the company and the chairman guilty and liable.

2.3 Management and employees

Management theory places a clear division of duties between the board and management with the board in charge of policies and the management responsible for executing them. The senior management of banks is appointed by the state who is the controlling shareholder and they take orders from and make corporate decisions to favour the state. Corporate governance structures are often viewed by management as an obstacle to be put in place only when the entity is about to get listed. However, good corporate governance levels are associated with good earnings management (Liu and Lu 2007) and good corporate governance supports firm performance and market valuation (Bai *et al.* 2004). That is why the International Finance Corporation has called on SOEs to establish sound governance mechanisms early.

Skills and experience of management are an indication of the degree of professionalism and studies by Tenev and Zhang (2002) indicated that about 60 per cent of directors of listed companies have a graduate or higher degree. According to a survey carried out by the Centre for Financial Market Integrity (China Corporate Governance Survey 2007) the 'skills & experience of management has improved somewhat over the previous 3 years'. This bodes well for the future development of corporate governance. Nevertheless there are still shortcomings. Management often pay lip service and set up the various management committees in accordance with the Code of Corporate Governance but these management committees exist on paper and often do not meet or carry out the duties expected of them.

Employees play a key role in the success of a corporation and the structures and mechanisms of corporate governance should recognize this fact (Lower 2009). This can be done by having employee representation on key boards and committees, namely pensions, benefits and human resource committees. This is not currently the norm but Chinese Company Law tries to address this issue by legislating for the board of supervisors to have at least one-third of its representation from employees. In addition employees should be rewarded adequately according to industry standards. In the twenty-first century, knowledge-based industries and intellectual property are increasingly important which means that employees are crucial to a company's success. This paradigm shift must be reflected in the corporate governance of companies.

2.4 Ethical standards

Business ethics face an array of daunting challenges in China and most observers agree on an urgent need to address these ethical challenges. Some perceive China as an example of a country where management has failed the test of ethics (Chen and Chen 2005; Pedersen 2006). Shi and Weisert (2002) write about 'Enron-like' cases in China. An example widely reported is the case in 2008 involving the management of the Sanlu Milk Company where melamine, an industrial chemical, was knowingly added to milk 'to increase its protein content'. The tainted milk products were subsequently sold in the marketplace causing severe kidney problems to thousands of babies and infants. The culprits have since been given the death sentence and the company liquidated.

Ethics are part and parcel of corporate governance and the ethical standards of a people play an integral role in the execution of governance practices. One view holds that elements of Chinese culture tend to encourage unethical business decisions (Jing *et al.* 2007). Yet another more accurate perspective is that China has ethical issues in business because of transformational and transitional changes (Hulpke and Lau 2008). The changing rules of the economic model create business ethical problems and the large amount of new wealth creates incentives to cut corners to get rich.

Confucius (551–479 BC) has been the most powerful influence shaping Chinese culture and Chinese society. He emphasized benevolence, goodness and humaneness. Confucian teachings also place a high priority on hierarchy, where the senior makes the decision, while the junior follows instructions. This happens in both private and government organizations. However, it has a disastrous effect on corporate governance as opportunistic CEOs and government officials overstep their authority and take advantage of their powers. Within the framework of 'Confucian values', the subordinates would keep silent and be disinclined to reveal such misconduct to the higher levels because most believe that their career will be severely affected if they do so.

Confucian philosophy presupposes that the life of each individual is only a link in that person's family lineage and that each individual is a continuation of his or her ancestors. This is the main reason why Chinese officials are often involved in corruption together with their families. Moreover, the transfer of illegal wealth by corrupt officials to their distant relatives makes punitive claims extremely difficult. Lu (1997) and Rarick (2008) both write about the pervasive influence of Confucianism in business ethics in China.

Other factors impacting on business practices are Marxist philosophy; the impact of the economic reforms; and the influence of business practices from abroad. While traditional Chinese values were strongly influenced by Confucianism, after 1949, Marxist theory and philosophy gained prominence. Marxist theory does not denigrate good business ethics, but its denunciation of religion as being the 'opiate of the masses' (Marx 1843) coupled with various state-orchestrated campaigns critical of traditional Chinese values resulted in a rejection of the moral teachings that religions represented.

When economic reforms began in 1979, Deng Xiaoping declared that 'to be rich is glorious'. This slogan stirred the Chinese population enormously and they were happy to take up the challenge. Being rich during the days of the Cultural Revolution meant being a 'capitalist' and a fate worse than death awaited them. However everything has changed since then. The road to riches for the Chinese was aided by overseas investors who brought along not only capital and expertise but also their own business practices.

To blame the overseas investors for the current lack of business ethics in China would be totally wrong but fierce competition for Chinese contracts did result in corrupt practices from overseas investors. It was reported in 2008 that Siemens, Europe's largest engineering company, would be shut out from World Bank financed projects for two years and the company agreed to pay US$100 million to support anti-corruption work. Siemens had also agreed to pay total fines and penalties of US$1.4 billion in Germany and the United States for bribing officials in several countries including China. Between 2001 and 2007, the company bribed government officials in return for business around the world. For instance, Siemens paid approximately US$22 million to business consultants who used some portion of those funds to bribe officials in connection with seven projects for the construction of metro trains and signalling devices in China. The company also paid approximately US$25 million in bribes for high voltage transmission lines in South China and approximately US$14.4 million in bribes for medical equipment in that same country. Poor business ethics is a severe problem that has spread throughout China and it must be addressed quickly. Good corporate governance is part of the solution.

3 Problems of governance at the macro level

Conventional theory indicates that corporate governance at the macro level impacts heavily on the economies of emerging markets (Adeoye 2009) and yet in spite of the general acknowledgement that China lacked good corporate governance at the macro level, it continued to attract strong and increasing FDI over the decade from 1993 to 2003 (Fan *et al.* 2007). The answer perhaps lies in the fact that China developed a set of transitional institutions that were able to meet the needs of a transitional economy and while it did not possess strong private ownership and a comprehensive legal system to protect shareholders' rights, it possessed them in sufficient quantity to reassure foreign investors that the situation would improve. However, let us examine the institutions that impact on corporate governance at a macro level and analyse them in the context of China, comparing them with four other countries in Asia. It will be seen that China lags far behind Japan, South Korea, Singapore and Taiwan but it must be remembered that China is both a transitional economy and a developing country as well. The other four countries are clearly not transitional economies. That goes a long way to explaining the differences in scores.

3.1 Voice and accountability

Accountability in any economic system depends on transparency and acceptance of the notion that all (including political leaders, state and political party) are subject to the rule of law and that none is above the law. A free press is necessary in order that transgressions are publicized. In the free market economies, such practices are not only theorized but also practised; hence the impeachments of Presidents Nixon and Clinton in the United States and a jail sentence for the former President of Taiwan Chen Sui Bian. In China, transgressions by CCP officials tend to be subject to the Disciplinary Committee of the CCP and the lack of a free press hinders transparency.

In China, there is also a lack of corporate accountability. Senior management and executive directors are appointed by the largest shareholder – the state – and they report to the state (Tenev and Zhang 2002). However, these political appointees are rarely held accountable for their performance as the appointments are made by bureaucrats who do not have the objective of profit maximization (Clarke 2003). The management's accountability is not to all shareholders per se, but purely to the controlling shareholder. Thus there is no equitable treatment of minority shareholders. One result is that a majority of the investors in the stock exchanges are speculators and not long-term investors. China's two stock exchanges had a total of 70 million investor accounts of whom over 95 per cent were individuals and investors' shareholdings were held on average less than six months (CSRC 2004 Annual Report).

The Company Law came into effect in 1994 and it was based on the UK and US model – it is a document with corporate governance mechanisms in place and allocates rights, duties and responsibilities to the directors, managers and shareholders. These were further enhanced in the 2005 amendments to the Company Law. The accountability factor in theory is there but in practice it is lacking.

Table 5.1 shows the results of a World Bank survey into the voice and accountability factor for China compared to four other Asian countries, namely Taiwan, South Korea, Singapore and Japan. It shows that China lags far behind. There have been recent moves, however, to improve voice and accountability in China with investigative journalism becoming more commonplace now. With a growing middle class, China, like other developing countries, has an increasingly inquisitive press, electronic media and calls for transparency are often heard. The increasing adoption of Western business models in China has also resulted in corporate governance playing an important role in abetting and improving voice and accountability. Calls for accountability are more common now and Li (2002) writes that unless accountability is implemented and practised, it will be difficult to have effective corporate governance.

A somewhat different view is proposed by Jacobson who wrote 'Speech & Harmony: An Experiment'. He writes about why 'voice' and the 'press' are often viewed differently in China (2010). The people desire freedom of speech but also want civility and respect. This is best exemplified in the Confucian ideal

Table 5.1 Voice and accountability

Governance indicator	*Year*	*China percentile rank (0–100)*	*Taiwan percentile rank (0–100)*	*South Korea percentile rank (0–100)*	*Japan percentile rank (0–100)*	*Singapore percentile rank (0–100)*
Voice and accountability	2007	6	68	67	75	35
	2006	6	69	67	76	36
	2005	7	77	72	80	51
	2004	7	77	71	82	49
	2003	8	76	69	77	48

Source: adapted from Kaufmann *et al.* (2008).

of harmony, a cultural tradition which is very real among average Chinese citizens, including scholars, and implies, among other things, civility and respect. And that is why the Western concepts and indices of voice and accountability cannot be applied *in toto* to China.

3.2 Government effectiveness

Government effectiveness in the free market economies is based on the practice of meritocracy, equal opportunity employment laws and a level playing field to ensure that the best and most deserving get promoted. In China, promotion is based more on the length of membership of the CCP. This does not result in efficient government administration although steps are being taken to redress the situation. For example, the State Assets Supervision and Administration Commission (SASAC), the government body that manages and directs China's SOEs has embarked on several rounds of large-scale global recruitment for senior managers of SOEs.

The effectiveness of government impacts on corporate governance. When it can take up to three months for a business to be registered and lengthier times to get various permits the effectiveness of the Chinese government is called into question.[1] In comparison Singapore claims that foreign businesses can start up in a week if not sooner. Singapore also scores 100 per cent on government effectiveness in this survey. And yet businesses continue to be attracted to China as provincial governments scramble over one another to attract new investments into their locality promising to expedite applications and approvals. One of the reasons, perhaps, lies in *guanxi* (for details please refer to Chapter 6, Section 5) and provincial authorities promise the earth to entice new investors. But there is a catch to all this as such practices lend themselves to rent-seeking activities and point to weak institutions.

Table 5.2 shows that China passes the test of government effectiveness, scoring 61 per cent in 2007. This is a respectable credit and is due to the

Table 5.2 Government effectiveness

Governance indicator	*Year*	*China percentile rank (0–100)*	*Taiwan percentile rank (0–100)*	*South Korea percentile rank (0–100)*	*Japan percentile rank (0–100)*	*Singapore percentile rank (0–100)*
Government effectiveness	2007	61	82	86	89	100
	2006	58	83	85	90	100
	2005	56	85	79	85	100
	2004	57	88	79	85	99
	2003	57	84	79	85	99

Source: adapted from Kaufmann *et al.* (2008).

entrenched power of the bureaucracy. When there are goals and objectives to be achieved, the Chinese bureaucracy responds quickly and effectively in spite of limitations.

3.3 Regulatory framework

The main regulatory body for banks is the CBRC which was only established in 2003. Prior to that, regulatory functions were carried out by the PBOC. For listed entities, the CSRC is the main regulating body. One of the criticisms of the CSRC is that it performs the dual functions of approval and regulation including delisting which are contradictory in character. In the United States and UK the listing procedure is a market driven process and the regulatory work is separate. In the United States, the Securities Exchange Commission (SEC) supervises the stock markets and in the UK similar work is done by the Financial Services Authority (FSA). Another criticism of the CSRC is that it is burdened by conflicting policy missions (Heilmann 2002) who wrote that the CSRC's first and foremost mission is dedicated to market growth and only to a lesser degree to the enforcement of strict regulatory standards. Jia (2009) identifies the regulatory bodies in China as one of the main external 'stakeholders' impacting on corporate governance in China's CCBs.

Table 5.3 shows that China's regulatory framework has improved its performance over the years although it is far behind Singapore. It must be borne in mind though that the CBRC was established in 2003 and has substantially increased staff numbers to 23,345 in December 2008, establishing training centres in Beidaihe, Shenyang, Sunde and Wuhu (CBRC 2008 Annual Report).

In China the CSRC has taken enforcement actions but much remains to be done.[2] Alan Cameron, the former Head of the Australian Securities Investment Commission (ASIC – which is the Australian equivalent of the CSRC) at the 2nd International Round-table Conference on Securities Markets in China in June 2002 made the observation that the best way to ensure good corporate

Table 5.3 Regulatory quality

Governance indicator	*Year*	*China percentile rank (0–100)*	*Taiwan percentile rank (0–100)*	*South Korea percentile rank (0–100)*	*Japan percentile rank (0–100)*	*Singapore percentile rank (0–100)*
Regulatory quality	2007	46	80	79	83	99
	2006	42	78	71	86	98
	2005	46	80	73	86	100
	2004	44	83	75	82	99
	2003	39	78	72	79	99

Source: adapted from Kaufmann *et al.* (2008).

governance was to ensure strong enforcement measures. This view on enforcement is echoed by Kim Yongboem, Senior Economist at the World Bank who wrote that 'fair and prompt enforcement without favoritism is vital since drafting laws and regulations will not in itself produce an honest and fair market' (Kim *et al.* 2003).

For more details on regulatory bodies in China, please refer to Chapter 6, Sections 2 and 3.

3.4 Rule of law

There is much debate about the legal framework in China: what kind of system does it practice and how does it compare with Western democracies? To understand the legal framework in China, we refer to Chen (2003) who explains the legal tradition of China; how it existed over the last 2,000 years as an extension of the legislative and still does to this day. According to La Porta *et al.*, the legal system is of paramount importance in determining the breadth and depth of capital markets, with the implication that for capital markets to progress, they need to evolve means of protecting shareholders and private ownership (La Porta *et al.* 1997, 2000a). The implication here is that rule of law is essential for economic systems to progress. So the question we ask is: does China possess the rule of law? According to Peerenboom, China does enjoy a form of rule of law – a thin rule of law (Peerenboom 2002). However, it does not enjoy the rule of law as construed and understood in the Western democracies. China's rule of law is certainly different from Westminster's version. However, the CCP in drafting the State Constitution in 1982 committed the state and the party to the basic principles of rule of law; that all must abide by the law and that none is above the law. This concept was further strengthened in March 1999 when the constitution was amended to incorporate the new policy formulation of 'to govern the country in accordance with law and to establish a socialist rule of law state' [依法治国, 建设社会主义法治国].

Generally speaking the presence of strong property rights is an indication of strong rule of law and this is an area that has shown improvement in China. For example Shanghai in the mid 1980s granted only 30-year leasehold lands for the construction of hotels but by the mid 1990s was prepared to lease land on 70-year leasehold tenure (the Mandarin hotel in Shanghai was built on a 30-year lease in 1988 and later CapitaLand's property projects in Shanghai were granted 70-year leasehold in 1997).[3] Freehold land ownership is not available as all land belongs to the state. A new Property Rights law was also enacted in March 2007 where the individual's right to property ownership was recognized and commits China further to the market economy (Allens Arthur Robinson Report 2007). According to Cohen (2010), the most formidable challenge to China's establishment of a credible rule of law is neither the quality of its legislation nor the professional competence of its judges, prosecutors, lawyers and police. The real challenge to the administration of justice in China is, rather, the intrusion of politics and, even more broadly, of *guanxi*, the network of interpersonal relationships.

Table 5.4 Rule of law

Governance indicator	*Year*	*China percentile rank (0–100)*	*Taiwan percentile rank (0–100)*	*South Korea percentile rank (0–100)*	*Japan percentile rank (0–100)*	*Singapore percentile rank (0–100)*
Rule of law	2007	42	70	75	90	95
	2006	44	70	69	90	94
	2005	43	79	75	90	96
	2004	43	76	71	89	96
	2003	41	77	68	90	93

Source: adapted from Kaufmann *et al.* (2008).

According to the World Bank survey conducted by Kaufmann *et al.*, China scores poorly in the rule of law index and is way behind the four Asian countries on the table. However, as pointed out by Peerenboom, China is a developing country and should not be measured by the same yardstick as developed countries. Research shows that there is a dualist regime in the application of the rule of law with different bodies of laws and regulations applying to Foreign Invested Enterprises (FIEs) from those that apply to domestic firms. In general, the legal and regulatory treatments of FIEs are superior to those that pertain to domestic firms, especially domestic private firms (Huang 2003). In addition, CCP members appear to be treated more leniently. Critics argue that the CCP must be tougher on its errant members who are responsible for much of the fraud and corruption. Statistics show that of the 170,000 Communist Party members disciplined for wrongdoing in 2004, barely 3 per cent of those disciplined were prosecuted. Of the corrupt officials convicted in 2003–2005, 52 per cent received suspended sentences and served no jail time (Pei 2006). As Feng (2009) wrote: 'much deeper reforms to the legal structure are needed – such as introducing a truly independent judiciary and removing the influence of the Communist Party over the appointment and discharge of judges and lawyers.'

3.5 Control of corruption

Corruption impacts at both the micro- and macro-economic levels: at the micro level by adding on a layer of transaction costs and at the macro level by deterring new investments and thus impeding economic growth. It is an insidious practice which has threatened the very existence of the CCP: after all, the Tiananmen crackdown in 1989 was triggered by widespread disaffection with perceived rampant corruption. Corruption is a common occurrence in China and often occurs when licences or permits are applied for or approved.

What are the causes of corruption? Are the Chinese as a people more corrupt than others or is the system to be held accountable? China is evaluated by Standard & Poor's to be in the same category as Brazil and India. It fares better than many countries including Russia but scores lower than the developed economies. We studied the issue of business ethics in Section 2.4 of this chapter and concluded that there were a host of reasons, the most important of which are the fact that it is a transitional economy, because of the generally low per capita income and that temptations are many. Corrupt practices are further exacerbated by the Chinese traditions of *guanxi* and *renqing*. These two practices are considered in detail in Chapter 6, Section 5.

In the Western democracies, authorities fight corruption with a combination of transparency, an independent judiciary, an unfettered press and strict enforcement of the legal penalties for those convicted on corruption charges. These ingredients exist in China only in prescribed dosages. Table 5.5 shows an inability by authorities to reduce corruption in China with the Control of Corruption Index falling from 43 per cent in 2003 to 31 per cent in 2007 compared with Singapore's 96 per cent. Recent media reports indicate authorities meting out death penalties and stiff jail sentences for bribery and corruption. In another action to deter corruption the Chinese government recently unveiled a database of names of all companies and individuals convicted of bribe giving since 1997.

Powerful bureaucrats who have been prosecuted include Chen Liangyu, former Communist Party secretary of Shanghai and then member of China's powerful Politburo; Xu Zongheng, former mayor of Shenzhen and China's former richest tycoon, Huang Guangyu, founder of the electronics retailer Guomei.

Large multinational companies operating in China must beware as even Rio Tinto, the global mining giant, has found that its employees are not immune from prosecution. Stern Hu, a senior Rio Tinto employee, was sentenced to ten years' imprisonment for bribery. The Chinese government is increasingly clamping down on the corrupt activities of foreigners as a warning to local officials.

Table 5.5 Control of corruption

Governance indicator	*Year*	*China percentile rank (0–100)*	*Taiwan percentile rank (0–100)*	*South Korea percentile rank (0–100)*	*Japan percentile rank (0–100)*	*Singapore percentile rank (0–100)*
Control of corruption	2007	31	70	68	85	96
	2006	35	72	65	90	97
	2005	31	73	69	85	98
	2004	33	76	64	86	98
	2003	43	74	65	85	99

Source: adapted from Kaufmann *et al.* (2008).

4 Results of lack of corporate governance

One of the results of the lack of corporate governance is the concentration of wealth amongst a few who then manipulate the capital resources of the economic system through the use of pyramidal structures (Fan *et al.* 2005; Morck *et al.* 2005) to control more corporations. This can skew the allocation of resources as more resources are made available to the pyramidal group of companies. Morck *et al.* call this 'Economic Entrenchment' (2005). This economic entrenchment has obviously happened in Russia where in the transition to a free market economy, an oligopoly has emerged, gathering enormous wealth and becoming economically entrenched (Reardon 2004). What happened in Russia did not happen in China because the SOEs were not privatized but corporatized. Nevertheless there has been misallocation of resources as these SOEs and their affiliated entities have gained access to financial resources which others more deserving have been deprived of.

A more debilitating effect of lack of corporate governance is the presence of high NPLs. NPLs in commercial banks should generally be kept well below 5 per cent but during the early years of the twenty-first century, NPLs in Chinese banks were well in excess of 5 per cent (see Table 5.6). High NPLs in Chinese banks were due to all those problems mentioned in earlier sections of this chapter; they resulted from the confluence of both micro- and macro-level inadequacies of corporate governance. Micro-level governance inadequacies manifested themselves in poor lending policies and a lack of internal controls and poor risk expertise (Guo 2007). Coupled with this was the fact that the large banks (SOCBs) had a preferred bias to lend to SOEs. Lu *et al.* (2005) use a set of data of publicly listed companies in China to empirically explore the relationship between banks' lending behaviour and NPLs. Their research showed that listed SOEs got more loans than other firms; other things being equal, SOEs with high default risks were able to borrow more than others. This suggests that Chinese banks have a systemic lending bias in favour of SOEs. The causes are socio-political. Chinese SOEs are noted for their low productivity and high employment numbers. This is due to the need to maintain high employment (20 million enter the workforce every year) and with the private

Table 5.6 NPLs of China's total commercial banks (including CCBs)

Year	*Amount (RMB 100 millions)*	*% loans outstanding*
2008	5,635.4	1.76
2007	12,701.9	4.57
2006	11,703	4.91
2005	12,197	5.90
2004	17,176	9.11
2003	21,045	12.40
2002	22,793	23.50

Source: adapted from CBRC Annual Reports (2002–2008).

sector economy being profit-oriented, only the SOEs can take up the additional burden of providing employment. Furthermore SOEs that are making losses still continue to be given loans by state-owned banks as authorities fear the spectacle of large numbers of unemployed and retrenched staff who may create social unrest.

NPLs in the banking sector in China have been reduced substantially in recent years and, as Brandt and Zhu (2007) note, this came about through a combination of transferring out NPLs into Asset Management Companies (AMCs) and the injection of substantial new capital into the SOCBs in the form of cash and government backed debt securities. Thus Table 5.6 shows the steady decline of NPLs in the banking sector over the years.

Table 5.7 shows a detailed analysis of NPLs of various sectors of the banking industry as they strove to reduce their NPLs. The progress made was due to the combination of injection of government funds, of strong regulatory actions by the CBRC, and through adoption of governance standards by the banks themselves. NPLs of the various banking sectors in China for the years ended 31 December 2002 through to 2008 showed a steady decline. For the CCBs, the NPLs dropped from 4.78 per cent in 2006 to 2.3 per cent in 2008 while for the Rural Commercial Banks, the NPLs dropped from 5.90 per cent to 3.9 per cent. Foreign banks had the lowest NPLs and their ratio was 0.78 per cent in 2006 and 0.8 per cent in 2008. The NPLs of the various categories of financial institutions are shown in the Table 5.7.

Boudriga *et al.* (2009) wrote that to reduce NPLs, the effective way is through enhancing the legal system, strengthening institutions and increasing transparency, rather than focusing only on regulatory and supervisory issues. This study provides an interesting perspective as with the recent Global Financial Crisis, there is a danger of NPLs arising again. A report that Chinese banks have started using trust companies to shift loans off balance sheets of banks has raised some concern among analysts.

Table 5.7 Detailed analysis of NPLs of banking institutions in China

Type of financial institution	*% of NPL 31 December 2006*	*% of NPL 31 December 2007*	*% of NPL 31 December 2008*
State-Owned Commercial Banks (SOCBs)	9.22	8.0	2.8
Joint Stock Commercial Banks (JSCBs)	2.81	2.1	1.3
City Commercial Banks (CCBs)	4.78	3.0	2.3
Rural Commercial Banks (RCBs)	5.90	4.0	3.9
Foreign Banks (FBs)	0.78	0.5	0.8

Source: adapted from CBRC Annual Reports (2006–2008: Appendices).

5 Conclusion

The problems of corporate governance are many and relate to conflicts arising from ownership and control, abuse of shareholding power and a lack of business ethics. At the micro level they can be traced to the relationships affecting rights, duties and responsibilities between shareholders, managers, employees and at the macro level to institutional determinants like government effectiveness, regulatory framework, a weak judiciary and corruption. Much of the problems of governance arose because of the transition from planned to market economy with its many attendant changes.

China has weak institutions as shown by the World Bank Survey on Governance Indicators and yet China has managed consistently high economic growth over the last three decades. As Qian (2000) observes, the main lesson learned is that considerable growth is possible with sensible but not perfect institutions, and that some unconventional transitional institutions can be more effective than best practice institutions for a limited period of time.

As pointed out by various academics, Chinese values also differ from Western practices. When evaluating Voice & Accountability, one must remember that the Chinese practice is to avoid 'washing dirty linen in public' that the Western media often do when discovering misdemeanour or corruption, preferring instead the civility and respect that comes with a harmonious society. However, in fighting corruption, China has shown determination and handed out death sentences to several high officials and compiled a national database of bribe givers. The database is open to the public and reinforces the view that bribe donors have some responsibility for the problem. When considering the rule of law, as Peerenboom (2002) has pointed out, China has a 'thin rule of law' which compares favourably with other developing countries and should not be put in the same basket as the developed economies. However, we also learn from Cohen (2010) that the greatest challenge to China establishing a credible rule of law comes from the intrusion of politics and *guanxi*. Thus the evidence is clear. China must do more to strengthen its institutions at the macro level and the structures and mechanisms at the micro level so that the economic system in China can function more efficiently.

Although the term corporate governance insinuates a reference to corporations only, the reality is that it also applies to all organizations large and small, and equally to both government and private sector organizations. In addition to the corporate entities, it also applies to clubs, associations, societies, charities, professional firms, NGOs, etc. When there is full and proper practice of corporate governance by all the participants in the economic system, there is little corruption, proper accountability, strong rule of law, and all this helps in the efficient allocation of economic resources. This book does not research them, but my point is that all segments of society, all players in the economic society, must practice good governance, otherwise there will be disconnects and a breakdown in the practice of good corporate governance.

6 External determinants of corporate governance

1 Introduction

In this chapter we investigate the external determinants of corporate governance in China. Whereas in Chapter 5 we considered the problems of corporate governance from a micro and macro point of view, in this chapter we specifically consider the role of regulatory bodies which impact on corporate governance. We read in Standard & Poor's (2008) that China has made 'enormous strides in company transparency over the past decade thanks to government and regulatory policies' and here we analyse what was done. We study the role of two regulatory bodies, namely the CBRC and CSRC. As its name implies, the CBRC regulates all banks in China and the CSRC supervises all securities and listed companies. We also examine the Code of Corporate Governance, the rules for listing on the Shanghai Stock Exchange and how they impacted on the corporate governance of Chinese banks. Business networks are also considered for their impact on corporate governance and finally we consider the role of the CCP.

2 The China Banking Regulatory Commission

The People's Bank of China (PBOC) was initially both the Central Bank of China and also the regulator for the entire banking system. As NPLs ballooned to massive levels in the early years of the twenty-first century, it was obvious that the PBOC was not capable of supervising the banking system properly. The CBRC was thus set up in April 2003 when the regulatory functions of the PBOC were hived off from the central bank. According to the CBRC's 2008 annual report, its objectives are 'to promote safety and soundness of the banking system; to promote public confidence in the banks and to encourage fair competition' (CBRC Annual Report 2008).

The CBRC has to regulate and supervise all banking institutions in China. This is a tall order, especially considering that, as of the end of 2008, there were 5,634 banking institutions with approximately 193,000 outlets employing a total of 2,718,857 employees (CBRC Annual Report 2008). To carry out all of the tasks mandated, the CBRC had, in 2008, a total of 23,345 staff working in 2,074 departments spread all over China. This may seem a lot, but critics still argue that the staff numbers may be inadequate as enforcement actions appear somewhat lacking.

The main responsibilities of the CBRC are set out in the above objectives but an unstated objective is 'to transform the domestic banking system and enhance the international competitiveness of the Chinese banking sector'. Bureaucrats hope to achieve the twin goals by commercializing the banks and listing them on the stock exchanges of Shanghai, Hong Kong, London or New York. This can only be done when the existing NPLs are substantially reduced, additional cash injected as capital reserves and corporate governance improved to meet listing standards.

The NPLs reduction exercise began in 1999 when the first round of NPLs totalling RMB1.4 trillion (US$173 billion) were transferred out of the SOCBs into Asset Management Companies (Ma 2007). Subsequently cash injections were made in 2003/2004 totalling US$60 billion into the three SOCBs (ICBC, CCB and BOC). The three major SOCBs were later listed in the Hong Kong Stock Exchange in 2005 and 2006. (The Agricultural Bank of China was listed in July 2010 after a similar restructuring exercise involving the transfer of NPLs.) As for the third tier CCBs, the CBRC coordinated with the local government to assist in the clean-up of their balance sheets and this was done by injecting RMB36 billion (US$6 billion) into them (Ma 2007). In addition foreign banking shareholders have invested a total of US$1.604 billion into various CCBs (see Chapter 10, Table 10.1).

So how has the performance of the CBRC been since inception in 2003? It appears to have done well as Table 6.1 indicates. NPLs for the SOCBs have decreased from 23.5 per cent in 2002 down to 1.76 per cent in 2008. These are figures provided by the CBRC and sceptics may question the veracity of the figures. However, the trend is self-evident and even critics acknowledge that major progress has been made in combating NPLs (Trumpbour 2007). The CBRC has urged all banks to meet the capital adequacy requirement of 8 per cent and worked actively with other government agencies to realize this goal.

One of the reasons for the rapid decline of the NPLs was the CBRC's strong insistence that all banks in China meet the Basel 1 Banking Regulations whereby the Capital Adequacy Ratio (CAR) was to be at a minimum of 8 per cent. In 2003 only eight banks in China, owning 0.6 per cent of banking assets, met that requirement, but under the push of the CBRC, the majority of banks in China met that criteria by 2008 (CBRC Annual Report 2008). Of course all this was made possible with the help of government measures: transfers out of massive NPLs and transfers in of very substantial cash injections. The weaknesses in

Table 6.1 NPLs of major commercial banks 2003–2008

NPLs	*2002*	*2003*	*2004*	*2005*	*2006*	*2007*	*2008*
% total loans	23.50	12.40	9.11	5.90	4.91	4.57	1.76

Source: adapted from CBRC Annual Reports (2002–2008).

China's banking industry are not confined to NPLs and capital inadequacies only. Other glaring problems relate to acute shortages of well trained and professional staff, weak internal controls, poor management information systems and lack of operational experiences in new areas of risk management, foreign exchange, etc. All these shortcomings are partially reflected as corporate governance problems.

2.1 Other regulatory initiatives by the CBRC

The CBRC conducted specific studies on medium sized commercial banks and worked out 'Opinions for Improving Corporate Governance in Small and Medium Sized Commercial Banks', which CCBs were urged to adopt. This included further steps to improve board election, optimize equity structure and standardize shareholder meetings. Banks were also urged to set up incentive schemes for staff and to improve entry requirements of senior management. The CBRC also urged all banks to improve their internal control systems and provided guidance through information dissemination for the enhancement of this system. At the same time accountability aspects of all senior management was emphasized. Through the enhancement of the accountability system, the role of the directors and the senior managers was highlighted to ensure effectiveness of internal controls.

The EAST (Examination And System Technology) System was implemented by the CBRC in 2008 to facilitate quicker examination of commercial banks' performances which permitted on-site examination of banks by collecting raw data online directly from the various banks' headquarters. This resulted in quick and rapid action by the CBRC. During 2008, the CBRC examined 46,100 banking institutions, amongst which 873 banks were penalized and 78 persons barred from senior banking positions (CBRC Annual Report 2008).

The CBRC also has a role in pre-vetting banks before listing. Apart from meeting the regulations of the CSRC, CCBs wanting to list on stock exchanges also have to meet the seven basic conditions set by the CBRC which are as follows: first, NPLs should remain at or below 5 per cent; second, CAR should be above 8 per cent; third, NPL provision coverage rate should reach 100 per cent; fourth, profit should continue to grow; fifth, all information should be fully disclosed; sixth, the ability to prevent market risk and operational risk should be in place; and, seventh, operation features, operation mechanism, corporate management, corporate culture and quality of employees should all have shown improvement.

Thus the Bank of Nanjing was the first CCB to go public when it listed on the Shanghai Stock Exchange on 19 July 2007 and the Bank of Ningbo listed on the Shenzhen Stock Exchange on the same day. Following that the Bank of Beijing listed on the Shanghai Stock Exchange on 19 September 2007. The Hangzhou City Commercial Bank (name later changed to Bank of Hangzhou), the Chengdu City Commercial Bank (name later changed to Bank of Chengdu) and the Bank of Shanghai have all expressed interest in getting listed on the local exchanges.

But they have to meet the criteria set by the CBRC and the CSRC. The general conclusion thus is that the CBRC has been an effective regulatory body executing the government's directives and policy lending initiatives and that progress has been made in improving corporate governance and reforming China's banks (Hwa 2008).

3 The China Securities Regulatory Commission

Mandated in 1992 by the State Council to regulate the securities markets, the CSRC supervises the Shanghai Stock Exchange, the Shenzhen Stock Exchange, the two Commodity Exchanges (Dalian and Zhengzhou) and the two Futures Exchanges (Shanghai Futures Exchange and China Financial Futures Exchange).

3.1 Duties and responsibilities of the CSRC

The duties of the CSRC are laid out in Article 170 of the Securities Law and may be summarized in one sentence: to formulate the supervision and administration of the securities markets and exercise the power of approval. There are thus two main responsibilities of the CSRC: to supervise and to approve. To carry out the supervisory duties, the CSRC is enabled to conduct on-site investigations, to examine the accounts, securities accounts and bank accounts of any party concerned and to restrict trading of the party concerned pending investigation. It can thus be seen that the CSRC is armed with formidable powers of supervision bearing in mind that it virtually has unlimited powers as such powers include 'other functions prescribed by administrative ordinances'. Unfortunately there is no mention of corporate governance in either Articles 179 or 180 of the Securities Law which designates the scope and duties of the CSRC.

The other major duty of the CSRC is to approve the listing of companies. Getting listed in China is a stringent and rigorous procedure that can take SOEs years to prepare for. Nevertheless it is an objective that many aspire to. Senior management of banks aspire to their corporation being listed because it is recognition that the corporate governance in the company has improved substantially and this translates into improved access to finance. It can also mean more branches and regional expansion as these governance improvements are welcomed by the CBRC. Another result of listing is that a market value is placed on the company often substantially higher than its net asset value. All of this obliges the management to operate the entity on a commercial basis. There are some basic requirements that companies have to meet before listing and the first criterion is that it must have made continuous profits for the last three years; its financial statements must be prepared in accordance with 'Accounting Standards for Business Enterprises' (ASBE) which are based on International Accounting Standards; its internal controls systems are comprehensive and effective and finally systems for shareholders' meetings, directors' meetings, supervisory meetings and independent directors are in accordance with the law. This last point is important as they form the basis of good corporate governance in the listed entity.

Once the corporate entities are listed, they then have to adhere to the rules and regulations of the Shanghai or the Shenzhen stock exchanges which are also rigorous. An example is the rule relating to directors and senior officers' duty of 'guaranteeing that the listed company discloses information in a timely and fair manner and that information is truthful, accurate and complete' (Rules of Listing on the Shanghai Stock Exchange, Chapter 2 clause 2.2). Other provisions concern related party transactions and delisting procedures. All these provisions place pressure on directors and senior management to ensure that high standards of corporate governance are established and maintained.

One of the main criticisms of the CSRC is that it performs the dual functions of approval and regulation including delisting, which are contradictory in character. In the United States and UK, the listing procedure is a market driven process and the regulatory and supervisory work is done by the Securities Exchange Commission (SEC) in the United States and by the Financial Services Authority (FSA) in the UK. The contention is that once approval is granted to the corporate entity to list, the CSRC is reluctant to delist it despite its transgressions. Hence enforcement is often slow and inadequate. This criticism is also underscored by the fact that enforcement measures undertaken by the CSRC have to be coordinated with the Ministry of Public Security before seizures and arrests can be made. The Shanghai Stock Exchange started operations in 1990 and the first delisted company was PT Narcissus in April 2000. Despite the many corporate collapses since then (Shi and Wesert 2002) there were only six companies under temporary suspension as of the end of December 2004. That is one of the reasons why enforcement by the CSRC has been perceived to be less than stringent. Another example of a lax case undertaken by the CSRC related to the Sanjiu Pharmaceutical Co. The CSRC uncovered Sanjiu's troubles in mid 2001. The listed company, which was reportedly China's largest pharmaceutical group, had misappropriated RMB2.5 billion (US$302 million) on behalf of a few major shareholders and related business partners without the consent of other shareholders or the public. These diversions amounted to a major portion of the company's net assets, posing considerable threat to the company's operations. The CSRC merely reprimanded the senior principals and fined the company RMB150 million (US$18.1 million).

The Shanghai and Shenzhen stock exchanges were established to facilitate the growth of capital markets and both have grown in size and importance with the Shanghai exchange ranking as tenth largest in the world by market capitalization in 2007. However, the CSRC has been criticized for failing to regulate the stock markets adequately as both exchanges exhibit high volatility. Is the CSRC responsible for the high volatility on the stock markets? It is responsible if the volatility is due to inaction from the CSRC, but there are many reasons for stock volatility in Chinese stock markets and not all of them relate to lack of corporate governance. One reason is that, being a new and developing stock market, new companies are constantly being added and despite stringent entry/listing conditions some will fail. This contributes to volatility. Another is the nature of the investors: most of the initial local investors were speculators and not long-term investors at all. This contributes to volatility too. However, the CSRC has announced the introduction of new financial products to allow investors to hedge against volatility in the Chinese stock market.

3.2 Financial performance and corporate governance after listing

So how have companies performed after listing on the Shanghai and Shenzhen markets? Have they performed better financially? Have they shown better corporate governance? Studies show that this has not happened. In a study funded by the World Bank, Wang *et al.* (2004) found that between 1990 and 2000 the financial performances of SOEs did not improve after listing. Table 6.2 shows that average return on assets dropped from 19.6 per cent before listing to 2.7 per cent in the sixth year after listing. The average return on sales also dropped from 16.6 per cent before listing to 0.2 per cent in the sixth year after listing. Leng (2009) found that many listed companies' financial performances declined after listing because in order to qualify for an IPO, they had to submit inflated figures which obviously they could not meet.

In addition, although the CSRC issued a set of guidelines in June 2000 called 'Announcement Regarding Listed Company's Loan Guarantees for Others' prohibiting listed companies from giving loan guarantees for other companies, a year later it was reported that 159 such new cases totalling RMB23.1 billion were discovered (Leung *et al.* 2002). This indicates the disregard that many listed companies have for the directives of the CSRC and the kinds of corporate governance problems encountered.

3.3 Regulations issued by the CSRC to improve corporate governance

The CSRC issued a series of regulations in order to improve corporate governance. In August 2001, it released the 'Guidelines for Introducing Independent Directors to the Board of Directors of Listed Companies' (CSRC 2001; hereafter referred to as the Guideline) According to the Guideline, listed companies should have at least two independent directors of the board of directors by 30 June 2002, and at least one-third of board members shall be independent directors by 30 June 2003. Although it is called a guideline, the CSRC has stipulated that all listed companies must adhere to it. The Guideline spells out clearly what

Table 6.2 Selected mean performance statistics of listed SOEs

	Year –1	*Year 0*	*Year 1*	*Year 2*	*Year 6*
Return on assets (%)	19.6	15.4	9.7	19.6	2.7
Return on sales (%)	16.6	16.2	19.6	13.76	0.2
Sales growth (%)	28.7	47.8	19.6	10.5	16.5

Source: adapted from Leung *et al.* (2002).

constitutes 'independence' and stresses that such directors must meet 'independent' requirements and possess qualifications to perform their duties for the position nominated. The nomination and election process of independent directors is also clearly spelt out and their roles clarified.

So does the presence of independent directors improve the financial performance of companies? Research seems not to indicate this (Clarke 2006; Tian and Lau 2001) and in some instances appear to deteriorate. The reasons are quite baffling and can only be surmised. Why don't independent directors seem to work? Surveys conducted indicated that over 50 per cent of independent directors were tertiary education professors and researchers, over 30 per cent were accountants, lawyers and other professionals and about 5 per cent had banking experience (Clarke 2006). So it is possible that the majority of independent directors, being professors and researchers, were less than qualified for the role. Another possible reason is that the independent directors are reluctant to oppose those who appointed them in the first place because of the high director fees received (Clarke 2006). Be that as it may, the concept of independent directors has taken root in the corporate landscape in China although it is unlikely in the short term to evolve towards the Western model where independent directors constitute the majority of the board.

3.4 The Qualified Foreign Institutional Investor scheme and corporate governance

The Qualified Foreign Institutional Investor (QFII) scheme was established by the CSRC in 2003 with the objective of liberalization of China's securities markets. There was also a secondary objective: to improve corporate governance in the listed companies in the stock markets. This scheme granted certain quotas to foreign institutional investor enabling them to buy stocks and shares on the two Chinese stock exchanges. As of the end of 2007, a total of 52 foreign institutions had been granted quotas totalling US$9.95 billion (CSRC Annual Report 2007).

Originally, China's stock market was segregated into A share and B share market with A shares being quoted in RMB and B shares being quoted in foreign currencies. Only domestic persons or domestic corporations were allowed to deal in A shares and foreign persons or foreign corporations were allowed to deal in B shares. In 2001 the law was changed to allow domestic corporate entities and domestic domiciled persons, under certain conditions, to acquire B shares which were normally reserved for foreigners. H shares are the shares of companies incorporated in Mainland China listed on the Hong Kong Stock Exchange and are available for investment in the open market.

In 2002 the CSRC announced the QFII scheme. This scheme allowed foreign institutional investors to deal in A shares. The rationale for the scheme was that foreign institutions would be long-term investors and would only invest in those firms which practised good corporate governance. Firms listed on the Chinese exchanges would also benefit from having well-known foreign institutions on their share registry. The view that the QFII scheme would improve corporate governance in the listed firms was shared by many including Ferguson and McGuinness (2004), Hu (2005) and Ward (2002).

My other research findings (Tan 2009b) indicate otherwise, however, as foreign institutional investors under this scheme base their investment decisions mainly on the profitability of Chinese companies and not on its corporate governance structures. Furthermore, the foreign investors do not play any role in the management of the Chinese companies they invest in. Hence there is no direct impact on corporate governance and their contribution to governance is through indirect means like training sessions and advisory services.

4 Code of Corporate Governance

The Code of Corporate Governance was promulgated on 7 January 2002 by the CSRC and it applies to all listed companies in China. This is the most important document for improving corporate governance and it covers every aspect of corporate governance from shareholders to directors, and from specialist committees to stakeholders. The Code sets out the basic principles of corporate governance for the protection of investors' interests and rights, governs the behaviour, rules and moral standards for directors, supervisors and managers. It has been called 'Corporate Governance with Chinese Characteristics', but it is in fact largely based on the US model.

Shareholder rights are paramount in any corporate governance model and China's Code starts off by stressing the primacy of the shareholder. Section 1 of Chapter 1 of the Code stresses that 'all shareholders are to enjoy equal rights' and calls on the corporation to 'ensure fair treatment to all shareholders especially minority shareholders'. Section 3 provides for all shareholders to participate in major decisions of the company and Section 4 allows the shareholder to protect their interests and rights through civil action. The Code further stipulates that every listed company shall use modern technology to 'increase the number of shareholders attending the shareholders meetings' (Article 8). We see therefore that shareholders' rights are enshrined and protected in the Code but a criticism is that it reads well and sounds good but the enforcement is somewhat lacking. An example is the provision for redress for shareholders via legal action, but when the judicial system is itself weak and stacked against the minority shareholder, not many minority shareholders take up the challenge. Chinese courts have shown themselves to be unreliable enforcers of relatively clear standards (Clarke 2008).

4.1 Controlling shareholders, related transactions and independence of entity

Transactions between listed companies and their related parties have plagued the Chinese corporate landscape and this is as much a legacy of the centrally planned economic system as it is of corporate malfeasance. When SOEs were corporatized and companies selected for listing, initially on a regional basis, usually the most profitable company was listed. Often the listed company was part of a stable of companies and it continued to trade with them after listing. The listed company was often under pressure to enter into related party transactions to help the less profitable companies in the group.

Clause 13 of the Code of Corporate Governance addresses this issue and allows such transactions on condition that they 'observe commercial principles'. Furthermore, listed companies are to 'adopt measure to prevent related parties from interfering in the operations of the company' and clause 19 states that 'the controlling shareholders owe a duty of good faith to the listed entity and other shareholders'. Clause 27 states that 'a listed company shall be completely independent from that of its controlling shareholders'.

4.2 Duties and responsibilities of directors

The Code requires the company to have transparent procedures for selecting directors (Articles 29–32). This is important as it adds to the transparency process in listed companies, an objective of corporate governance. There is also provision for cumulative voting mechanism for minority shareholders and this cumulative voting mechanism is important as it increases the probability of minority shareholders' board representation. The position of independent director is also restricted to persons not holding any position or related to the company in any way (Article 49). The board is also entrusted with the task of establishing sound financial and accounting management systems (Article 25). This is an important clause as some SOEs were believed to keep two sets of accounts, one set for the tax office and another set for shareholders. Board committees are the norm in listed companies as they provide avenues to ensure the proper execution and follow up of board policies and directives. Hence the Code specifically directs the board of the listed company to set up a corporate strategy committee; audit committee; nominations committee; remuneration and appraisal committee. These committees are to be chaired by independent directors too (Article 52).

We can see from the above that the Code is a very detailed document that sets out clearly the requirements for good corporate governance. It was designed to meet the needs of the Chinese corporate landscape. Critics allege that it is merely a Code and not law. As such it does not go far enough; for example, there is no specification of fines and penalties for non-observance nor does it indicate whether such breach would result in criminal or civil penalties. Thus, while the Code has undoubtedly helped improve corporate governance, it is merely a Code for the guidance of listed companies. It needs teeth in the enforcement area which would have made it more effective.

5 Business and informal networks

Networks form an important part of business dealings in China and one often hears of *guanxi* 关系 and *renqing* 人情. Perhaps the closest English synonym to *guanxi* is *interpersonal connections* while *renqing* can be interpreted as *reciprocity*. *Guanxi* is a kind of special relationship. This concept suggests that people exist in relationship with others. Chinese business people devote a significant amount of time and energy to cultivating close *guanxi* with powerful people. People who have *guanxi* can accomplish what they want even when such behaviour is against the rules. The main point is the consequences of *guanxi* in business. *Guanxi* has been identified as one of the most important factors in doing business successfully in China where many entrepreneurs have extensive networks of connections with senior government officials. Research by Djankov *et al.* found that China's successful entrepreneurs were those who took risks, exhibited greed traits and had strong social networks (2006).

The Chinese cultural explanation is that *guanxi* is based on Confucian ideology which teaches filial piety, loyalty, harmony and reciprocity as the basis for relationships. *Guanxi* may be based on blood ties, geographical ties, linguistic and cultural ties that bind what may otherwise be different groups together. Dating back as far as the Sung dynasty, the Chinese networks appear to be established to facilitate exchange of personal and knowledge based resources, for mutual aid and for protection (Hendrischke 2003). The need to deal with institutional insecurity has also stimulated the evolution of an alternative form of social organization that provides this security – business networks.

These relationships have carried into the economic sphere in China where they provide a substitute for weak institutions and property rights. McNally *et al.* (2007) found that in spite of stronger formalization of private sector institutions, informal networks form a key component in a firm's success. The most significant of these are the political networks that connect private entrepreneurs to the political hierarchy. On the one hand legal, political and market structures are being institutionalized; on the other hand the use of political networks to further success is essential.

Informal networks exist in all kinds of areas. At the corporate level, senior management may meet over a meal where they will discuss agenda items on forthcoming board meetings and sound out each other's position before making their own minds up. Again at inter-organizational levels, the head of the CBRC may meet with senior CCP members in Beijing to propose certain candidates for CEO positions of various banks. Positions of CEO and chairmanship positions have to be sanctioned by the CBRC but they may want to consult with various bodies including the CCP before a decision is made.

6 The role of the state and the Chinese Communist Party

What influence does the state and the CCP wield today in the corporate arena? How does it impact on the governance of banks and listed companies? In China, the role of the state and that of the CCP is blurred. In the early years of economic transition to a market economy, the influence of the CCP was strong. In subsequent years, with the transition to a market economy, the influence has declined and continues to decline. This is because the Chinese authorities recognize themselves that for the transition to a market economy to be successful, the role of extraneous bodies like the CCP must be reduced. In fact the Code of Corporate Governance stresses the independence of the listed company and clause 27 states that 'a listed company shall be completely independent from that of its controlling shareholders'. Of course the state and not the CCP is the controlling shareholder in most of the SOEs, but the CCP exerts its influence through informal channels linking it to the controlling shareholder. Research has shown that in spite of all these recent ameliorative developments, the CCP still wields influence (Opper *et al.* 2002, 2004; Huang and Orr 2007).

This may be due to Article 19 of the Company Law of 1994 (Amended 2005) which states that:

> an organization of the Chinese Communist Party shall, according to the Charter of the Chinese Communist Party, be established in the company to carry out activities of the Chinese Communist Party. And the company shall provide necessary conditions for the activities of the Chinese Communist Party.

Critics argue that as a result of this clause the local committee of the CCP was able to cling on to vestiges of its former power. In addition, Article 31, subsection 7 of the CCP constitution explicitly assigns the local party committee to 'supervise party cadres and any other personnel to ensure that they strictly abide by the state laws and the administrative disciplines'. As practically all senior management of listed SOEs are CCP members, this clause gives the local party units the right to interfere and supervise personnel in the companies. There thus appears to be a conflict between the Code of Corporate Governance, the Company Law and the CCP constitution and this is something that foreign shareholders must be aware of when they invest in Chinese listed SOEs.

Research has shown that direct intervention by the state into the governance of firms is likely to yield negative economic effects. Nee *et al.* (2007) and Chang and Wong (2004) and Xu *et al.* (2005) find in their studies that reducing politician control positively correlates to a firm's reform success. Another interesting study into the economic progress of Jiangsu and Zhejiang provinces over two decades reveals the negative effects of government intervention. Although Jiangsu has received far more foreign investment and public-works spending than Zhejiang, it has also endured far more government intervention in economic affairs. Within 20 years it was surpassed economically by Zhejiang, where government involvement was less and entrepreneurship was encouraged (Y.S. Huang 2009).

At a practical level, the forces of commercialization, market forces and the profit incentive will result in gradually reduced influence from the CCP. Nevertheless the CCP will continue to exert some influence at both local and board level where the appointment of the Chairman and the CEO will continue to be sanctioned by the state.

7 Conclusion

There are many factors impacting on corporate governance in China and some of the more important factors are external determinants like the regulatory bodies, their codes and informal networks. It is important to note that the Chinese regulatory bodies play both a regulatory and enforcement role. We study the work of the CBRC set up in 2003 to regulate the banks and the CSRC established in 1992 to regulate the listed entities. The CSRC sought to improve corporate governance by promulgating various codes pertaining to governance. The CSRC also established the QFII scheme under which large foreign institutional investors would be allowed to invest in China's listed companies. The objective of the scheme was a first step towards the opening up of China's securities markets, but a secondary aim was to help improve corporate governance in the listed companies.

Both the CBRC and the CSRC have strong regulatory powers but are often criticized for lacking strong enforcement resources. Enforcement actions by the CSRC have to be coordinated with the Ministry of Public Security which complicates the issue. China has a weak judicial system and a multi-layered bureaucracy makes it hard for corporate grievances to get legal redress.

The Code of Corporate Governance is a very detailed document laying down guidelines for good governance for listed entities. The code is based on the US model and indeed if all the Chinese listed companies were to abide by it, corporate governance would take a quantum leap forward. However, this has not happened and there are many reasons. A good explanation is that China is a transitional economy and many of its institutions are also transitional institutions. Both managers and shareholders are learning how to apply the structures and mechanisms provided under the Code to improve corporate governance. China is in transition to a model which is based more on that of the United States and UK than that of France, Germany and Japan. It is also a model of corporate governance with Chinese characteristics. These Chinese characteristics relate to *guanxi* and *renqing* and also to the fact that informal networks including the state and the CCP play an important role in the economic arena. The CCP may have a diminished role in the management of corporate entities but it is still a relevant role.

7 Financial systems and economic growth

1 Introduction

This chapter is relevant to the text content as studies have indicated that there are two systems of finance that facilitate economic growth: bank based and free market based financial systems. I mentioned in the conclusion to Chapter 5 that corporate governance should apply to all sectors of society and this ensures that there is little corruption, proper accountability and strong rule of law, which helps in the efficient allocation of resources. A bank based financial system is one where most of the new investment capital is provided by banks (as in France, Germany and Japan) and a free market based financial system is one where the capital and stock markets are well developed and hence most of the new financing and investments come from the stock markets (United States and UK). China has relatively underdeveloped stock markets and hence most of its corporate financing comes from the banking system. And that is why corporate governance in the banking system is important. It must be mentioned, however, that funds raised through the stock markets via IPOs (initial public offerings) are becoming increasingly common and popular.

Do developments in banking and finance contribute to economic growth or do they occur simultaneously? We have proponents for both sides of the argument with one view that economic development are the result of advances in finance and banking (Schumpeter 1911) and the opposing view that financial and economic development occurred simultaneously (Goldsmith 1969). Adam Smith wrote in 1776 that the invisible hand of the free market forces brought about the optimum allocation of scarce resources by adjusting for equilibrium in the production equation of supply and demand and in so doing facilitated economic growth. His book espoused free trade, capitalism and laissez-faire and provided much of the theoretical basis for the study of modern economics. Another Englishman (Bagehot 1920) observed that the London financial markets were able to raise substantial amounts of capital to finance a variety of large and long-term projects, e.g. long sea voyages to the East for the spice trade, construction of innovative manufacturing facilities, production of steam engines, infrastructure projects, etc. In this manner long-term illiquid investment opportunities were financed and these investments resulted in increased economic growth. In other words, he indicated that capital markets contributed to economic growth.

Schumpeter theorized that economic development was the result of advances in finance and banking. He argued that the basic services provided by financial organizations, which included gathering savings and deposits from the local communities and then lending them out as loans, facilitated economic development. This was because the financial intermediaries brought with them a whole chain of processes that stimulated economic development – these included project evaluation, risk control, the monitoring of projects and the facilitation of transactions. These processes were basic to banks but were a necessary corollary to technological innovation in the communities which these institutions served. For many years, Schumpeter's views were unreservedly accepted and it was not until Goldsmith (1969) examined the relationship between finance and growth that a new era began. His seminal work on *Financial Structure and Development* illustrates the close ties between financial growth and economic development.

First of all he defined 'financial structure' as the mixture of financial instruments, markets and institutions operating in an economy. Second, he used the value of financial intermediary assets relative to GNP as a measure of financial development. Third, he studied the financial data on 35 countries over 103 years from 1860 to 1963 and came to the conclusion that financial and economic development occurred simultaneously. Goldsmith's views on finance and economic development were confirmed by McKinnon (1973) and Berger *et al.* (2004) who studied the impact of community banks on economic growth using data from 1993–2000 in 49 countries.

2 Measurement of the development of banking and finance

There are various measures of the degree of development of banking and finance in an economy and obviously the banks and the stock markets play key roles. Traditionally, loans from banks are the most important source of finance for businesses and it is only in the more developed economies that the stock markets and investment banks play an increasingly vital role. Stock markets raise funds from ordinary households and investors by selling shares to investors in the expectation that future earnings will justify their investment. The stock markets therefore only thrive when all the ingredients associated with a successful free market economy are present: fiscal transparency, rule of law, corporate governance and accountability.

How much credit is extended by the banks compared to the economy's GDP is one measure that shows the activity of the banking system and another measure is the stock market capitalization in an economy compared to its GDP. An acceptable method of measuring the degree of financial development in an economy is to compare and add the two percentages. Added together the number gives an indication of the degree of financial penetration in an economy.

Table 7.1 Extent of financial development 1990–1995

Country	*Bank credit as fraction of GDP*	*Stock market capitalization as fraction of GDP*	*Extent of financial development*
France	0.64	0.33	0.97
Germany	0.66	0.24	0.90
Japan	1.91	0.79	2.70
Great Britain	0.96	1.13	2.09
United States	0.60	0.80	1.40
Hong Kong	1.63	1.96	3.59
Singapore	1.12	1.37	2.49

Source: adapted from Demirguc-Kunt and Levine (2001).

Demirguc-Kunt and Levine conducted research into over 100 countries for the period 1990–1995 and the results were used to measure the extent of financial development of an economy and also to indicate whether the economies are 'bank based' or 'market based'. Where the bank credits and stock market capitalization of the economy (as a fraction of the GDP) exceed 1 on both measurements, it denotes that it is a banking and financial centre as borne out by the statistics on Hong Kong and Singapore. Where the banking credits as a fraction of GDP is much higher than the stock market capitalization to GDP fraction, this indicates that the financial system is bank oriented (Japan, France and Germany). Where the stock market capitalisation to GDP fraction is more closely aligned to the bank credit to GDP fraction, this is indicative of a well developed stock market as shown by the United States and the UK.

3 Bank based and market based financial systems

Economists have studied bank based and market based financial systems using as examples the data collected from Germany and Japan as being examples of the bank based financial systems and the data from the UK and United States as being examples of market based economic systems (see Table 7.1). In the market based systems, the stock markets are more developed and the main arbiters of how financing for corporations is enabled whereas in bank based economies, the main portion of corporate financing comes from banks.

Allen and Gale (1999) and Stulz (2000) have produced research that shows that the four countries show very similar long-term growth rates so that it is difficult to correlate differences in financial structure to differences in long-term economic growth rates (Beck *et al.* 2000). Proponents of the bank based financial system highlight the positive role of the bank in mobilizing savings, identifying commercially viable projects, monitoring managers and curbing risk. The bank based financial systems proponents also criticize the market based systems as having a surfeit of information (some of which may be irrelevant and misleading) and thus reduce investors' desire to acquire information. Thus greater market development may result in highly liquid markets and a myopic investor climate as investors have few incentives to monitor managers rigorously. Bank based financial systems on the other hand, with their robust risk management techniques, can force firms to reveal information and act as corporate citizens (Rajan and Zingales 1998). This helps economic growth in the long run.

The market based system of financial system stresses the important role of markets in promoting economic growth (Beck and Levine 2000). In particular free markets promote diversification and innovation. Banks are by nature conservative as they have to protect depositors' monies and this tendency reduces their desire to finance high risk, high return projects. Thus bank based financial systems may retard innovation and growth (Morck and Nakamura 1999; Weinstein and Yafeh 1998). In addition powerful banks may collude with oligarchies against other investors, hindering competition, effective corporate control and economic growth. Proponents thus claim that market based systems will reduce inefficiencies associated with banks and promote economic development.

4 How financial systems impact on economic growth

We define financial system as the term given to ... *any structure, financial or otherwise that acts as an intermediary between savers of funds on the one hand, and borrowers of funds on the other*. In other words, the financial system facilitates the monetary savings from thousands of households and saves them the time and costs associated with lending out these funds to the borrowers. The borrowers would be the firms and businesses who in turn do not have time to approach the thousands of small savers to convince them of the commercial viability of their projects. The financial system therefore facilitates information flow and reduces transaction costs that would otherwise be incurred. A second way that the financial system promotes economic growth is by determining who gets to borrow the funds deposited with the financial institutions by household savers. Banks and financial institutions have access to commercial and economic information that the normal household savers would not have and in this manner the banks help to allocate scarce resources in the economy.

The third way that the financial system helps promote economic growth is by spreading the household savings across many different investment opportunities. Normally the financial institutions would be governed by their charter, which will ensure risks are mitigated by stipulating that loans must be diversified across a range of business sectors. In this way, the risks associated with lending to any particular sector of the economy and to any particular group of companies is minimized. This reduction in risk will help bolster confidence in the financial system. Yet another important role of the financial system is to provide liquidity. Households deposit their savings with financial institutions because they have no immediate use for these funds, yet at some time in the future the need will arise. Financial institutions over time and through a process of trial and error are able to gauge the needs of their depositors from the duration of their deposits, etc. At the same time, these financial institutions allocate their loans and structure the loan portfolio to meet their own internal depositor's requirements. In this manner, the overall liquidity of the financial system is maintained.

The financial system also facilitates trade and commerce in an economy. This is done by guaranteeing payments through the issuance of cheques, credit cards, letters of credit, letters of guarantee, etc. Goods and services therefore are exchanged with the help of financial institutions without having to resort to barter. Thus economic growth is enhanced. We know that financial markets can increase the efficiency of resource allocation in an economy and hence increase the income of households and the profitability of firms by reducing transaction costs and facilitating information flow.

The nexus between economic growth and financial development has always been contentious. As mentioned above, the Schumpeterian view that economic growth is the result of financial development is contested by those who believe that economic growth and financial development go hand in hand. Yet another contending theory is that of La Porta *et al.* (1998) who wrote that it was the legal system that was the primary determinant of the effectiveness of the financial system in facilitating innovation and economic growth. La Porta *et al.* reject the entire bank versus market based financial system and instead put forth the view that the efficiency of the legal system positively correlates to innovation and economic growth.

5 Corporate governance and economic growth

One important, often unrecognized, factor impacting on economic growth is corporate governance. Business corporations are mainly responsible for the capital investments and employment in any economy and these corporate decisions drive economic growth. Thus, how these corporations are governed and the corporate governance models adopted will impact on economic growth.

There is broad consensus that the corporate governance framework within an economy does impinge upon the development of equity markets, innovative activity, entrepreneurship, and the development of an active SME sector which impacts on economic growth (Mayer 1998; Knack 2002). However, there is no single model of corporate governance that can be described as ideal and each country must over time develop a variety of mechanisms of corporate governance (Maher and Andersson 1999). Pierre-Gauillaume and Weill (2005) found that better governance is associated with greater efficiency, with the two most important aspects of governance being government efficiency and rule of law while control of corruption and quality of regulatory institutions play secondary roles.

There are various models of corporate governance that policy-makers can choose to emulate and we read in Chapter 2 the various theories of corporate governance. Most of the Western democracies practise either the Shareholder Value or the Stakeholder model where free market forces play the determining role in corporate governance. With the former centrally planned economies of China, Russia and Eastern Europe, they are in transition to market economies.

However, these countries cannot be described as fully practising either the Shareholder Value or the Stakeholder model. In these transitional economies, the state plays a strong role in determining the regulation and implementation of corporate governance (Paredes 2005). This model of corporate governance depends on the state to promulgate various laws in which the state rather than the marketplace plays the central role in regulation and enforcement. All of these transitional economies are in transition to free market based economies but a market based corporate governance regime cannot be achieved overnight. As Nobel laureate Douglass North[1] puts it, 'institutions are the result of long gestation periods and the process of institutional change is overwhelmingly incremental' (Paredes 2005).

6 Why aim for economic growth?

Politicians and economists alike proclaim the desirability of economic growth, which after all is the avowed objective of most governments in power. We ask why economic growth and in particular why long-term economic growth? The answer lies in the implied benefits of higher standards of living, higher per capita income, more leisure and the consumption of more material goods and services. These are all worthy objectives which mankind as a whole understandably aspires to.

An example is China and India. Both countries have in recent decades experienced sustained economic growth and, in so doing, uplifted hundreds of millions of their population from poverty. For example, China has seen double-digit economic growth since economic reforms began in the late 1970s and in 2005 the real per capita income of China was estimated at PPP US$6,600 while for India it was PPP US$3,460. Compared to the rich countries like the United States (US$41,950), Germany (US$29,210) and Japan (US$31,410), of course the per capita income of India and China is much smaller. Nevertheless, if these two countries maintain their high economic growth over the next 25 years, they have every chance of narrowing the gap between them, given the fact that the Western industrialized economies are mature economies growing at some 2–4 per cent each year.

7 What causes long-term economic growth?

Economies grow sometimes by fits and spurts and sometimes gradually. In a year, there may be quarters when growth may be positive or even negative and these short-term fluctuations are the subject matter of economists who study business cycles. These business cycle variations may be fairly volatile and can result in massive unemployment and corporate failures, and it is the work of economists to advise governments on how these cyclical downturns can be mitigated, if not completely consigned to the garbage bin.

There are many measurements of economic growth and there is broad agreement on the various measures used: they may be real per capita GDP, or income growth per annum in a country. We are concerned more with long-term economic growth because these are the trends that will profoundly affect the welfare and well-being of the population. To give an example, Johnson (2005) writes that the real GDP of the American economy (adjusted for inflation) grew by 2.7 per cent each year from 1979 to 1999. If the American economy had grown during the period by an extra 0.6 per cent each year, i.e. by an average of 3.3 per cent each year instead of 2.7 per cent each year, the 1999 GDP would have reached US$9.152 trillion instead of the US$7.552 trillion worth of goods and services. That means that the income of the average American household in 1999 could have been 21.2 per cent higher than it actually turned out to be, if only a way could be found to marginally increase the trend rate of economic growth.

So what causes long-term sustained economic growth? Economists agree that it is complex. They further agree that these theories may be technical, ideological and cultural. There is, however, generally broad agreement on what causes economic growth. Broadly speaking, economic growth is driven by investments in capital plant and equipment and also investments in research and development. From R&D we get technological innovation which leads to production efficiencies and new products which facilitate the economic production process. Investment in human capital is also very important and impacts very strongly on the long-term economic growth. Various measures of literacy, enrolment ratios, average life expectancy, general health, proportion of university graduates: all these impact on long-term economic growth. Mr Lee Kuan Yew, Prime Minister of Singapore during the formative years, wrote in his autobiography (2000) that he stressed the importance of education and spent a substantial portion of the state budget on education. This investment in human capital has been more than paid off as Singapore today is a wealthy nation with high, long-term sustained economic growth rates.

8 Conclusion

What are the financial institutions that mobilize savings and surplus funds from households, individuals and corporate entities and arrange for their transfer of these surplus funds to borrowing households, individuals and corporate entities? The two major financial systems that perform this function are the banks and the stock markets with the United States and UK being examples of the stock market dominated system and Germany, France and Japan being representative of the bank based systems. In the United States and UK based systems, the stock markets are more developed and the main providers of finance, while in France, Germany and Japan, financing for corporations is mainly through banks.

Banks and stock markets perform the same function as repositories of surplus funds from households and individuals and channelling them out to corporate enterprises. The risk element is however different in that the banks shoulder the main burden of risk in the former while in the latter case, the risks are borne by individual shareholders. In so doing it fosters economic growth. A financial system promotes economic growth by mobilizing savings and allocating it to borrowers and in so doing the financial system decides who gets to borrow money, what projects are financed and which are rejected. In other words, the financial system is the final arbiter on the allocation of the most important resource: finance. Banks and stock markets thus assist in the efficient allocation of capital.

Many economists agree with the view that financial institutions foster growth while others contend that these financial institutions are the result of economic growth. There is controversy on the causality – what causes what and which comes first. Whatever their views, policy-makers strive for long-term economic growth because their citizens will have higher per capita income and higher standards of living.

There are many reasons for economic growth, amongst which are investments in capital plant and equipment and also investments in research and development. Investment in human capital is also very important and impacts strongly on the long-term economic growth but another little recognized, indirect factor impacting on economic growth is corporate governance. This is because corporate entities are mainly responsible for the capital investments and employment in an economy and these corporate decisions drive economic growth. There is consensus that how capital investment decisions are made impact on economic growth. That is why it is important for China and other transitional economies to establish good corporate governance standards in their economies so that there can be efficient allocation of resources which facilitate economic growth.

8 A historical perspective of City Commercial Banks in China

1 Introduction

Barry Naughton and Nicholas Lardy are two academics who have written extensively about the economic reforms in China. Both present views which are clearly divergent and yet entirely plausible. Naughton (1995) sees the gradualist approach adopted by the Chinese authorities as a strategy for combating the massive bad debts and NPLs of the SOEs and state-owned banks while Lardy (1998) concentrates on financial reform and the development of a modern banking sector in China. His conclusions are clear. Disagreeing with Naughton, who argues that economic reforms arising from the natural growth of the non-state sector will cure the ills of the state-owned sector, Lardy insists that unless the current reform programme is speedily and thoroughly implemented, there is a serious danger of financial collapse of the banking sector and by implication the entire Chinese economy.

CCBs form the third tier of China's banking system. As of 2008, there were 136 such banks. They were all formed from the mid 1990s to the early years of the twenty-first century from the Urban Credit Cooperatives (UCCs) which were restructured. The UCCs underwent restructuring because of their many problems faced: high NPLs, low CARs, poor risk control and incompetent management. Another reason was the desire by the central government to exert control over their lending policies so that on an overall basis the economic development of the country could be better controlled through guidelines on lending policies and adjustments of interest rates. Following the promulgation of 'The PRC Law on Commercial Banks' in May 1995, the first CCB was formed in June 1995 when the Shenzhen City Commercial Bank was registered. It was an amalgamation of ten urban credit cooperatives operating in Shenzhen; and was followed by other CCBs throughout China and today practically every large town and city has its own City Commercial Bank.

The history of CCBs is fairly short – most of them are about a decade or so old. In order to understand the history of China's CCBs, we need to understand the history of China's UCCs from which they all emerged.

2 Background of China's Urban Credit Cooperatives

Authorities in China adopted a phased approach to the reform of the financial sector. Initially the first tier in China's banking system, the SOCBs were protected from both internal and external competition and the vast majority of their loans were to the SOEs. In the 1980s and 1990s, a new class of financial institution was allowed to be established to lend to the fast-growing private sector and to foreign commercial enterprises. These institutions were the Joint Stock Commercial Banks (JSCBs) which did not have the backing of the state. They did not compete with the SOCBs as their main targets were the private and foreign sector. The 12 JSCBs are CITIC Bank, China Merchants Bank, Minsheng Banking Corp, Huaxia Bank, Shanghai Pudong Development Bank, China Everbright Bank, Shenzhen Development Bank, Guangdong Development Bank, Industrial Bank, Evergrowing Bank, China Zheshang Bank and China Bohai Bank. After allowing for the formation of the JSCBs, authorities considered that there was still room left for other non-bank financial institutions in the overall financial picture.

There was room because the 1980s saw a dramatic increase in Town and Village Enterprises (TVEs). TVEs are business enterprises owned by village and township governments (including those leased to individuals) and their need for loans and finance was not met by the SOCBs and JSCBs. These TVEs played an extremely important economic role. In 1978, there were 1.5 million TVEs employing 28.2 million workers, but by 1996 the figure had increased to 23.4 million TVEs employing 125.1 million workers (Da Costa and Carroll 2001). The SOCBs and the JSCBs were not bothered about lending to these TVEs, many of which had no track record and no security to offer as collateral. JSCBs steered clear of such businesses – wary of their political connections. It was therefore not surprising that, under the circumstances, Chinese authorities allowed the formation and emergence of a new category of non-bank financial institution – the Urban Credit Cooperatives (UCCs) to service the small business enterprises in the towns and Rural Credit Cooperatives (RCCs) to service the small village enterprises in the rural areas. We shall concern ourselves with the UCCs only.

3 The emergence and development of UCCs

UCCs are collectively owned urban financial institutions which were under the supervision of the PBOC. Originally all banking and deposit-taking institutions were under the purview of the PBOC but, in 2003, the CBRC was formed and banking institutions were transferred to their supervision. Supervision of the credit cooperatives, both urban and rural, remained with the PBOC.

There are two main types of UCCs – Urban Credit Cooperatives and urban credit affiliates with the UCCs being located in large or middle sized cities. Their main business is to take deposits, grant loans and undertake settlement and remittance transactions. On the other hand, the UCC affiliate is probably a financial organization owned by the UCC, but with independent and separate accounting, operations and financial accountability.

The first UCC was set up in Luhoe county, Henan province, in 1979 (Giradin and Xie 1997). From a standing start in 1979, the number of UCCs increased dramatically to 1,600 in 1987 and 4,800 in 1993. However, during the economic slowdown in the aftermath of the Tiananmen crackdown, many of the UCCs got into trouble with high NPLs and there was a real danger of their collapse. As this would have caused social unrest in the cities, authorities acted quickly to prevent this happening. Subsequently, UCCs in each city were forced to amalgamate to become CCBs and thus the numbers of UCCs fell dramatically to about 2,000 in 2003, 681 at the end of 2005 and 22 at end of 2008. UCCs grew very quickly during the 1980s in terms of numbers, employees, volume of deposits taken and loans granted. Table 8.1 shows their amazing growth. As can be seen from the table, the number of employees grew from 26,500 in 1987 to 122,900 in 1993, a growth of 363 per cent.

The growth rate of assets of UCCs was also very rapid as Table 8.2 shows (row 'r'). The assets of the UCCs increased year on year, by 225.1 per cent in 1987, 111.2 per cent in 1988, before tapering down to 26.8 per cent in 1990 and then growth picked up again to 57.3 per cent in 1993 and 85.6 per cent in 1994. These are very substantial figures and confirm the explosive growth of the UCCs during the 1980s and 1990s.

Table 8.2 shows that the growth rate of assets of UCCs (r) and the growth rate of production of urban private-owned enterprises (R) was closely related. This shows that UCCs financed mostly SMEs in the private sector of the urban economy.

The UCCs play a diminishing role in the Chinese banking system. At the end of 2006 there were a total of 78 UCCs with a share of total assets of the banking

Table 8.1 UCCs staff and number of UCCs in thousands

Data	*1987*	*1988*	*1989*	*1990*	*1991*	*1992*	*1993*
Staff	26.5	49.7	60.3	68.6	77.3	90.9	122.9
UCCs (numbers)	1.6	3.2	3.4	3.4	3.5	4.0	4.8

Source: adapted from Giradin and Xie (1997).

Table 8.2 Comparison of growth rate of assets of UCCs (r) and growth rate of production of urban private owned enterprises (R) data in percentages

Data	*1987*	*1988*	*1989*	*1990*	*1991*	*1992*	*1993*	*1994*
R	31.7	41.5	22.9	12.3	22.4	44.7	55.7	69.2
r	225.1	111.2	46.6	26.8	27.0	57.3	56.3	85.6

Source: adapted from Giradin and Xie (1997).

Table 8.3 China's banking institutions: share of total assets (31 December 2006)

	Number of institutions	*Share of assets (%)*
City Commercial Banks	113	5.9
Urban Credit Cooperatives	78	0.4

Source: adapted from CBRC Annual Report (2006).

Table 8.4 China's banking institutions: share of total assets (31 December 2008)

	Number of institutions	*Share of assets (%)*
City Commercial Banks	136	6.62
Urban Credit Cooperatives	22	0.13

Source: adapted from CBRC Annual Report (2008).

system of about 0.4 per cent (Table 8.3). By the end of 2008, the number of UCCs had further dropped to 22 and the assets of UCCs had dropped further to 0.13 per cent of total banking assets while CCBs had increased their numbers from 113 in 2006 to 136 in 2008 and their share of bank assets increased from 5.9 per cent in 2006 to 6.62 per cent in 2008 (Table 8.4). This was mainly due to the fact that the majority of the UCCs had, with the active encouragement of the authorities, converted into CCBs.

4 The unique features of UCCs

The UCCs have generally reflected the spirit and intention of the original founders of cooperative movements which was to look after the interests of their members. These interests are usually spelt out in the objectives and governing articles of the cooperatives and all the Chinese UCCs spell out three dimensions which are crucial for their success: economic, social and moral. These UCCs reflect the cooperative as being an example of a democratic institution of its members, for the members and by the members. They practised the principle of one member, one vote in their decision-making.

Although the UCCs have had a relatively short history in China, they saw tremendous growth initially. This is because, as Table 8.2 shows, they mirrored the growth of the urban collective enterprises. These UCCs also enjoyed advantages over the much larger SOCBs and JSCBs because of their smaller scale of operations, larger numbers, accessibility and greater flexibility in operations. They also had better knowledge of their clients and businesses as the management was very much locally based and locally oriented.

The 'Regulation on UCCs' issued by the PBOC in 1988 defined the UCC as 'a financial membership institution whose shareholders can be collectively owned urban enterprises, individual businessmen and individual citizens'. The capital of the UCCs comprise shares purchased by enterprises and by individuals. The shares can be transferred and inherited but not withdrawn. Membership is normally based on certain qualifications which may be based on industry, geographical locality or even employment. The original UCCs usually allowed membership based on the fact that one or more of the family members were resident in the city. The UCCs have an executive body that is appointed by the member shareholders. The management of the UCC is democratic and the Shareholder Representative Council of the UCC elects the Council of the UCC as an Executive Body of the UCC engaging in supervision over operations. The directors of the UCC are appointed by the Council and are responsible for daily management. Staff are normally employed under contract. In principle UCCs enjoy much autonomy in personnel, finances and management of material resources. Voting is based on the 'one member, one vote' principle.

Although the management structure is purportedly democratic, the reality belies the theory and in practice, the members' meetings comprise party cadres who get elected and use these UCCs as financiers for local government projects (Ong 2006). UCCs are usually more nimble and flexible in their operations than the SOCBs who cater to the large SOEs and the state-owned sector and the JSCBs who cater for the large business enterprises operating in the private sector. UCCs are also more numerous in the towns that they operate in. For example, UCCs have deposits with the right to withdraw interest if necessary (not allowed by banks) and these UCCs may even pay wages on behalf of their clients and sometimes even collect debts on behalf of their customers. All that flexibility makes the UCCs very convenient for SMEs to bank with them.

5 Origins of CCBs

China's CCBs have had a short history and were created through the active merging and restructuring of the approximately 5,000 UCCs that existed around 1995. The first CCB formed was Shenzhen City Commercial Bank, created in June 1995. By December 1998 the roughly 5,000 UCCs had been reduced to 3,240 and in their place there were 89 CCBs. At the end of December 2008, the UCCs had been further reduced to 22 and the number of CCBs increased to 136. The vast majority of the UCCs have thus been absorbed into the CCB system.

Why did the authorities merge and restructure the UCCs? The reason was because of the need to bring them under the control and supervision of the central government. Once the UCCs were restructured into CCBs, they came under the supervision of the CBRC and they were subject to the same rules as other commercial banks. There are regulatory requirements for the CCBs to be met, with the minimum capital requirement set at RMB100 million; the necessity to maintain a CAR of 8 per cent; to reduce the NPLs to the levels periodically set by the CBRC and to comply with PBOC's rules on 'Information Disclosure for Commercial Banks'.

Previously, under the old system, the UCCs were part of the city government's economic planning apparatus and were controlled by them. They operated under the credit cooperatives umbrella which was loosely under the umbrella of the PBOC. Although the CCBs are under the supervision of the CBRC now, they still have strong ties to the local government economic apparatus as the local government authorities often hold a majority of the shares of the banks. The result of this close nexus is that apart from being the financiers of the SMEs and urban enterprises, the CCBs are also the financiers for the local government's projects. There is thus a looming local government debt. This has come about because of the lack of clear-cut lines of authority and inadequate corporate governance structures in the CCBs that were restructured. Often they just inherited the old management models of the UCCs and took their orders from the local government. Loans were made by the CCBs to government related SMEs, often on highly inflated asset values and securities, and more often against guarantees provided by the local government. What this meant was that if the SME enterprises were liquidated, the collateral would be insufficient to pay off the debts and the local governments would be liable for the difference (Ong 2006).

Although the CCBs play an important role in the provision of loans to the SMEs in the urban areas, they may be considered as small fish in a very large pond. However, they are not that small. Typically a CCB operating in a large city would have about 50 branches although some have over 200. And when you consider the cities of Shanghai, Beijing and Chongqing, which have populations in excess of 15 million each, their CCBs are operating in the equivalent of small countries. CCBs have also carved out niche positions in the cities they serve and usually occupy a prominent position in terms of bank size and assets.

5.1 Assets of China's CCBs

China's CCBs have shown consistently high growth as the Table 8.5 shows. In 2003, CCB assets totalled RMB1,462.17 billion, which increased by 16.6 per cent to RMB1,705.63 billion in 2004 and then gradually to RMB2,036.69 billion in 2005. From 2006 onwards, the CCBs grew their assets by over 20 per cent per annum. This was in part due to the overall economic growth and may also have to do with the presence of foreign strategic shareholdings in some of the larger CCBs.

The future looks bright for the CCBs as national economic growth continues at a rapid pace. Since 1978 China has seen average real growth of more than 9 per cent per year with several peak years of more than 13 per cent (Hu and Khan 1997). However, it must be remembered that these figures are national figures –

Table 8.5 China's CCB assets (RMB billions)

Bank assets	*2003*	*2004*	*2005*	*2006*	*2007*	*2008*
RMB 100 million	1,462.17	1,705.63	2,036.69	2,593.79	3,340.48	4,131.97
Percentage increase		16.6	14.4	27.2	28.8	23.7

Source: adapted from CBRC Annual Reports (2003–2008).

traditionally, economic growth in the urban areas is often double the national average as economic growth in the rural areas is much lower. In addition much of the growth has been along the eastern coastal belt and the inland and western regions have seen much lower growth.

5.2 NPLs of CCBs

What are the NPLs of the CCBs like? We know that the NPLs of the SOCBs were very large throughout the 1990s into the early years of the twenty-first century and had to be rescued by massive injections of cash into their balance sheets and the simultaneous transfer out of NPLs into Asset Management Corporations (AMC). The UCCs, which were the precursors of the CCBs, also had their fair share of NPLs during the 1990s, which resulted in their being restructured into CCBs.

Although the NPLs of the CCBs were high, being 14 per cent of outstanding loans in 2004 (KPMG 2006), depositors did not believe that the government would allow any to fail and that was why they continued to bank and to support the CCBs. However, it must be stressed that there is no deposit insurance scheme in place but this does not appear to bother bank depositors. Pressure from the central government on the provincial and city authorities to reduce the NPLs resulted in a reduction of NPLs in the CCBs to 7.73 per cent at the end of 2005. The NPL ratios of the CCBs have since been substantially reduced to 3 per cent in 2007 and to 2.3 per cent in 2008 (CBRC Annual Report 2008).

As mentioned earlier, local government authorities currently are majority shareholders in many of the CCBs and thus are in a position to exert strong influence over the lending decisions of these banks. This has resulted in many of the CCBs becoming the financiers of the local government enterprises. What happens at the national level with the SOCBs being directed to make loans to the SOEs is replicated at the provincial level with the provincial authorities directing the CCBs to lend funds to state related projects. This practice however appears to have abated as we see from the CBRC 2008 Annual Report that 71.16 per cent of all loans from CCBs are now directed to SMEs (CBRC Annual Report 2008).

5.3 The CAR of CCBs

The CAR of the CCBs remained in the low single digits during its early years after formation and was well below acceptable banking limits. However, with restructuring and loan write-offs there has been a gradual improvement. This has come about with some assistance from the local government authorities. The CBRC reported that China's local governments had put in as much as US$4.3 billion into the CCBs in 2004 to offset their losses from NPLs and help them overcome their problems.

Many of the CCBs did not initially meet the recommended CAR of 8 per cent. At the end of 2005 the average CAR of the CCB sector was 5.13 per cent, an increase of 3.82 per cent over the previous year. The number of CCBs which had attained the CAR of 8 per cent rose from 18 in early 2005 to 36. By the end of 2005 (CBRC Annual Report 2005) and in 2008, the total number of banks that had met this ratio (i.e. CCBs including SOCBs, JSCBs, RCBs, etc.) rose to 204 owning 99.9 per cent of the total banking system's assets (CBRC Annual Report 2008). The continuing improvement of the CAR was maintained and the average CAR of the CCB sector has since increased to 12.58 per cent as of the end of 2008.

6 Foreign investor interest in China's CCBs

The Banker magazine chronicled in their April 2006 issue 'Best Banks to Buy in China' and identified several leading CCBs (*The Banker*, April 2006). Most, if not all, of these CCBs are largely owned directly or indirectly by the local government authorities and many of them have problems of low CARs, high NPLs and poor risk management. Given the negatives mentioned above, what is the attraction for foreign banks to take up shareholdings? After all, the maximum that foreign banks can hold in total in a domestic bank is only 25 per cent and the maximum that anyone can hold is 20 per cent. The attraction lies in that currently this is the only cheap option available to gain entry into the Chinese banking sector (see Chapter 10, pp. 101–102). While the rules may seem strict now, it is conceivable that they may be relaxed in the years ahead in which case the current prices paid on these investments may turn out to be very profitable investments in the future.

The time is now right for foreign participation because the CCBs themselves are open to the idea of foreign partnerships and this is crucial for the success of such ventures – that both parties want to make it work. However, both parties must be clear about what they want so that expectations can be met. On the Chinese side they are clear – they need capital injection and technical expertise in many areas including corporate governance. And in return there is the expectation of capital and value appreciation when the bank is listed on the stock exchange.

Foreign banking institutions wishing to invest in China's CCBs must remember that there are many problems to be faced. The main challenges facing foreign entrants into the Chinese CCBs relate mainly to a poor credit culture. From this deficiency arise a host of other problems including high percentages of NPLs, related party transactions, poor internal controls and lack of supervisory procedures. Other problems relate to obsolete equipment and processes and lack of professionalism among the staff. The resolution of these problems will take a long time and foreign financial institutions must be prepared to invest for the long term, otherwise they will be disappointed.

The opportunities that the CCBs bring to the table are considerable. As mentioned earlier many of the larger cities have huge populations. Table 8.6 gives an idea of the three major cities in China and their respective statistics. The ANZ Bank of Australia based part of its decision to invest in the Shanghai Rural Commercial Bank and the Tianjin City Commercial Bank on these statistics.

Table 8.6 Statistics of three major cities in China

Details	*Tianjin*	*Shanghai*	*Beijing*
Population (million)	10.2	16.7	13.9
GDP US$ billion	36.3	92	53
GDP growth (%)	+15.7	+13.6	+13.2
GDP per capita (US$ 000s)	3.6	5.5	3.8

Source: adapted from ANZ Bank Report (2005).

Investment in any one of the large CCBs therefore brings along with it the expectation of a large and growing population as China's rural farmers migrate to the cities in ever increasing numbers, bringing with them strong and sustained economic growth. Cities along the east coast belt will continue to show sustained economic growth and increasing economic activity as the population become more affluent and increase consumption. There is also the possibility of ongoing banking deregulation and the reducing reliance on government can only augur well for the future.

7 Foreign investments in CCBs

Liu Mingkang, head of the CBRC, has called on the CCBs to pursue strategic relationships with foreign investors in order to strengthen their balance sheets, accelerate their development of customer service, risk management and the introduction of new products. At the end of 2008, 13 have already entered into agreements with foreign partners with more at the negotiations stage. Although foreign banks have answered this call, they must be aware that there are substantial differences in how banking business is conducted in China compared with overseas markets and they must be aware of the pitfalls. Hawes and Chiu (2007) have written on the cultural differences that matter and suggest ways of how both parties may work together for mutual benefit.

The International Finance Corporation (IFC), the private sector arm of the World Bank Group, was the first foreign financial institution to invest in a CCB, the Bank of Shanghai, in 1999. Subsequent negotiations concluded an investment in 2001 for the IFC to invest US$27 million for a 15 per cent stake in the Nanjing City Commercial Bank (since renamed the Bank of Nanjing). Nanjing is the capital of Jiangsu province and the Bank of Nanjing was set up in 1996 through a merger of 40 UCCs. About 90 per cent of the bank's total lending is to the SME sector. Since its entry into the bank, the IFC has helped the Bank of Nanjing to improve its credit and risk management policies and transformed it into a relatively well run commercial lender by bringing its management in line with international practices. The bank's NPL was reduced to 3.32 per cent by June 2004, which was much lower than the 14.8 per cent average for the country's 111 CCBs at the same time (*The Banker:* Nanjing City Commercial Bank Edition 2nd May 2005). The bank also had a CAR of 9.59 per cent which was above the 8 per cent minimum requirement.

The IFC partnership was very successful and, in October 2005, BNP Paribas announced that it would acquire a 19.2 per cent stake in the Bank of Nanjing for US$87 million. The IFC's stake of 15 per cent, which it bought for $27 million, became valued at US$68 million and the IFC Group sold down its 15 per cent stake to 5 per cent and realized a handsome profit. The Bank of Nanjing listed on the Shanghai Stock Exchange in July 2007.

In 2001, the HSBC Banking Group, together with the IFC and the Shanghai Commercial Bank (Hong Kong), concluded a deal for the consortium to take a 18 per cent stake in the Bank of Shanghai with the IFC taking 10 per cent, HSBC Bank 8 per cent and the Shanghai Commercial Bank (HK) taking 3 per cent. The Bank of Shanghai was established in 1995 and as of 31 December 2000 had assets of US$11.64 billion and 196 branches. With its expertise and connections to the CCBs, the IFC became a focal point for outside investors wishing to invest in China's CCBs and so again in 2004 the IFC joined the Bank of Nova Scotia to take up a stake of 24.9 per cent in the Xian City Commercial Bank. The Xian City Commercial Bank was established in 1997 through a consolidation of 42 UCCs and it provides a full range of banking services directed primarily at SMEs.

In September 2004, the Commonwealth Bank of Australia (CBA) concluded an agreement to invest US$17 million in the Jinan City Commercial Bank (JCCB) and took up 11 per cent in the bank with an option to raise it to 20 per cent of its shareholding. Jinan City Commercial Bank, which has since changed its name to Bank of Qilu, was set up in 1996 and has its branches throughout Jinan, the capital city of Shandong province. Shandong has a population of over 90 million. This initial investment was further increased by the CBA in April 2005 when it agreed to invest US$78 million for a 19.9 per cent stake in the Hangzhou City Commercial Bank. Hangzhou City Commercial Bank, which has since changed its name to Bank of Hangzhou, is ranked at number two overall amongst all CCBs according to the KPMG Research Report on China (Appendix 6). The attraction of Hangzhou is that it has a large population of over six million and is the capital of Zhejiang province. It has also been named as a top investment destination by Forbes. The attractiveness of the bank was further evidenced in August 2006 when the Asian Development Bank (ADB) signed an agreement to take up a 5 per cent stake for US$30 million. The Australian interest in China's CCBs was furthered demonstrated by the ANZ Banking Group when it signed an agreement to take 19.9 per cent of the shareholding of Tianjin City Commercial Bank (TCCB) for US120 million in December 2005. Tianjin City Commercial Bank has also changed its name to Bank of Tianjin.

Hong Kong's Dah Sing Bank and the US private equity firm Carlyle Group have also agreed to pay US$130 million for a 25 per cent stake in Chongqing City Commercial Bank, a small lender in south-west China. The Bank of Beijing (formerly known as Beijing City Commercial Bank) has, as its foreign shareholder, the Dutch Banking & Insurance Group ING which bought a 19.9 per cent stake in November 2005 for US$215 million. The IFC also bought a 5 per cent stake in the Bank of Beijing. ING appointed two senior bankers to work with and advise the Bank of Beijing on implementation of new technologies and management know-how.

Table 8.7 shows the largest 20 cities in China and those CCBs that have foreign investors. Of the remainder, many are in discussions with foreign banks for strategic alliances. The table gives an indication for prospective investors.

Amongst the top 50 CCBs there are some city banks which are quite attractive and which do not have foreign shareholders yet. Among them are Suzhou City Commercial Bank and Wenzhou City Commercial Bank. However, foreign partners have shown interest in both banks. Wenzhou City Commercial Bank is a small thriving bank because the town itself is a thriving centre of private commerce. Suzhou is also a rapidly expanding light industrial city that has benefited its own CCB.

8 China's CCBs

Most CCBs have the provincial government or one or more of their SOEs as major shareholders. Restructuring was promoted to make these CCBs more viable, competitive and market driven. They have shown tremendous growth in China over the last few years as Table 8.8 shows.

Table 8.7 China's top 20 largest cities

City	*Population million 2003*	*GDP US$ billion 2003*	*City Commercial Banks*	*Foreign share hldg (%)*
1 Shanghai	12.8	76	Bank of Shanghai	18
2 Beijing	10.2	44	Bank of Beijing	25
3 Chongqing	10.1	27	Chongqing City Com bank	25
4 Wuhan	7.8	20	Wuhan City Com bank	
5 Tianjin	7.6	30	Tianjin City Com bank	20
6 Guangzhou	5.9	42	Guangzhou City Com bank	
7 Xian	5.1	11	Xian City Commercial bank	5
8 Nanjing	4.9	19	Nanjing City Com bank	15
9 Shenyang	4.9	19	Shenyang City Com bank	
10 Shantou	4.8	6	–	
11 Chengdu	4.5	23	Chengdu City Com bank	20
12 Hangzhou	3.9	13	Hangzhou City Com bank	20
13 Foshan	3.4	4	Foshan City Com bank	
14 Jinan	3.3	17	Jinan City Com bank	11
15 Harbin	3.2	17	Harbin City Com bank	
16 Changchun	3.1	16	Changchun City Com bank	
17 Tangshan	3.0	16	Tangshan City Com bank	
18 Dalian	2.7	20	Dalian City Com bank	10
19 Zibo	2.7	11	Zibo City Com bank	
20 Huaian	2.7	5	Huaian City Com bank	

Source: adapted from KPMG Report (2006).

Table 8.8 Data on City Commercial Banks (RMB 100 million)

	2003	*2004*	*2005*	*2006*	*2007*	*2008*
Total assets	14,621.7	17,056.3	20,366.9	25,937.9	33,404.8	41,319.7
Growth (%)		16.6	19.4	27.3	28.8	23.7
Total liabilities	14,122.5	16,472.7	19,540.2	24,722.6	31,521.4	38,650.9
Growth (%)		16.6	18.6	26.5	27.5	22.6
Owners' equity	499.1	583.6	826.7	1,215.3	1,883.4	2,668.7
Growth (%)		16.9	41.6	47.1	54.9	41.7
After tax profits	54.2	87.4	120.7	180.9	248.1	407.9
Growth (%)		61.2	38.1	49.9	37.1	64.4
NPLs (% of total loans)	n/a	n/a	7.73	4.78	3.0	2.3
Number of staff	n/a	n/a	n/a	113,999	123,380	150,920
Number of banks	n/a	n/a	n/a	113	124	136

Source: adapted from CBRC Annual Reports (2006–2008).

Total assets and liabilities have grown year on year, showing a 16.6 per cent increase in 2004, 19.4 per cent in 2005, 27.3 per cent in 2006, 28.8 per cent in 2007 and 23.7 per cent in 2008. Owners' equity has also increased year on year from 16.9 per cent in 2004 to 54.9 per cent in 2007 before dipping to 41.7 per cent in 2008. These figures were matched by pre-tax profits which also increased substantially over the years to 2008. NPLs were also reduced from 7.73 per cent at the end of 2005 to 2.3 per cent at the end of 2008.

9 Conclusion

China's CCBs evolved from the UCCs which were mostly set up in the 1980s and early 1990s in response to the tremendous growth of the TVEs which proliferated as a result of the economic reforms. The UCCs were restructured because of the many problems faced: high NPLs, low CARs, poor risk management and inadequate financial products. Many of the CCBs still suffer from the same problems faced when they were credit cooperatives. Although the CCBs play a minor role in the overall scheme of things, accounting for about 6 per cent of total banking assets, their influence on the SMEs is substantial.

CCBs form the third tier of the PRC banking system and are currently being encouraged to further restructure by taking in foreign banking partners who will provide capital injection and banking expertise. It is also hoped that they will help to raise the levels of the local banks to international standards. Foreign banking institutions are keen to invest in this sector because it provides a relatively cheap entry into China's booming banking sector. Most of the top ten CCBs already have foreign shareholdings in place and potential investors will have to look further down the scale. However, those CCBs further down the scale are bogged down by continuing problems of NPLs, state interference and poor corporate governance.

The restrictions placed on the banking shareholdings that foreigners can hold are also onerous: 25 per cent in total and for any single foreign shareholder not to exceed 20 per cent These limits, together with the lack of free market forces in the corporate marketplace, mean that the potential for substantial gains on their foreign investments is limited and may be curtailed in the future. Under the WTO accords, as from the end of December 2006, China's banking industry was considerably opened to foreign competition and foreign participation. However, there was not a plethora of foreign banks and branches opening up all over the country because of stringent conditions placed on such activities by the CBRC. When conditions have been met by foreign applicants, approval has been given. Recently the ANZ Bank opened its fourth branch in Chongqing, China (*Sydney Morning Herald*, 7 May 2010). The ANZ Bank already has branches in Beijing, Shanghai and Guangzhou.

The opportunities in CCBs are still there but both parties will have to be clear on their expectations and proceed on the basis of a long-term relationship. Only in this scenario can the benefits and objectives be achieved by both parties. The warnings sounded by Lardy regarding the systemic risks of the banking system however should serve as a reminder to foreign banking institutions wishing to invest in CCBs in China.

9 Government policies affecting City Commercial Banks

1 Introduction

China's planners have traditionally used the banking system as an extension of economic planning and hence a tool for the attainment of national economic goals and objectives. During the central planning era until the late 1970s, the banking system handed out loans to SOEs without little regard to profitability or repayment capacity. In fact many of these loans were merely regarded as disbursements and were never repaid and many enterprises were kept afloat for socio-economic reasons, such as maintaining high employment and preventing social unrest. Other reasons were strategic, such as keeping loss-making military industrial enterprises afloat. The soft budget constraint (Kornai 1986) was in constant usage. From the late 1980s onwards, the banking system was slowly reformed to be more commercial and profit oriented but still retained many of its old failings with the SOCBs still being instructed to direct their lending to often bankrupt SOEs regardless of creditworthiness.

There were two main types of policies impacting on the banks in China and they emanated from both the central and the provincial government. At the central level the economic policies were those promulgated by the NDRC, i.e. the National Development and Reform Commission of the State Council and various economic planning targets as enunciated from time to time by the provincial governments. This chapter describes how government policies have impacted directly and indirectly on the CCBs.

2 National policies of the National Development and Reform Commission

The State Council (the CBRC and the PBOC both report directly to the State Council) is the Chinese equivalent of the Westminster-style ministerial Cabinet and the NDRC is one of the most powerful departments within the State Council. It is responsible for the macro-planning and control of the national economic targets, goals, and objectives. It draws up the country's Five-Year Plans and broadly outlines the means of achieving these goals. Its stated objectives are to organize and implement national economic and social development strategies, long term, medium term and annual plans; propose goals and policies for national economic development and optimization of important economic structures; put forward proposals for various economic measures and policies; make reports on the national economic and social development plans to the National People's Congress on behalf of the State Council.

Because it has successfully steered China's economic reform process over the last 30 years, this department's plans and policies carry weight and credibility. Some of the policies that best describe the NDRC's plans appear as slogans but their policies are real and they are assiduously implemented by bureaucrats. Throughout the 1980s to the present, there have been many economic policies and here we shall consider some of them insofar as they impact on CCBs.

2.1 Touching stones to cross the river

This policy of 'touching stones to cross the river' [摸 石 过 河] was used to describe the economic policy in the early reform years when China's planners gradually introduced economic changes to open up the economy to private enterprise while still retaining the structures of a centrally planned economy (Nolan 1994). The policies adopted were incremental and experimental, much like a person trying to cross a river by feeling for stones on the river bed. Whichever policies worked were adopted, whichever did not were discarded. The reason for this gradualism was obvious – there was no model to follow as China was the first socialist country to introduce market reforms. The Big Bang theory of economic reform had yet to make its debut. Deng Xiaoping had visited Thailand, Malaysia and Singapore in early 1978 and had seen how prosperous those countries were when compared to China. He came back determined to implement market reforms. The result was the 'walking on two legs' policy. Naughton has described this policy in his book *Growing Out of the Plan: Chinese Economic Reform 1978–1993*. This policy describes the dual-track approach adopted by Chinese authorities. Initially, in accordance with central planning policies, the state-owned sectors of the economy in both agriculture and industry continued to be assigned certain production targets. Any excess over the planned targets was sold in the free marketplace and profits generated were shared by the workers and the peasants. The result was dramatic and economic growth picked up sharply.

The process of economic reform continued with new experimental steps being undertaken. Peasants were leased land plots for private farming and the beginnings of private ownership in the commercial sector appeared. Initially the private sector ownership appeared as TVEs. The rapid growth of these TVEs created a new demand – their need for financial services which resulted in credit cooperatives being allowed to be established in both rural and urban areas. UCCs were thus set up in the cities and RCCs were set up in the rural areas. The numbers of UCCs flourished as Table 8.1 shows.

With the influx of FDI, it was necessary to attend to foreign investors' special needs of infrastructure and other supporting services. Special Economic Zones

(SEZ) were thus set up in the coastal provinces, in Shenzhen, Xiamen and Shanghai as these were cities with historical links to the Chinese diaspora who were the main initial investors. At the same time, the national banking system was reformed and the SOCBs were created: the Agricultural Bank of China, Bank of China, China Construction Bank and Industrial & Commercial Bank. (The Bank of Communications was later added on as one of the SOCBs.) These SOCBs initially lent most of their funds to the state-owned sector and, in keeping with the policy of 'walking on two legs', other national financial banks were allowed to be established to fund the private sector. These were the JSCBs and were all founded and funded by the private sector.

2.2 Seize the large and release the small

During the 1990s, in the aftermath of the Asian Financial Crisis, authorities decided to further reform the economy by tackling the SOEs. The large SOEs were reorganized, repackaged and listed on the two local stock exchanges and the small SOEs were privatized. At that time, there were about 300,000 SOEs, of which about one-third were loss-making, about one-third were profitable and the balance were borderline. With the implementation of this policy, the vast majority of the small and medium SOEs were privatized and were no longer a burden to the state. Those remaining were reorganized and some became profitable. The larger SOEs were listed on the Shanghai or Shenzhen stock exchanges. This policy of keeping the large SOEs and selling off the small enterprises [抓大放小] was the brainchild of the then Premier Zhu Rongji and was generally deemed an economic success (Yeung and DeWoskin 2001).

In terms of the banking industry, the authorities concentrated their efforts on restructuring the main SOCBs. These SOCBs were huge banking enterprises each with tens of thousands of branches. The Chinese authorities' priority was to introduce corporate governance, commercial principles and risk management so that these SOCBs could increasingly meet the demands of a market economy. The JSCBs, on the other hand, which were newly set up, were much smaller and were allowed a free hand to expand and compete with the SOCBs. At the same time, UCCs were restructured into CCBs with the expectation that they provide banking services to the SMEs in the urban areas. At the same time, CCBs were encouraged by the CBRC to seek our foreign partners who would not only introduce capital into the CCBs but, more importantly, help them introduce proper risk management techniques and raise banking standards to international levels.

2.3 Opening of the West

In 2000, the 'Opening of the West' [西方大开发] policy was announced and special tax and other fiscal incentives were announced to encourage FDI to flow to the western regions of China. The then President of China, Jiang Zemin, declared that the development of the west was crucial to China's stability, the

Communist Party's hold on power, and the 'revitalization of the Chinese people' (Moneyhon 2003). Infrastructure expenditure in the western regions was accelerated and substantial increases in investments in roads and railways were made by the central government in subsequent years. An example was the Beijing–Tibet Railway opened in July 2007.

In terms of banking institutions, they were also accorded similar favourable treatment if they opened branches in the western regions. Overall the policy has had mixed success as both local direct investment and FDI have been slow to relocate to the remote western regions in spite of incentives being given to banks and businesses to relocate there. CCBs set up in the western regions include Urumqi City Commercial Bank in Xinjiang and, in Inner Mongolia, Hohhot City Commercial Bank and Baotou City Commercial Bank.

2.4 A harmonious society

Establishing a harmonious society [和谐社会] is the slogan of the current political leadership and this means the attainment of several objectives including reducing the disparity in economic development between coastal provinces and the western regions/central provinces; reducing the income disparity between rural/urban population and finally reducing the high unemployment in the poorer provinces. When Hu Jintao came to power, he inherited an increasingly divided society, widening regional disparities, a tattered social and welfare system, massive unemployment, structural poverty and rising environmental concerns (Zheng and Tok 2007).

One of the best methods of promoting economic growth and employment in the poorer regions is to facilitate the growth of SMEs. However, in China, SMEs have traditionally been starved of bank funds. Their sources of funding have been friends, business associates, rotating credit associations, credit cooperatives and private money lenders. Insofar as the banking industry is concerned, both local and national banks have been directed to lend to SMEs in both rural and urban areas. In May 2006 the CBRC sent out 'Guidelines on Due Diligence of Commercial Banks in Lending to Small Businesses' to all banks encouraging credit to SMEs. The directive has been successful and, as of 31 December 2008, 71.16 per cent of all loans outstanding in the CCBs were classified as being loans to SMEs (CBRC Annual Report 2008).

In the wake of its success in Bangladesh, through the Grameen Bank founded by Dr Mohamed Yunus (winner of Nobel Peace Prize 2006), microfinance has also been introduced to China and there is a concerted effort to make it work as the government, NGOs and commercial banks begin to explore ways to provide the country's most impoverished people with greater access to credit. According to research there is potential for microfinance to succeed in China especially in the area of structured microfinance (Bystrom 2007). The China Association of Microfinance is moving into the phase of from 'experiment to large-scale commercial development'. The development of microfinance is not likely to impact heavily on CCBs as they lend mostly to SMEs while microfinance lenders will direct their activities at the farmers and peasants who comprise the lower end of the market. Typically, loans for microfinance range from RMB10,000 to RMB50,000. *The People's Daily* recently reported (18 July 2010) that the Agricultural Bank of China (which listed on the Shanghai Stock Exchange on 16 July 2010) had expanded its mircofinance loan programme in the rural areas with microfinance loans comprising 2 per cent of all new loans disbursed in 2009.

2.5 The challenge of WTO commitments

The government negotiated for China to enter the WTO and, as from December 2006, the banking industry has been opened up to foreign banks so they can compete on a more level playing field. Foreign banks were invited to participate in the NDRC's initiatives and open branches in the interior and the western regions. In coastal areas, which are already overbanked, there are restrictions but banking services once denied to foreign banks are now being permitted (an example is the opening up of RMB services to foreign banks).

However, there is the fear that with the WTO accords, the Chinese SOCBs and the JSCBs will be overwhelmed by the foreign banks, most of which are global banks with deep pockets, superior services and innovative products. The growth of market share by foreign banks has been phenomenal in the last few years and while still small overall by comparison to the local banks, it is growing rapidly and could pose serious competition in future. For example the foreign banks' share of total bank assets bank assets grew 223 per cent over a five-year period between 2003 and 2008 from RMB415.9 billion to RMB1,344.8 billion whereas local banks only increased by only 125.6 per cent (CBRC Annual Report 2008). One result of this fear is that the Chinese banks have modernized themselves in many ways and invited foreign banks to become shareholders. The impact of WTO entry on corporate governance was summarized by Guo (2008) who found the result being 'a reduction of the Party-state's control of economic activity and improved legal regulation and increasing transparency of trade-related rules and rule-making'.

3 Preferred lending policies directed by the government

The degree of interference in the lending policies of banks differs from province to province and from bank to bank. At the ground level, the SOCBs are most vulnerable to pressure from the central government agencies like the NDRC and, to a lesser degree, to pressure from the provincial governments. Many of these bank managers are aspiring bureaucrats and CCP members who approve credit facilities to SOEs to gain favour with senior colleagues. The NDRC has also made it clear that the SOCBs' main lending should be to the SOEs and the reasons are not only economic but also socio-political.

In the execution of lending policies at the provincial level, however, the following Chinese saying sometimes applies – 天 高皇帝远 (The Sky is High and the Emperor is Faraway). This pithy saying merely means that the further the province is away from the capital Beijing, the less closely are the central government's policies likely to be followed. An example of this relates to the strict environmental laws enacted years ago but a decade later pollution and land degradation is still problematical.

Insofar as the CCBs are concerned, they are under pressure to fund the local government's infrastructure spending and development projects. Provincial governments are responsible to a large extent for the economic development, employment situation, revenues and expenditures of the province and hence are keen to see economic development and new FDI in their province. The central government cannot sensibly and speedily approve new investments all over the country and hence has given provinces limited approval authority for new investments. A recent preferred lending sector is the housing sector as China becomes a home ownership country. Home loans are one of the fastest growing loan categories of all banks now. Home prices have also rocketed in recent years and the home property market in China appears to be over-inflated with the former chief economist of the IMF, Kenneth Rogoff, on record as predicting a collapse of property prices in China (*Bloomberg*, 5 July 2010).

4 Bridging the urban–rural and rich–poor divide

The relationship between the central and provincial government has come under strain in the reform period and the prevalent view is that economic reforms have reduced the political control of the centre. Huang (1996) disputes this view. His findings show that economic decentralization has been accompanied by a strengthening of China's unitary political system. This relationship has changed over time and this is clearly exemplified by the urbanization policy, which once was discouraged by central authorities but later reversed (Brada *et al.* 2009).

China, while not impoverished, is still a developing country with wide income and wealth disparities between the rich and poor. A report by the Chinese Academy of Social Sciences (CASS) shows that China's worrisome income gap shows no signs of narrowing despite government efforts to bridge it (*Xinhua*, 7 January 2007). The central government in Beijing is well aware of the huge income/wealth disparity between urban and rural areas and the rich and poor and is determined to alleviate the situation. This is reflected in its determination to promote and modernize rural financial institutions and encourage lending to SMEs. Traditionally RCCs have serviced most of the financial needs of the farmers and peasants but they have been stymied because of poor management, poor governance and weak financials. In the past these RCCs merely served as deposit collection points and these funds were then lent out in the urban areas or to SOEs. To address this disparity, the CBRC has restructured the RCCs so that they can better meet the banking needs of the farmers and peasants. This was completed in 2006 when reforms were rolled out. Of the 30 provinces, 27 chose to establish integrated provincial credit cooperatives, two chose to become rural commercial banks and one chose to become a rural cooperative bank. The CBRC arranged for the newly reformed RCCs to report to the provincial government but responsibility for their supervision and regulation would rest with the CBRC. The rural credit cooperatives would however be responsible for lending out loans and retain risk control.

5 Conclusion

Government policies that impact on local banking in China emanate from two sources: the NDRC of the State Council and various economic planning units within the provincial government. Central government policies have obviously taken a macro-level approach to national economic problems while the provincial governments concern themselves with local and regional issues. We study these national and provincial policies adopted insofar as they impact on the banking system.

The first major economic policy adopted during the late 1970s and early 1980s was an experimental one: where tentative market reforms were introduced initially with elements of private enterprise being allowed to co-exist with state ownership. Later on the beginnings of private ownership were allowed and this made its appearance as TVEs. Gradually, a series of other incremental steps were taken to reform the economy. This is best described as 'Touching Stones to Cross the River' [摸石过河]. This policy also was also responsible for the growth of the financial institutions in the towns and villages where various financial structures including credit unions and small local banks were allowed to be established. Another national policy practised in the late 1990s was 'Seize the Large and Release the Small' [抓大放 小] where the large SOCBs were restructured through cash massive injection and transfers out of NPLs into AMCs. Simultaneously the UCCs were restructured into CCBs with encouragement from the CBRC to seek foreign equity partners. The policy of 'Opening of the West' [西方大开发] has had mixed response as businessmen hesitate to invest in the far western regions even though the central government has offered incentives for banks and businesses to locate there. The policy of 'A Harmonious Society' [和谐社会] focuses on reduction of income and wealth disparity between the rich and the poor. This policy sees implementation by the central government through large investments in infrastructure spending in the poorer provinces. Efforts by authorities to bridge the rural–urban divide concentrate on the reform of rural financial institutions as these are seen as key to the alleviation of poverty and the creation of wealth and employment in the rural areas. Microfinance in the rural areas is seen as an area of great potential.

Government policies at the provincial level focus on the local banks that are under their control. These are the CCBs, which in the majority of cases have the state or SOEs as majority shareholder. As such, they exert influence on its lending policies and thus the CCBs were under pressure to finance the provincial government's projects and enterprises. However the CBRC has also stepped in and directed these CCBs to lend to SMEs as well and this directive has taken root. The CCBs have also had much success in reducing their NPLs and this is because banks are becoming more commercial driven and profit oriented. Some of that success in reducing NPLs and increasing CARs is attributable to the foreign shareholders who have injected not only capital, but more importantly, introduced expertise in risk management and good corporate governance practices. This trend is being actively encouraged.

The CCBs have seen rapid expansion over the last decade as they amalgamated, restructured and took on new shareholders, both local and foreign. In the process of doing so, they have become stronger, more cohesive and more commercialized. The CBRC has removed the geographical restrictions imposed on some of those CCBs as they improved their corporate governance regime and they will begin to pose a challenge to the JSCBs. The CCBs accounted for over 6 per cent of total banking assets at the end of 2008 but this percentage will increase in the years ahead.

10 Foreign partners in China's City Commercial Banks

1 Introduction

Corporate governance is a topic of interest to both international investors and Chinese regulatory bodies. International investors invest in the Chinese local banks with a view to financial gain and the CBRC has encouraged CCBs to seek foreign partners with the aim of raising their skill set and expertise levels. Both of these objectives find congruency in corporate governance.

As of the end of 2008, there were 136 CCBs in China. Of the 136 CCBs, 13 of them had foreign shareholdings (Table 10.1) and this chapter focuses on those banks with foreign shareholders. The author was successful in interviewing ten[1] of these banks with foreign shareholdings. This number (ten out of 13) represents 77 per cent of the total number of CCBs with foreign shareholders. Interviews were conducted with senior personnel from the banks and included CEOs, executive directors, general managers, heads of department, senior vice presidents and others involved in the acquisition and administration of the Chinese shareholdings. Their views were sought on a range of issues relating to corporate governance before and after they invested. Interviews were based on the questionnaire in Appendix 7. It is emphasized that all ten of the foreign partners are banking institutions, most of which are large financial banking organizations. They were not sleeping partners who merely invested capital in the CCBs and, possessing banking expertise themselves, were able to play an active role in the management of the banks they invested in.

Our findings indicate that foreign equity participation has impacted on and improved the corporate governance of Chinese CCBs. The findings also indicate that, with improved corporate governance, some CCBs had financial performances which exceeded similar corporate governance statistics in JSCBs and this obliged the CBRC to grant regional operating branch licences to them. The CBRC announced in 2004 the criteria for CCBs to be granted regional licences: their key financial performance such as NPL and CAR ratios must exceed the average performance of the JSCBs.

Research confirms that the model of corporate governance in Chinese banks is trending towards the United States and UK model but with Chinese characteristics. This model is however based on best practice although it will take some years to get there. In the words of Alex Thursby, the managing director ANZ Bank, Asia and the Far East, 'corporate governance in China is not like instant noodles – it will take time, effort and goodwill to attain best practice'.

2 Foreign investors in China's CCBs

In the aftermath of the Tiananmen crackdown and the ensuing economic slowdown in the early 1990s, many UCCs accumulated huge NPLs and were encouraged by the authorities to amalgamate into CCBs. They became the third tier of China's banking system. Subsequently, the CBRC encouraged them to seek foreign banking partners who could provide access to intellectual capital and help them modernize and 'grow stronger'.

The foreign investors in China's CCBs come from all over the world but in terms of value of investment; most of them are from Europe (34 per cent), Australia (29 per cent), Asia (28 per cent) and others (9 per cent). The European investors are diverse, coming from the UK (HSBC Banking Group, Rothschild), the Netherlands (ING Group), France (BNP Paribas) and Italy (Intesa Saopaolo SpA). The second

Table 10.1 Foreign investment in City Commercial Banks

City/bank	*Foreign investor*	*Date*	*Share (%)*	*US$ millions*
Bank of Shanghai	HSBC	Dec 01	8.0	63
	IFC	Sept 99	7.0	47
	Shanghai Commercial Bank	Dec 01	3.0	23
Bank of Nanjing	IFC	Nov 01	5.0	27
	BNP Paribas	Oct 05	19.2	87
Xian City Commercial Bank	International Finance Corp	Oct 04	2.5	7
	Bank of Nova Scotia		2.5	7
Qilu Bank	Commonwealth Bank of Australia	Sept 04	11.0	17
Bank of Hangzhou	Commonwealth Bank of Australia	Apr 05	19.8	78
	ADB	Aug 06	5.0	30
Nanchong City Commercial Bank	DEG	Jul 05	10.0	5
	SIDT		3.3	
Bank of Beijing	ING	Oct 05	19.9	215
	IFC	Oct 05	5.0	54
Bank of Tianjin	ANZ Bank of Australia	Dec 05	19.9	120
Shanghai Rural Commercial Bank	ANZ Bank of Australia	Nov 06	19.9	252
Bank of Ningbo	OCBC of Singapore	May 06	12.2	75
Chongqing City Commercial Bank	Dah Sing Bank	Dec 06	17.0	89
Qingdao City Commercial Bank	Intesa Saopaolo SpA	Jul 07	19.9	135
	Rothschild	Jul 07	5.0	33
Bank of Chengdu	Hong Leong Bank (M'sia)	Oct 2007	19.9	240
13 in total			TOTAL	US$1,604

Source: adapted from KPMG Report (2007).

Table 10.2 Investments in City Commercial Banks (by origin – percentage of total value 2009)

Origin	*Percentage of total investments*
Europe	34
Australia	29
Asia	28
Others	9
Total	100

Source: data adapted from Table 10.1.

largest group of investors by value come from Australia – namely the ANZ Banking Group and the Commonwealth Bank of Australia. The third largest foreign investor group by value come from Asia and originated from Hong Kong (Dah Sing Bank), Malaysia (Hong Leong Bank) and Singapore (OCBC Bank). Other foreign investors include the Bank of Nova Scotia from Canada and the International Finance Corporation (IFC). The IFC is part of the World Bank Group and was the first foreign institution to invest in a CCB in China when it took a 7 per cent stake in the Bank of Shanghai for US$47 million in September 1999.

Foreign banks invested in China because they had reason to believe that they would do well and research had indicated that foreign equity participation helps improve financial performance significantly. Berger *et al.* (2009) studied the efficiency of Chinese banks from 1994 to 2003 and findings suggested that the SOCBs in China are by far the least efficient; foreign banks are the most efficient; and that minority foreign ownership is associated with significantly improved efficiency. Another study by Laurenceson and Qin (2008) found a positive correlation between foreign investment and cost efficiency.

2.1 Summary of foreign investments in China's commercial banks

With China's admission into the WTO in December 2001, foreign banks stepped up their interest in Chinese banks. The Chinese banking system was the last sector of the economy to undergo thorough reform and foreign investors were quick to seize the opportunity. The CCBs themselves sought foreign partners because of the need for their expertise – modern processes and best practice which are not easily transplanted into the Chinese banking system.

Foreign investors have to be careful in choosing their banking investments. They are allowed a maximum of 20 per cent of the bank equity with total foreign equity not to exceed 25 per cent. Thus foreign shareholders will never be able to take control of the CCBs. And yet they have to make the partnership work and ensure that the venture is successful as otherwise the reputation of the foreign bank will suffer.

Foreign banks however are keen to invest in China's relatively undeveloped banking industry – a 10 per cent stake in one of the big SOCBs can easily cost a few billion US dollars. The Bank of America paid US$3 billion for 9.1 per cent of China Construction Bank, the Royal Bank of Scotland Consortium paid US$3.1 billion for 10 per cent of the Bank of China and Temasek Holdings (Singapore) paid US$3.1 billion for a 10 per cent stake in the Bank of China. A similar stake in one of the 12 JSCBs may be somewhat less but would be still substantial. In comparison, a 20 per cent stake in one of the CCBs may cost anything from US$50 to US$200 million, a much more manageable figure.

2.2 Research

In this chapter we analyse the ten CCBs with foreign shareholdings that were interviewed by the author. Out of the ten banks interviewed, four of them had Australian banks as foreign partners, four had European banks as foreign partners and another two had Asian banks as their foreign partner. The analysis is divided for convenience into three parts. Part 1 details the Australian banks' experiences, Part 2 details the European banks' experiences and Part 3 details the Asian banks' experiences.

Regarding the research conducted, each section will investigate why the foreign partner chose to invest in the particular bank; what the Chinese bank hoped to derive from the partnership; what the foreign partner did to improve corporate governance and, finally, how successful the partnership has been.

3 Part 1: the Australian banks

Why did Australian banks choose to invest in China?

By the year 2000, the domestic banking market in Australia was very crowded with the four main Australian banks comprising the Commonwealth Bank of Australia (CBA), Westpac Banking Corporation (WBC), National Australia Bank (NAB) and The Australia New Zealand Banking Group (ANZ) competing very aggressively for market share. Coupled with the fact that the Australian domestic financial services sector had been largely deregulated in the mid 1980s, there was also stiff competition from international banks like Citibank, HSBC, ING, Credit Suisse, Deutsch Bank and UBS. Profit margins were extremely thin in Australia and Australian banks looked overseas for expansion. Investing in China's banking system was a natural progression.

The selection process by the Australian banks was relatively straightforward. China's stunning economic growth was concentrated in the cities along the eastern seaboard and Australian bankers naturally chose to invest in banks in these cities. As foreign banks were unofficially advised that they could take up stakes in two third-tier banks, ANZ and CBA both chose one target bank in the north and another in the south of China. In China, the Yangtze river is the demarcation that divides north and south China. Thus ANZ Bank chose the Bank of Tianjin in the north and Shanghai Rural Commercial Bank in the south whereas the CBA chose the Qilu Bank in the north and the Bank of Hangzhou in the south.

The list of attractive bank targets can be counted on the fingers of one's hands and the top dozen or so CCBs are easily identified by reference to various banking journals and publications. Almost all of the foreign banks have chosen Chinese coastal CCBs to invest in. Once identified, the target banks' financial reports were scrutinized and preliminary enquiries made through the CBRC and help was sought from Austrade (an Australian government agency). Other institutions were also asked for any information about these banks. Contacts were made and preliminary meetings arranged and, if initial discussions were fruitful, due diligence was proceeded with. In the case of the CBA, their man in Hong Kong made contact with and talked to 20 of the top CCBs before whittling the prospective list down to two.

3.1 The experience of the ANZ Bank

ANZ Bank's decision to invest in China was not a specific directive from the board of directors, rather, it was the continuation of an existing strategy that ANZ Bank already had in place. In the year 2000, the board of ANZ Bank had already agreed in principle to the then CEO John MacFarlane's vision to create a 'Super Regional Bank' and the decision to invest in China was part of that strategy. By 2005, the ANZ Bank had already invested in banks in Indonesia, the Philippines, Cambodia, and Vietnam. China was one of the missing pieces. The ANZ Bank chose to invest in CCBs in Tianjin and Shanghai. The reasons for the ANZ Bank choosing to invest in Shanghai are obvious: it is the largest and wealthiest city in China and is also the commercial and financial capital. Shanghai is a city that prides itself on having one of the best infrastructure and educational systems with international standard economic development zones in which many of the World's Fortune 500 companies are situated. The reasons for ANZ Bank choosing to invest in Tianjin are also clear – Tianjin is the fifth largest city in China with a population of 11.2 million. It is the port for Beijing and serves as the gateway for the Bohai Gulf area. The population has a per capita GDP that is more than twice the national average (RMB55,473 compared to the national average of RMB23,205). Like Shanghai, Tianjin is a well-developed infrastructure and educational hub with several high-tech economic development zones. In addition its hinterland has petroleum reserves, manganese, boron and salt mining which are buttressed by geothermal energy.

3.1.1 Why the Tianjin City Commercial Bank (TCCB)?

The Tianjin City Commercial Bank (changed its name to Bank of Tianjin in April 2007) started on 6 November 1996 when the city's UCCs merged and joined hands with several state-owned enterprises and individuals who became shareholders of the bank. Since then it has grown from strength to strength. In 2005, it was the fourth largest CCB in China by assets with five million customer accounts and 180 outlets. Its NPL, which stood at 25 per cent of total loan portfolio in 2002, was substantially reduced to 9 per cent in 2005 (ANZ Bank

Report, www.anz.com/documents/au/Investor, 6 December 2005). The ANZ Bank announced its decision to invest in the Bank of Tianjin on 6 December 2005, agreeing to acquire 19.9 per cent of the bank for approximately US$120 million. According to the media release the reasons were as follows: ranked number two amongst China's total CCBs, it has experienced local management and a large and well diversified branch network; the bank has strong underlying earnings with lending in financial year 2004 showing lending growth of 27 per cent and deposit growth of 19 per cent; Tianjin is also China's fifth largest city with a population of 11 million; it is the key city in Bohai region, which has a population of 300 million and a 27 per cent share of China's total GDP; Tianjin is the seaport for Beijing and is the fourth largest port with 19 per cent annual trade growth, second only to Shanghai.

3.1.2 Why the Shanghai Rural Commercial Bank (SRCB)?

The ANZ Bank also invested in the SRCB. The SRCB first started in 1951 as a credit union organization established to cater to the needs of the rural community in the outlying areas of Shanghai. There was steady growth from the 1950s through to the 1980s and 1990s. By the year 2000 the credit union organization comprised 14 'super regional credit unions' with a total membership of 234 rural credit cooperatives. The financial services provided comprised mainly deposit-taking facilities but with economic reforms in the late 1980s and 1990s, it was evident that this was inadequate and so, in 2001, the credit unions amalgamated and created a head office unit in Shanghai to look into strategic planning for the future.

In 2003, the ANZ Bank of Australia was chosen to commence a relationship with the then credit union organization (the ANZ Bank has had a representative office in Shanghai since 1986). A cooperation agreement, an MOU (memorandum of understanding) and a letter of intent was signed and the ANZ Bank started the process of helping the credit union modernize its operations. The Chinese management of the Shanghai credit union was forward looking and, in 2004, when the ANZ Bank proposed that a new management team be installed the suggestion was accepted. The ANZ Bank cooperation extended into many fields including risk management, credit lending practices and credit risk modelling.

Under the guidance of the ANZ Bank, the organization became licensed as a fully fledged commercial bank in 2005. In November 2006, the ANZ Bank was formally welcomed as a 19.9 per cent shareholder in the Shanghai Rural Commercial Bank (SRCB), the amount paid being US$252 million. The ANZ Bank chose the SRCB because it had an existing relationship with the bank and knew it well. The SRCB had developed rapidly and became the seventh largest bank in Shanghai with 330 branches, 380 ATMs and over 5,000 staff. It had also strong underlying earnings lending growth increasing by 19 per cent over 2004 and deposit growth rising by 11 per cent. Unlike many other CCBs, CAR was strong and stood at 8.1 per cent in December 2005 while NPL stood at 3 per cent in June 2006 which was low by Chinese standards (ANZ Press Release 2006).

3.1.3 Why the Chinese CCBs agreed to the partnership

Both the senior management of Tianjin City Commercial Bank (later renamed Bank of Tianjin) and the Shanghai Rural Commercial Bank (SRCB) agreed to the partnership because they realized their own shortcomings and decided that the best and quickest way ahead was to get a strategic long-term foreign partner. In the case of the SRCB, the ANZ Bank had been deeply involved in its modernization, reorganization and formation since 2003 and it was natural for the SRCB to welcome the ANZ Bank as its strategic foreign partner.

In the negotiations leading up to the partnership, the ANZ Bank had also agreed to provide technical resources and access to its intellectual property to both banks. This would be done by the ANZ Bank, providing a US$5 million 'Future Development Fund' to each bank to finance resource transfers, management training and skill building programmes. The ANZ Bank's assistance would focus on risk management and retail banking – these were areas that both the TCCB and the SRCB needed. Yet another reason why the two banks agreed to the partnership was because the ANZ Bank had a long history of successful investments in Asia underpinned by cross-cultural management. The bank also had award-winning products and well proven efficiencies.

3.1.4 What was corporate governance like before the ANZ Bank invested?

The managing director of the ANZ Bank for Asia and the Pacific, Alex Thursby, in an interview with the author enthused that the three main parties in the Chinese banking system, namely the city governments (who were the majority shareholders), the CBRC who regulated the banks and the board of directors of the CCBs, were all firmly committed to good corporate governance. They were committed to good governance because all parties wanted their banks to be financially profitable and successful.

He confirmed that both the Tianjin CCB and the Shanghai Rural Commercial Bank were lacking in strong corporate governance structures and measures before the ANZ Bank invested. On NPLs, the overall positions in the two banks have improved substantially in the last three to four years. The NPLs arose because of the lack of a strong credit culture and poor risk evaluation at both banks and were at fairly high levels: 6.92 per cent at the Tianjin CCB in 2005 and 4.07 per cent at the Shanghai Rural Commercial Bank also in 2005. Since then, because of the strict risk evaluation and credit controls established by the ANZ Bank, the rate had declined in 2008 to 1.59 per cent at the Tianjin CCB and to 2.29 per cent at Shanghai Rural Commercial Bank.

Both banks did not have independent directors before ANZ went in. However since then, two independent directors have been appointed to each bank. ANZ has also insisted on the establishment of various management committees, e.g. the audit committee, the investment committee, the risk committee and the remunerations and promotions committee with ANZ representation on the committees and ANZ has insisted on the appointment of an international firm of chartered accountants as auditors. Meritocracy within the banks is in the process of being implemented. Transparency is much better than what it was before ANZ went in because ANZ insists on information disclosure in all important matters. However, it is somewhat different to international standards. China is not like the United States where transparency often means the washing of dirty linen in public, the dismissal of CEOs and share values punished. In China, there is a veiled transparency. Regarding corruption, there has been progress. The Chinese authorities are cracking down severely on bribery and corruption and overall the situation is getting much better.

ANZ has a team of staff monitoring changes and processes at both banks in its headquarters in Melbourne. They also make frequent trips to China. The team has introduced new analytical tools, processes, banking technology and banking software. But cost and affordability are key issues. The two banks are being prepared for listing in a few years. ANZ expects that the value of its investment in the two Chinese banks will increase by two to three times upon listing.

The CCP is on the periphery insofar as management of the two banks are concerned. What is most encouraging is that all the important players in the corporate governance arena are committed to its improvement and it has been improving. Since the ANZ Bank went into the two banks corporate governance has improved a lot. Sometimes it is a case of 'two steps forward and one step backward' but that is still progress.

3.1.5 Corporate governance in the Chinese banks invested by the ANZ Bank

The ANZ Bank has been careful to ensure sound corporate governance structures and mechanisms were implemented in the two CCBs it invested in. This was facilitated by the partnership agreements with the two CCBs which provided for the secondment of foreign staff to key managerial positions. In the Tianjin CCB, the ANZ Bank seconded four appointees to help implement best banking practice and, for the SRCB, the ANZ Bank seconded seven appointees and local staff to help with the transfer and implementation of best banking procedures. Corporate governance in China has become an important issue and banks realize that the practice of good governance is integral to the operations and management of a bank. The ANZ Bank sees corporate governance as emanating from the board with important roles played by independent directors. Previously board meetings were held once or twice a year and the board rubber-stamped preordained decisions. Furthermore, the board members and the management team were all appointed by the state – there was no separation of ownership and control and the tendency was for power to be concentrated in the hands of key board members who made the decisions that were rubber-stamped by the board.

However, there are healthy changes in corporate governance and this is being driven mainly by the Chinese themselves – the CBRC and the CSRC. They use the carrot-and-stick approach, i.e. the threat of jail and severe punishment for corruption and non-compliance (stick) and the approval of new products, new branches, training courses and model employee awards (carrot). The ANZ Bank has a 19.9 per cent stake in each of the two Chinese banks and, not being a controlling shareholder, has to bring about the changes it wants through moral suasion and creative influence. ANZ found it best to explain the desired changes as being good governance practices which will have beneficial commercial results. Initially there was resistance to the governance measures introduced as senior Chinese management did not want to see a more inquisitive and active board of directors but gradually they realized that good corporate governance meant that all the stakeholders had a voice in how the bank could be better managed. The greatest driver for change for good governance came from the Chinese government authorities. A second agent of change is the foreign bankers but the third and very important agent of change came from the Chinese banks themselves: their desire to get listed on the local exchanges. An IPO requires a multitude of formalities, rules and regulations, annual accounts, reports, profitability, etc., and all of them concern good corporate governance. The result is that they realize they have to establish good governance structures and mechanisms before listing.

The old 'command and control' management style does not work anymore. An example of the old command and control policy being practised in the Tianjin CCB was when ANZ moved some key staff into the bank office in 2005/2006 and the desks and furniture arrived late because the purchase order had to be approved by the board chairman. This was totally unnecessary and showed the poor accountability structure in the bank. Banks in China also have structural problems which impact on governance. The most difficult problem is to resolve the role and responsibility of the branch manager. Currently the branch manager in each branch is responsible for everything that happens in that branch. The branch manager has the right to hire and fire staff and the granting of loans (within prescribed limits) is one power that the branch manager wields absolutely. This was international practice 40 years ago but in China this still holds true and although the Chinese CEO may want to change the structure, the CEO finds it difficult for the following reasons: the branch manager is usually a person with strong local contacts and *guanxi* which helps generate business for the branch. There is also a lack of credit evaluation companies like Moody's and Standard & Poor's to assist loan evaluations at head office level. China is a huge country and there are also major differences between regions which result in the need for local knowledge which normally only established local branch managers can possess.

Although AGMs for the TCCB and SRCB are generally low-key affairs, board meetings are becoming fairly robust. Although board meetings and discussions are robust, as the ANZ Bank has only two board seats, it has to be diplomatic and do things gently bearing in mind that 'face' is so important to the other board members. The board of directors does not hire and fire senior management, the state government does. The Chinese board meetings also tend to be more consensus based but the board realize they need to have directors who add value. The board also needs to devolve responsibility and management have come to realize that they cannot run the bank as their personal fiefdom. These are standards that have started to flow through.

The ANZ Bank appointed personnel to head key areas within the CCBs, including risk, treasury and investments. On the question of accountability, directors have yet to see themselves as acting in the interests of all shareholders; they see themselves as being representatives of the shareholders who appointed them. Transparency and the rule of law are not perfect but are generally acknowledged to be improving. Laws are sometimes loosely worded and interpretations can vary, so this can pose problems for foreign investors. These are problems for foreign investors – can this contract be relied on? Securities pledged to the bank are sometimes subsequently found to have conflicting ownership. The state and municipal government are playing a lesser role in management and looking to further step back. They realize they do not have all the answers to bank management and look to the experts and foreign investors instead. However, as soon as something happens, their knee-jerk reaction is to get involved. The CCP and the local party secretary still wield influence in the bank.

The implementation of high standards of corporate governance in Chinese banks is a time issue – it will not happen overnight. The most important thing though is that there exists the desire for change – from the government agencies, the foreign investors and the banks themselves.

3.1.6 The ANZ Bank approach to solving corporate governance problems

The above sections clearly state some of the corporate problems faced – so how did ANZ approach them?

The ANZ Bank adopted a low-key approach in getting the board to adopt principles of good corporate governance. Mindful of the fact that it is a minority and not a controlling shareholder, the bank's representatives at board meetings decided that they would not pound the table and demand answers. That does not mean that board meetings are mere pleasantries because robust discussions do occur. The ANZ Bank also sought to establish sound long-term relationships with senior management. This was important as the bank was aware that it would need to work with the Chinese management to achieve the goals and objectives that it wanted. This appears to be in line with the recommendation of Hawes and Chiu who advised foreign bankers to 'focus on legitimate relationship building rather than on legal rights and obligations' (Hawes and Chiu 2007).

The ANZ Bank arranged for selected Chinese management to go to Australia for training in various fields so that Chinese managers could learn best practice which they could implement on their return. The ANZ Bank also seconded staff to China who understood the Chinese mentality and who could speak the language. For instance the senior manager posted to the SRCB understands Mandarin and had been working with the ANZ Bank in Taiwan for many years prior to secondment. The head of retail banking in Tianjin CCB also speaks Mandarin fluently. The ANZ Bank sought to explain the importance of implementing good corporate governance by showing how such a new strategy would result in improved financial performance. This was an extremely effective way of convincing the board of directors and senior management on why various new governance structures had to be established. For example, in establishing new risk and credit procedures of the evaluation of loans for the banks, ANZ stressed its impact on NPLs and indeed subsequent figures confirmed its efficacy as NPLs at the SRCB were reduced from 4.07 per cent in 2005 to 2.29 per cent in 2008. This low NPL ratio has been achieved by maintaining a strict regime of loan credit evaluation and follow-up procedures.

The Chinese management of both the TCCB and the SRCB are both extremely keen to have their bank listed on the Shanghai Stock Exchange as this will establish a true market value of their banks. However, they understand that for this to happen both banks must uplift their corporate governance standards to meet the stringent conditions of the Shanghai Stock Exchange. The ANZ Bank has justified the many corporate governance changes in this context and this approach has certainly helped to make them acceptable. The ANZ Bank has also insisted on the appointment of an international firm of accountants as joint auditors so that best practices can be introduced gradually.

3.1.7 Summary

The ANZ Bank invested US$120 million for a 19.9 per cent equity stake in the Tianjin City Commercial Bank in December 2005. Since then ANZ Bank has worked hard to improve corporate governance in the TCCB bank and, over the last four years, it has improved. By and large the partnership has been successful and the ANZ Bank is satisfied with the results. It has not been smooth sailing, but as the managing director mentioned, sometimes one has to take one step backwards after having taken two steps forward. Such are the intricacies of partnership in China.

Under the guidance of the ANZ Bank, bank assets have increased year on year by 17.4 per cent in 2006, 35.5 per cent in 2007 and 11.6 per cent in 2008 (see Table 10.3). Net profits also increased by 19.2 per cent in 2006, 230.2 per cent in 2007 and 0.5 per cent in 2008. The substantial increase in net profits in 2007 was due to a change in treatment of various loan provisions and adoption of modern accounting standards. At the same time NPLs fell from 6.92 per cent in 2005 to 1.55 per cent in 2008, a substantial drop of 5.37 per cent while the CAR has increased from 8.64 per cent in 2005 to 12.2 per cent in 2008. State-owned shares have also been somewhat reduced while the loan deposit ratio has been kept at a healthy level of 47.27 per cent in 2008. The most important fact to note though is that related party loans have been reduced substantially from RMB1,128 million in 2005 to RMB270 million in 2008, a drop of 78.3 per cent.

In recognition of its corporate governance improvements and the fact that its NPL and CAR outperformed the relevant average ratios of the JSCBs a regional

Table 10.3 Tianjin City Commercial Bank financial performance

Details	*2005*	*2006*	*2007*	*2008*
Bank assets (000s, RMB)	69,118,980	81,163,660	110,011,936	122,819,854
Percentage increase		+17.4	+35.5	+11.6
Net profits (000s, RMB)	381,190	454,310	1,499,341	1,507,105
Percentage increase		+19.2	+230.2	+0.5
Return on equity (%)	10.03	10.17	20.07	16.2
Non-performing loans (%)	6.92	3.58	2.06	1.55
Capital adequacy ratio (%)	8.64	11.65	11.51	12.20
Loans to deposit ratio (%)	52.63	50.48	49.25	47.27
State-owned shares (%)	85.54	71.02	71.02	71.02
Related party loans (RMB million)	1128.22	832.44	718.00	270.00

Source: adapted from Tianjin City Commercial Bank Annual Reports (2006–2008).

licence was granted by the CBRC and the Bank of Tianjin has opened branches in Beijing, Shanghai and Tangshan. Opening up new branches in different localities, however, brings about a whole new set of problems as it requires more supervision and the recruitment of competent personnel.

The ANZ Bank invested US$252 million for a 19.9 per cent stake in the Shanghai Rural Commercial Bank (SRCB) in November 2006 (see Table 10.4). The ANZ Bank has been involved in the management of the SRCB since 2003 when the bank worked hand-in-glove with local management on their restructuring. After it became a partner in 2006, it focused on corporate governance reform in the SRCB and it has improved substantially. The partnership has been a success story and the ANZ Bank is happy with the results achieved thus far.

It can be seen from Table 10.4 that the financial results of the SRCB improved all round after the ANZ Bank became a partner. Bank assets increased by 6.8 per cent in 2006, 15.7 per cent in 2007 and 10.1 per cent in 2008. Net profits also increased by 9.2 per cent in 2006, 3.6 per cent in 2007 and 99.9 per cent in 2008. Over the same period, 2005–2008, NPLs, already low at 4.07 per cent in 2005, were further reduced to 2.29 per cent in 2008 and CAR was increased from 8.26 per cent in 2005 to 11.8 per cent in 2008. Another notable statistic is the fact that related party loans were reduced from RMB612.61 million in 2006 to RMB116.8 million in 2008, a drop of 80.9 per cent. This indicates better risk control and evaluation of the loan portfolio and growing commercialization of the bank. In May 2007 the SRCB was awarded the 'Outstanding Bank for Small Enterprises' award and in 2008 was ranked at number 18 overall amongst all commercial banks in China (2008 Annual Report of SRCB).

3.2 The experience of the Commonwealth Bank of Australia (CBA)

Earlier, in Section 3 of this chapter, we read that the CBA chose to invest in two CCBs in China: the Jinan City Commercial Bank (later renamed Qilu Bank) and

Table 10.4 Shanghai Rural Commercial Bank financial performance

Details	*2005*	*2006*	*2007*	*2008*
Bank assets (000s, RMB)	127,416,876	136,108,749	157,474,437	173,327,345
Percentage increase		+6.8	+15.7	+10.1
Net profits (000s, RMB)	327,567	357,591	370,572	740,805
Percentage increase		+9.2	+3.6	+99.9
Return on equity (%)	5.32	5.68	4.21	6.50
Non-performing loans (%)	4.07	2.91	2.34	2.29
Capital adequacy ratio (%)	8.26	7.32	9.16	11.80
Loans to deposit ratio (%)	54.43	58.89	62.15	63.06
State-owned shares (%)	74.65	74.65	79.4	79.4
Related party loans (000s RMB)	n/a	612,610	538,550	116,801

Source: adapted from Shanghai Rural Commercial Bank Annual Reports (2006–2008).

the Hangzhou City Commercial Bank (later renamed Bank of Hangzhou). Unlike the ANZ Bank, which had more experience investing in China, the CBA chose to invest in two smaller cities. However, the two banks that the CBA chose were also leading banks ranked in the top ten of the CCBs. What were the imperatives for their decision? Financial performance, the potential for growth and profitability of the target banks were the main reasons but why the CBA chose to invest in Jinan and Hangzhou can be summarized as follows. Both are fairly large sized Chinese cities which are provincial capitals and also manufacturing and logistics hubs for the surrounding areas. Both are also centres of growth for their surrounding regions.

The CBA paid US$78 million for a 19.9 per cent stake in the Hangzhou City Commercial Bank (HCCB) which was in the top five of China's CCBs by assets. Hangzhou is the capital of Zhejiang province, a province in east China with a population of 47 million. Like other cities along the eastern seaboard of China, it has experienced double-digit economic growth since the late 1980s. It is a light industrial centre and was named by *Forbes* as the top investment location in 2005. The HCCB has been consistently rated as one of the best managed CCBs in China and is ranked second in terms of overall competitiveness (see Appendix 6).

Established in 1996, the Jinan City Commercial Bank (JCCB) has grown rapidly. As of October 2004, the bank's total assets came to RMB22.8 billion and total loan liabilities amounted to RMB15.88 billion, making the JCCB one of the top ten CCBs in China in terms of assets. Another reason why the CBA invested in the JCCB was because the bank is the leading commercial bank in Shandong province, a province with a population of 94 million. The CBA paid

US$17 million for an 11 per cent stake in the JCCB. This stake was subsequently increased to 19.9 per cent in September 2008.

3.2.1 What was corporate governance like in the banks that the CBA invested in?

The general manager of strategy and development for the CBA confirmed that, in the beginning, measures and structures of corporate governance in the two Chinese banks were below average. Transparency, accountability, information disclosure, risk controls and protection of minority interests were not up to international standards, but after four years of partnership, these same measures have improved substantially. One of the main reasons for the substantial improvement was that the CBA set up model branches in each of the two banks to train and teach the Chinese banks on how to implement best practice.

Overall there have been substantial improvements in corporate governance because the Chinese banks were serious about achieving Western standards of corporate governance and they worked hard towards it. As an example, corporate governance scores on a scale of one to ten (with one being bad practice and ten being best practice) on accountability, information disclosure, minority interest protection and risk management at both Chinese CCBs were on a score of five when the CBA first invested, but after four years of partnership, all measures had substantially improved. The Bank of Hangzhou appears to have more responsive and alert senior management who have worked closely with the CBA on corporate governance restructuring whereas Jinan City Commercial Bank has been slower to respond. The CBA has made it clear to the two CCBs that as a foreign investor it is contributing to the well-being and reputation of their banks. If it was to walk away from its investment for whatever reason, it would have a very negative impact and the Chinese banks are aware of this.

3.2.2 Another view of corporate governance in the Chinese banks

The head of the CBA's operations in China confirmed that although financial performance was the main factor in deciding which CCB to invest in, corporate governance was also an issue at the final stage of due diligence. Corporate governance in Chinese banks is generally below international standards and the CBA found this to be true of the two CCBs it invested in. Since then there has been good improvement in corporate governance. Three specific areas showing substantial improvement were board functions, the operation of management committees and adherence to management processes.

Transparency is an area where the CBA has had a strong positive impact but at the same time there has been a big internal momentum to improve this aspect of corporate governance. Standardization and transparency in financial reporting is an area that the CBA has given strong input to, helping the Chinese banks remap and recast their ledger systems. Initially there were instances where there were matters that should have been brought to the attention of the board but were not. These matters were decided and resolved by key managers when the board should have been the final arbiter. On discovering such malpractice, the CBA immediately put in place procedures to ensure that these instances did not recur.

Corporate governance in China's CCBs may be considered to be trending towards a model of corporate governance with Chinese characteristics. An example of this would be the presence of the CBRC representatives on the board meetings of the CCBs. Another would be the close and continued influence of the local governments in the activities and policies of these banks. Yet another example of the close relationship between the local government and the CCBs is the fact that many of the quality loans on the banking portfolios relate to state projects. Where there were state projects that were NPLs, the state transferred them out at book value and replaced them with either cash or other assets.

3.2.3 The CBA bank approach to solving corporate governance problems

The above sections state some of the corporate governance problems faced: so how did the CBA approach them?

The CBA established two model bank branches, one each in Jinan and Hangzhou with model systems and processes so that both management and staff could learn best practice and where proposed changes of governance could be introduced easily. The CBA has also introduced a lot of new systems and processes and this resulted in efficiency and cost savings. This was implemented together with corporate governance changes which facilitated their acceptance. Like the ANZ Bank, the CBA also sent Chinese management to Australia for training so they could learn how systems and processes worked in the Australian head office.

The CBA ensured that they were in charge of the appointment of key personnel like the head of risk, information technology and finance. These provisions are part of the partnership agreements which also provide for training of Chinese management, technology transfers and secondment of Australian managers. These key managers report to the CBA office in Hong Kong that monitors the CCB operations. This is important as their head office in Sydney is too far away but from their Hong Kong office, the CBA can be and is very hands on.

3.2.4 Summary

The CBA invested in two CCBs – the Jinan City Commercial Bank and the Hangzhou City Commercial Bank. Both banks are ranked highly in China and since the CBA invested, corporate governance has improved. The CBA has seconded staff into key areas of the two banks and corporate governance structures and mechanisms have been strengthened. The Bank of Hangzhou has submitted an application for an IPO which is being evaluated by the CSRC.

The Hangzhou City Commercial Bank increased its banking assets by 115.3 per cent between 2005 and 2008 and net profits increased by 193.6 per cent over the same period (Table 10.5). At the same time NPLs have been kept low, standing at 0.84 per cent at the end of 2008, and CAR at 10.70 per cent was excellent. Return on equity increased from 17.58 per cent in 2005 to 26.56 per cent in 2008. The role of the state declined significantly as evidenced by state-owned shares dropping sharply from 71.91 per cent in 2005 to 37.48 per cent in 2008. This is important as it indicates that the state role and influence is declining. All these financial indications mean that the bank is progressing strongly forward as a fully functioning commercial bank with high standards of operational efficiency. In recognition of its corporate governance improvements and the fact that its NPL and CAR exceeded the relevant average ratios of the JSCBs, the bank was granted a regional licence in 2007 and has established branches in Shanghai, Beijing and Shenzhen and in 2008 was given permission to establish two new branches in Nanjing and Ningbo (Bank of Hangzhou Annual Report 2008). This is a mark of confidence by the CBRC in the Bank of Hangzhou and confirmation that its corporate governance is sound.

The Jinan City Commercial Bank (Table 10.6) increased its bank assets, year on year, by 28.9 per cent in 2006, 16.7 per cent in 2007 and 30.9 per cent in 2008, while net profits increased by 20.3 per cent in 2006, 67.6 per cent in 2007 and 46.8 per cent in 2008. These figures confirm the positive results of the partnership. The return on equity was 5.14 per cent in 2005 but it increased to 15.36 per cent in 2008 and the loan deposit ratio was well within limits at 63.42 per cent. CAR was 11.34 per cent in 2008 and the NPL ratio was reduced substantially from 6.66 per cent in 2005 to a low of 2.55 per cent in 2008. Related party loans were also reduced substantially over the period. State-owned shares were

Table 10.5 Hangzhou City Commercial Bank financial performance

Details	*2005*	*2006*	*2007*	*2008*
Bank assets (000s, RMB)	46,276,281	56,914,247	69,271,226	99,617,095
Percentage increase		+22.9	+21.7	+43.8
Net profits (000s, RMB)	435,030	595,397	847,659	1,277,434
Percentage increase		+36.8	+42.4	+50.7
Return on equity (%)	17.58	18.60	22.08	26.56
Non-performing loans (%)	2.03	1.40	0.82	0.84
Capital adequacy ratio (%)	8.84	9.54	9.04	10.70
Loans to deposit ratio (%)	63.43	64.86	65.51	668.331
State-owned shares (%)	71.91	61.87	35.93	37.48
Related party loans (000s RMB)	103,000	100,000	N/A	97,500

Source: adapted from Hangzhou City Commercial Bank Annual Reports (2006–2008).

Table 10.6 Jinan City Commercial Bank financial performance

Details	*2005*	*2006*	*2007*	*2008*
Bank assets (000s, RMB)	25,123,680	32,408,597	37,841,189	49,544,577
Percentage increase		+28.9	+16.7	+30.9
Net profits (000s, RMB)	118,641	142,740	239,179	351,142
Percentage increase		+20.3	+67.6	+46.8
Return on equity (%)	5.14	8.90	12.44	15.36
Non-performing loans (%)	6.66	1.57	1.33	2.55
Capital adequacy ratio (%)	n/a	10.40	10.13	11.34
Loans to deposit ratio (%)	n/a	59.60	63.80	63.42
State-owned shares (%)	78.55	80.26	80.15	65.9
Related party loans (000s RMB)	n/a	805,000	695,640	293,640

Source: adapted from Jinan City Commercial Bank Annual Reports (2006–2008).

reduced from 78.55 per cent in 2005 to 65.9 per cent in 2008 while related party loans were reduced significantly by 63.5 per cent between 2006 and 2008.

Unfortunately there has been a case of alleged fraud at the Bank of Qilu at the end of 2011 and the financial institution is believed to have accepted forged commercial bank bills to the value of around RMB1.5 billion (US$240 million). The case is under investigation and highlights the problems and challenges that foreign partners have to be aware of.

4 Part 2: the European banks

The author contacted four European banks that had invested in China's CCBs. They were the HSBC Banking Corporation from the United Kingdom, which invested in the Bank of Shanghai, the Dutch Financial Services Group ING that invested in the Bank of Beijing, the French Banking Group BNP Paribas that invested in the Nanjing City Commercial Bank and the German Savings Bank DEG that invested in the Nanchong City Commercial Bank. All four European banks that invested in the Chinese CCBs are very large international financial organizations with operations all over the world. China was the one country that they desired a presence in, or in the case of HSBC a greater presence. Another reason why these European banks invested in China was the same as the Australian banks who invested in China – the desire for profits and higher profit margins than they were getting elsewhere. Those same reasons propelled the European banks to go to China and invest in the third-tier banking sector.

4.1 The experience of HSBC Banking Corporation

Headquartered in London, HSBC is one of the largest banking and financial services organizations in the world. HSBC's international network comprises around 8,500 offices in 86 countries and territories in Europe, the Asia-Pacific region, the Americas, the Middle East and Africa (Facts about HSBC Group, www.hsbc.com). The Group has a long history in China dating back to 1865 and today it has a large presence in China with branches in all major cities. When the Bank of Shanghai reorganized and improved its corporate governance with the help of the IFC, the HSBC Banking Group became interested and, together with the Shanghai Commercial Bank of Hong Kong, bought an 11 per cent stake in the bank in December 2001. The HSBC Group took an 8 per cent stake for which it paid US$63 million and the Shanghai Commercial Bank (HK) took the balance 3 per cent stake for which it paid US$23 million.

In 2001, the HSBC Group already had its own branches in all the major cities in China, including Beijing, Shanghai, Guangzhou and Chongqing, and was looking for substantial acquisitions (HSBC subsequently bought a 19.9 per cent stake in China's fifth largest bank – the Bank of Communications – in August 2004). Why did it invest in a small CCB? It invested in the Bank of Shanghai because it was invited to do so by the board of the Bank of Shanghai, which realized that in order to improve and attain international standards of banking efficiency, it needed to have a world-class bank on board as a strategic investor.

4.1.1 What was corporate governance like before HSBC invested?

An executive director of the Bank of Shanghai advised that the Bank of Shanghai (BOS) was formally registered on 30 January 1996 from the amalgamation of 99 UCCs. In the early years of the bank, corporate governance, as we understand the term today, was poor. The bank was mainly owned by the local government and management decisions were made arbitrarily by powerful CEOs appointed by the local government. The board of directors met on an irregular basis, meetings were ad hoc and no detailed minutes were kept. There were no management committees, no board committees and no independent directors. The risk and loan evaluation skills were not there and loans were disbursed to state projects without project viability and proper feasibility studies. The bank management did not pay attention to the CAR. All this meant that the bank, like other banks in China, eventually accumulated a high proportion of NPLs.

HSBC's presence on the share registry gave the bank credibility as HSBC had an excellent reputation in banking circles within China. It also brought along with it an extensive training programme for the bank staff and a modern, efficient planning culture. Under the terms of the partnership agreement HSBC agreed to provide training over a five-year period. Having HSBC on board as a strategic shareholder was a big help. The BOS was also keen to eventually list on the Shanghai Stock Exchange and, knowing that listing is a rigorous exercise, hoped that HSBC would be able to assist. The process necessitated the BOS to improve its standards of corporate governance standards to meet listing regulations.

One of the biggest changes initially brought by HSBC was the management of the CAR, the idea that the business loans of the bank had to be determined by the CAR of the bank. Previously being a majority government-owned entity, there was no necessity for CAR management. As a result, CAR at the BOS in the past did not meet the Basel requirements. However, it has since exceeded the international standard of 8 per cent set by the Basel Committee on Banking Supervision (11.3 per cent at end 2008). Although HSBC did not second any permanent staff to the Bank of Shanghai, many staff from BOS were sent to HSBC (HK) for training during the first five years. The bank itself spends a lot of money on staff training and sends its staff for short-term courses to Singapore and the United States.

4.1.2 Results of HSBC's presence on corporate governance

At the BOS, the corporate governance structures and mechanisms are now sound and solid. For example, shareholders' meetings are held in accordance with CBRC guidelines, shareholders are provided with adequate notice and they are allowed to bring up matters for discussion. Properly submitted resolutions are voted upon and directors are subject to questioning. Even extraordinary general meetings can be requisitioned in accordance with the company regulations when necessary by shareholders.

All shareholders enjoy one vote per share – there are no shares with special voting rights. The board currently comprises 12 directors whose composition comprises one-third from representatives of shareholders, another third are independent directors, and the remaining third are the executive directors. The independent directors are highly experienced professionals with banking experience or are university professors with relevant experience and they participate actively in policy discussions and investment decisions of the bank. Representatives of shareholders include one director each seconded by HSBC Group and IFC. The directors' meetings minutes are very detailed and record decisions taken and how the decisions are arrived at.

HSBC helped establish a strong credit culture at the bank, especially at the credit evaluation and approval level. Levels of authority are established for approving loans and approving management is held responsible and accountable for their actions. Previous NPLs were tackled firmly and legal action taken against delinquent borrowers. This resulted in the NPL ratio dropping substantially since HSBC became a partner. The CBRC sends observers to attend board meetings and this ensures that board meetings are conducted with a high degree of professionalism and according to CBRC guidelines. Board members sometimes seek the views of the CBRC representative and their suggestions are often accepted.

The following committees report directly to the board of directors and HSBC has representatives on all six committees; audit, risk control, remunerations, strategy, related transactions and nominations. The nominations committee has the responsibility for nominating directors and all senior management positions from vice president upwards. There are three independent directors and they chair four of the above management committees including audit, risk control, nominations and related transactions.

In regards to accountability, information disclosure and transparency the BOS has reached international standards. In addition, having a reputable international firm of accountants helped ensure that internal controls and accounting standards meet international standards. Another important change was the stress on risk and credit control. HSBC brought along with it a strong credit culture and management and stressed the commercial aspects of banking – cash flow, liquidity and profitability. As a result of the emphasis on risk and credit control, the NPLs at the BOS have been at low levels and as of 2008 stood at 2.23 per cent. Corporate governance standards at the BOS have improved substantially and a main reason is HSBC's contributions and presence.

4.1.3 Summary

The HSBC Banking Group brought world-class standards to the Bank of Shanghai and through its training and skills transference programme was able to uplift standards of corporate governance. The BOS was voted the 'Best Retail Bank in China' by *The Asian Banker* for the third consecutive year in 2008 (Bank of Shanghai Annual Report 2008). The partnership between HSBC and the BOS has been very successful – bank assets increased by 10.6 per cent in 2006, 17.5

Table 10.7 Bank of Shanghai financial performance

Details	*2005*	*2006*	*2007*	*2008*
Bank assets (000s, RMB)	237,631,191	262,902,617	308,986,012	367,735,975
Percentage increase		+10.6	+17.5	+19.0
Net profits (000s, RMB)	2,138,686	2,843,946	3,796,439	3,454,264
Percentage increase		+32.9	+33.5	–9.0
Return on equity (%)	20.73	19.32	19.88	16.33
Non-performing loans (%)	3.92	3.57	2.41	2.23
Capital adequacy ratio (%)	11.11	11.97	11.27	11.27
Loans to deposit ratio (%)	57.17	57.33	61.37	63.58
State-owned/legal entities shares (%)	57.71	57.71	57.72	57.72
Related party loans (RMB million)	3,774	3,921	3,059	1,100

Source: adapted from Bank of Shanghai Annual Reports (2006–2008).

per cent in 2007 and 19 per cent in 2008 while net profits increased year on year by 32.9 per cent in 2006 and 33.5 per cent in 2007 but dropped by 9 per cent in 2008. This was due to the write-offs of some NPLs. NPLs were reduced from 3.57 per cent in 2006 to 2.23 per cent in 2008 while CAR was maintained, being 11.97 per cent in 2006 and 11.27 per cent in 2008.

The BOS has clearly followed and met the guidelines 'Enhancing Corporate Governance for Banking Organisations (July 2005)' set by the Basel Committee on Banking Supervision. It has also met the various Chinese guidelines and governance codes. More important, the BOS's key financial performances in CAR and NPL have bettered the average of similar statistics of the JSCBs and as a result the CBRC has awarded it regional licences to open new branches in Tianjin, Chengdu and Shenzhen in 2008 (Bank of Shanghai Annual Report 2008). CCBs are normally only allowed to operate in the city of origin and for permission to be granted simultaneously in three different provinces is an accolade for the bank management. The bank has also submitted an IPO to the CBRC for listing on the Shanghai Stock Exchange and it expects a quick approval process.

4.2 The experience of ING

ING is a global financial institution of Dutch origin offering banking, investments, life insurance and retirement services to more than 85 million private, corporate and institutional customers in Europe, North and Latin America, Asia and Australia (Profile of ING Group, www.ing.com/group/index). It invested in the Bank of Beijing together with the IFC in 2005 when it took a 19.9 per cent stake for US$215 million and the IFC took a 5 per cent stake in the bank for US$54 million.

The reasons for ING investing in the Bank of Beijing are obvious. Beijing is the capital of China and the Bank of Beijing was the second largest CCB in China, employing over 3,600 staff serving retail and corporate clients through 116 branches. It also had a network of 272 ATMs and a fast-growing e-banking business. At the end of 2004, the bank had total assets of RMB209 billion (US$29.9 billion).

ING planned to leverage its own retail banking expertise to work closely with the Bank of Beijing on the development and expansion of its suite of products to customers. ING looked to further support the bank in improving corporate governance, risk management, human resources and management functions in anticipation of the fact that the bank would be a distribution platform for ING's insurance and wealth management products.

4.2.1 What was corporate governance like before ING invested?

The author interviewed the executive director at the Bank of Beijing who has been its director since 2005 when ING first invested. When he first arrived, the bank had a chairman and management team who were very receptive to change.

As a result ING was able to implement many corporate governance changes easily. The bank had a young and progressive management team who wanted a stock exchange listing and they were ready for the bank to make the leap from city to national status. The foreign partners in the Bank of Beijing consider themselves very lucky in this regard.

However, there was no proper risk culture in many areas and the first thing ING did was to put in place a risk framework so that loans and other banking operations could be properly evaluated. This resulted in the NPL ratio dropping significantly from 4.38 per cent in 2005 to 1.55 per cent in 2008. The risk management procedures put in place included asset and liability management, currencies, foreign exchange and corporate business.

Initially, there was a basic framework of corporate governance but that framework was based on a different set of criteria and circumstances. The bank was not listed then, there were no minority shareholders and the bank was wholly owned by the state and municipal governments. The state and the CCP had all along wielded strong influence over its operations and of course that situation was not acceptable to ING. ING worked diligently to implement corporate governance mechanisms and structures, being careful to solicit views and preferred course of action from the local management. Over time, bank assets almost doubled between 2005 and 2008 and related party loans were also reduced. The state and party influence diminished as exemplified by the reduction of state-owned shares from 65.4 per cent in 2005 to 52.9 per cent in 2008.

Initially, the board of directors was unclear as to its role and responsibilities and ING put in place rules and documentation to educate directors to ensure that all members could play the role expected of them. ING was concerned not so much as to what happened at the board meetings but what was recorded and to ensure that the board minutes were accurate, analytical and actions taken to follow up board decisions. Previously the Chinese board minutes merely consisted of board resolutions and sketchy minutes of directors' meetings – totally inadequate by international standards.

When the shareholding in a bank changes substantially or when a bank is listed, there will usually be changes in some rules and objectives. In some instances, these may result in different structures of corporate governance. What the ING Group did was that after it became 19.9 per cent shareholder in the Bank of Beijing, it gradually reformed the framework of corporate governance to one that was more transparent, with more information disclosure and accountability.

4.2.2 How has corporate governance changed at the Bank of Beijing?

Standards of corporate governance at the Bank of Beijing have improved substantially over the last five years and insofar as transparency and information disclosure is concerned it is now equal to international standards. The active participation of foreign shareholders like ING and IFC is one reason but the commitment and positive attitudes of the Chinese management is another. Both the

IFC and ING play crucial roles at both the board and management committee level.

The bank also listed on the Shanghai Stock Exchange in September 2007 and this also required the bank to uplift its governance standards. Furthermore the bank has plans to list on the Hong Kong Stock Exchange and this will help improve governance standards even more. The external auditor and accountant is an internationally renowned firm and it also contributes to good governance through its high standards of audit and internal control and the enforcement of international accounting standards. There are six independent directors on the board of 17 directors and they play a very important role in the bank. They dominate the nominations committee and they chair the audit committee and the related transactions committee. The independent directors are approved by the CBRC and have proven themselves to be independent and competent. They have not hesitated to take opposing positions when necessary.

Reporting lines of authority at the bank were clearly redefined so that management decisions at the bank were more structured. An example was the change of reporting authority from all branch managers to various departmental heads for different matters. Previously the branch managers were used to reporting and getting all decisions from the chief operating officer. ING also ensured that various management committees were established at the Bank of Beijing. These include the following: audit committee, new products committee, credit/risk committee, operational risk committee, strategies committee, related transactions committee and the remuneration committee. ING has appointed four key persons to work full time at the Bank of Beijing including the executive director and the deputy chief risk officer.

The establishment of an audit trail as a management tool was stressed by the external auditors PwC and accepted by the bank's board as desirable. In other words all important decisions made must have a sequence of documentation showing who made the decisions. This is important as then there is accountability. This is all part of corporate governance. ING has also implemented a series of 'stress testing' to see how the Bank of Beijing would react if there was a run on deposits at the bank and what actions the bank should adopt. The results indicate that the Bank of Beijing is very strong and solid and passed the 'stress tests' extremely well. When problems arise ING will call upon expert advice and assistance from ING headquarters. For example, banking experts will fly in to conduct training for the bank staff.

At the distribution level, ING has worked hand in hand with the management for the expansion of the distribution network. ING has also worked hard to redesign existing branches for the Bank of Beijing. New products have also been introduced to the bank and these have been welcomed by customers. New products include credit cards and new branded accounts. One of the focus areas of ING is also information technology and ING has much expertise in the IT area. ING does a lot of training for the Chinese staff, sending about 50–60 Chinese staff annually for training overseas to Amsterdam and Romania. They are trained on risk, retail banking, head office training and information technology. ING also provides other in-house training on various topics including corporate governance and banking experts are hired to conduct specialist seminars for the staff. Training is a very important aspect of the partnership agreement and plays a key role in the bank's efforts to attain international standards.

4.2.3 Summary

When ING first arrived at the Bank of Beijing, it did not do so with fixed ideas on how things were to be done or how operations could be improved. It arrived with an open mind, an understanding of Chinese culture and a willingness to view any problem from different angles so that a satisfactory solution acceptable to the Chinese and ING was arrived. Thus when ING found deficiencies in risk management and control, it held a series of meetings with local management, explained the problems, pointed out the dangers, proposed remedies and the desired results. When the local managers clearly understood the challenges and problems faced, it was easy to put in a risk framework so that loans and other banking operations could be properly evaluated. Standards of corporate governance at the Bank of Beijing in this manner improved substantially over the last five years.

The Bank of Beijing has done well since ING became a strategic shareholder: between 2005 and 2008 net profits increased 221 per cent while NPL also dropped from 4.38 per cent to 1.55 per cent over the same period. The CAR also increased from 12.06 per cent to 19.66 per cent. Bank assets also increased by 78.9 per cent between 2005 and 2008. The percentage of state-owned shares has

Table 10.8 Bank of Beijing financial performance

Details	*2005*	*2006*	*2007*	*2008*
Bank assets (000s, RMB)	233,043,818	272,968,890	354,222,941	417,021,019
Percentage increase		+17.1	+29.8	+17.7
Net profits (000s, RMB)	1,685,595	2,140,408	3,348,197	5,417,165
Percentage increase		+27.0	+43.8	+61.8
Return on equity (%)	22.00	24.21	18.34	17.91
Non-performing loans (%)	4.38	3.58	2.06	1.55
Capital adequacy ratio (%)	12.06	12.76	20.11	19.66
Loans to deposit ratio (%)	52.22	46.72	57.77	57.98
State-owned shares (%)	65.4	65.4	65.4	52.9
Related party loans (000s)	N/A	2,195,500	2,110,812	1,750,792

Source: adapted from Bank of Beijing Annual Reports (2006–2008).

also dropped from 65.4 per cent in 2005 to 52.9 per cent in 2008 (see Table 10.8). The partnership between ING and the Bank of Beijng has been an outstanding success and the Bank of Beijing has been allowed by the CBRC to open branches in Shanghai, Tianjin, Shenzhen and Hong Kong. Corporate governance has improved substantially and in many areas has reached international standards. The Bank of Beijing has won numerous awards and in 2008 it was awarded 'Best City Commercial Bank in China' (Bank of Beijing Annual Report 2008).

4.3 The experience of BNP Paribas

BNP Paribas is a European leader in global banking and financial services and one of the six strongest banks in the world according to Standard & Poor's. It has one of the largest international networks with operations in 83 countries and 202,300 employees, including 160,200 in Europe, 15,200 in North America and 10,200 in Asia (*BNP Paribas* – About Us – www.bank.bnpparibas.com/en). In October 2005, BNP Paribas took a 19.2 per cent stake in the Nanjing City Commercial Bank (later renamed Bank of Nanjing) for US$87 million. Earlier on in 2001 the IFC had taken a stake of 5 per cent in the same bank for US$27 million.

The author interviewed a senior manager representing BNP Paribas at NjCCB. As its name indicates, the bank is situated in Nanjing, one of the most important cities in China. Nanjing has a population of about 7.6 million and is the capital of Jiangsu province in eastern China. It is approximately 300km north-west of Shanghai and NjCCB itself is the eighth largest CCB in China, with total assets of RMB42.7 billion (US$5.3 billion), a loan portfolio of RMB22.5 billion (US$2.8 billion) and RMB35 billion (US$4.3 billion) in deposits (end September 2005). The NjCCB network comprises 58 branches in the city of Nanjing and employs nearly 1,500 people. It is active in corporate lending, trade finance, mortgage lending as well as securities dealing. The city has a per capita GDP income of RMB50,327, which is more than twice the national average of RMB23,205. These are some reasons for BNP Paribas to invest in the NjCCB.

BNP Paribas also agreed in the partnership agreement to establish close cooperation in certain operational areas, including retail banking, fixed-income transactions, consumer finance, wealth management, risk management, information technology and organization. The objective was to further develop and enhance NjCCB's core competitiveness as well as to capture new business opportunities in the fast-evolving Chinese banking market. BNP Paribas also agreed to second to NjCCB a number of executives and experts, including a senior vice president who will be a member of NjCCB's executive office, for the purpose of implementing the strategic alliance and providing technical assistance and guidance in the areas of governance, risk management and consumer banking. BNP Paribas also appointed a member to the board.

BNP Paribas' decision to invest in the NjCCB was a purely commercial one. The annual reports had been made available and its own projections on future growth and profitability were optimistic. BNP Paribas knew that IFC had been a shareholder since 2001 and so when BNP Paribas invested in 2005, it felt fairly comfortable and knew that corporate governance would have improved somewhat at the bank. Corporate governance in the Chinese bank thus was a factor for BNP Paribas but not the most important factor. More important factors were commercial and financial. BNP Paribas had investigated several other Chinese CCBs and found that the corporate governance regime at NjCCB was relatively better than most of the other Chinese banks. BNP Paribas chose to invest in a CCB because it could have relatively more influence (19.2 per cent of the equity) with a relatively small capital outlay (US$87 million) in a CCB rather than in a JSCB. That same amount of money would probably buy less than 10 per cent in one of the larger JSCBs.

4.3.1 What was corporate governance like before BNP Paribas invested?

When BNP first arrived, it found a basic governance framework that was quite comprehensive. There was a board of directors, board committees and management committees and there were independent directors. There was transparency and information disclosure to a certain degree. All that BNP Paribas did was to make suggestions for improvements and supervised its implementation. BNP Paribas was lucky in that the NjCCB was also getting ready for listing on the Shanghai Stock Exchange and this necessitated that corporate governance be lifted to meet listing standards. The process was already in motion and BNP Paribas helped to expedite it. The bank was listed on 16 July 2007.

When BNP Paribas first came on board, it worked very hard to reduce the level of NPLs. That was the first issue of concern. The percentage has been substantially reduced and it was due to a combination of factors. The main reason was that the Chinese economy was expanding rapidly but another was the introduction of strong risk evaluation skills. There was no cash injection by the state or municipal government and the NPL situation in some problem loans sorted itself out with better cash flow and improvements in the economy.

On paper corporate governance at NjCCB seemed good initially but there were problems with the attitude of the staff and management. Sometimes, they did not understand the procedures and processes and concepts associated with good corporate governance. As a result they were reluctant to implement or enforce them. At the board level, BNP Paribas insisted on full and proper minutes being kept and proper procedures for the notification of board meetings and circulation of board minutes. Previously directors' minutes were scanty and incomplete. BNP Paribas also encouraged the board of directors to be open and robust in the meetings. For example when a director asks a question at a board meeting, it should be fully explained, duly recorded in the minutes and decisions made acted upon. The answer is important and all directors should know that the answer is not to be given at a private meeting later on.

Another important factor is the role of the CCP which plays a significant role in important management decisions. An example is the appointment of the CEO and the chairman of the board which has to be approved by the CCP. Another matter would be mergers and acquisitions and listing on stock exchanges. All these decisions require the tacit approval of the CCP. However, BNP Paribas did not want to discuss this matter in detail. BNP Paribas believes that of all the corporate governance priorities, accountability is the most important and BNP Paribas tries to ensure that both board and management are accountable to all shareholders, including minority shareholders.

4.3.2 How has corporate governance changed at Nanjing City Commercial Bank

Corporate governance at NjCCB has improved substantially over the last five years for many reasons. Improvements in corporate governance started in 2001 when the IFC became an initial shareholder and started to introduce basic practices of corporate governance. This encouraged BNP Paribas to become a 19.2 per cent strategic shareholder in 2005. Since then BNP Paribas has worked hand-in-glove with both the IFC and the local management to further improve corporate governance. When NjCCB listed on the Shanghai Stock Exchange in July 2007 this necessitated the adoption and practice of high standards of corporate governance. Issues of transparency and information disclosure were especially important. When PwC, a well-known international firm of accountants and auditors, was appointed the bank's auditor and accountant, it helped establish strong internal controls, transparency and information disclosure. At the same time, the bank adopted international standards of accounting which made for more transparency. In keeping with the Code of Corporate Governance, one-third of the bank's directors are independent and they have helped to ensure that minority shareholders are not oppressed or abused. And these independent directors helped establish and oversee various board and management committees established in accordance with the Code of Corporate Governance. All this has aided the governance process and finally as the board intends for the NjCCB to be listed on the Hong Kong Stock Exchange, this will necessitate even more transparency and disclosure and higher standards of governance.

BNP Paribas helped improve corporate governance in the NjCCB in many areas. Many of these improvements were simple but practical steps. An example is the board of directors, which is much more professional now than before. At the board level, BNP Paribas arranged for full and proper minutes to be kept, all matters recorded, minutes to be signed off, for adequate notices of board meetings to be given, for circulation of minutes, for signatures of attendees. BNP Paribas also insisted on the appointment of genuinely independent directors and ensured they were experienced and qualified directors. Board meetings became mandatory quarterly meetings and were no longer ad hoc.

Five staff were seconded by BNP Paribas to various departments including credit and risk evaluation, finance, consumer finance, corporate banking. They all report to the heads of the various departments. BNP Paribas also has representation on the senior management committee – this ensures that no important decision is taken without BNP Paribas knowing about it. Training is one area that BNP Paribas does a lot of and BNP Paribas regularly flies in banking experts to do training in various fields including corporate governance. There are also both short-term and long-term training programmes in place for the Chinese staff. Short-term training may be for a few days or a couple of weeks and this may be in-house or in other cities in China. Long-term training can be for two to three months and is usually conducted overseas in Paris or in the United States. BNP Paribas has trained a lot of staff locally and this has helped improve corporate governance because the Chinese staff are exposed to modern banking systems and procedures – it is as much about a change of mentality as the change in the actual process.

4.3.3 Summary

In October 2005, BNP Paribas took a 19.2 per cent stake in the NjCCB for US$87 million and worked hard to improve corporate governance and operational efficiency. It was lucky as corporate governance reforms had initiated when the IFC first became a minority shareholder in 2001 and the bank itself was preparing for an IPO which occurred soon after BNP Paribas' investment. The NjCCB was the first CCB to be listed on the Shanghai Stock Exchange in July 2007.

Corporate governance in China's banking system has improved a lot compared to five years ago. It is converging towards an international model of corporate governance but, because of the role of the state and the CCP, it has special features. China's corporate governance model is one where the major issue is how to accommodate the role of the state and the CCP. Whether one likes it or not, there will be some decisions that will be made by the state and/or the CCP. The BNP Paribas representative has observed several decisions at the NjCCB that were obviously made by the CCP and describes this as a model of 'corporate governance with Chinese characteristics'.

BNP Paribas' investment in the NjCCB has been a great success (see Table 10.9). Bank assets increased by 19.3 per cent in 2006, 31.2 per cent in 2007 and 23.2 per cent in 2008. Net profits increased substantially by 61.9 per cent in 2006, 52.9 per cent in 2007 and 60.1 per cent in 2008. NPLs also dropped from 2.47 per cent in 2006 to 1.64 per cent in 2008 while CAR increased from 13.1 per cent in 2005 to 24.12 per cent in 2008 while maintaining a healthy loan deposit ratio of 62.05 per cent in 2008. The bank was the first CCB to list on the stock exchange and has always been prudent and conservative, maintaining high CAR whenever possible. This was shown by the bank having a high CAR of 13.1 per cent in 2005 when most other CCBs had much lower CARs and the bank's CAR went up substantially in 2007 and 2008 as a result of capital injections from foreign investors and the substantial reduction of state-owned shares (see Table 10.9). The partnership between BNP Paribas and NjCCB can be described as happy and rewarding to both parties. The bank opened a branch in Shanghai in June 2008 and has applied to open a branch in Beijing. It also plans to open more branches next year.

Table 10.9 Nanjing City Commercial Bank financial performance

Details	*2005*	*2006*	*2007*	*2008*
Bank assets (000s, RMB)	48,593,266	57,987,003	76,063,711	93,706,071
Percentage increase		+19.3	+31.2	+23.2
Net profits (000s, RMB)	367,172	594,634	909,494	1,456,095
Percentage increase		+61.9	+52.9	+60.1
Return on equity (%)	17.45	22.66	9.15	12.89
Non-performing loans (%)	n/a	2.47	1.79	1.64
Capital adequacy ratio (%)	13.10	11.73	30.67	24.12
Loans to deposit ratio (%)	n/a	58.15	60.14	62.05
State-owned shares (%)	n/a	75.8	49.8	24.2
Related party loans (000s)	n/a	n/a	1,527,347	1,827,126

Source: adapted from Nanjing City Commercial Bank Annual Reports (2006–2008).

4.4 The experience of DEG (German Savings Bank) and SIDT

DEG is a member of Germany's largest banking group – KfW Bankengruppe which itself is one of Europe's largest development and finance institutions for long-term project financing. For more than 45 years, DEG has been financing and structuring investments in developing and transition countries. To date, DEG has worked with more than 1,500 companies and has committed financing of around 4.7 billion euros over the past five years (DWG website, www.deginvest.de/En_home).

DEG invested in the Nanchong City Commercial Bank in July 2005 taking a 10 per cent equity stake for US$3.8 million together with Sparkassen International Development Trust (SIDT) which took 3.3 per cent for US$1.2 million. Together with DEG and SIDT, the Savings Banks Foundation for International Cooperation (SBFIC) also agreed to provide technical assistance to the Chinese bank.

Nanchong City Commercial Bank (NcCCB) was established in 2001 through a merger of ten UCCs in Nanchong, a city of about 7.6 million in Sichuan province. Agriculture is the mainstay of the economy but there are SMEs in automobile parts, petroleum, textiles and building materials. With a mandate of helping local businesses access finance, NcCCB positions itself as a full-service bank to SMEs, private enterprises, self-employed entrepreneurs and individuals.

According to the Project Consultant of the Savings Banks Foundation for International Cooperation (SBFIC) appointed by DEG as project consultant, in 2004 DEG approached the CBRC expressing interest in investing in a Chinese CCB. The CBRC suggested four possible City Commercial Banks: in Inner

Mongolia, Heilongjiang, Hubei and Sichuan. The DEG chose the Nanchong City Commercial Bank because it looked the most promising of the four with its low NPLs, lack of hidden liabilities and relatively more manageable size. The fact that DEG and SIDT together only paid US$5 million for a 13.3 per cent stake in NcCCB indicates that the NcCCB is a small bank compared to other CCBs situated on the eastern seaboard for which much higher prices were paid by foreign banks for equivalent equity stakes.

4.4.1 What was corporate governance like before DEG and SIDT invested?

The project consultant engaged by DEG and SIDT opined that corporate governance in the Nanchong City Commercial Bank was at a below average industry standard in 2005 when DEG and SIDT first invested. This could be due to the fact that the bank had only come into existence in 2001 when ten UCCs in the city amalgamated under the patronage of the municipal government. The management was young and relatively inexperienced, did not have extensive banking knowledge or exposure and its structures were somewhat antiquated. For example, the bank had a CEO who was also the chairman of the board of directors. This would not normally be the case for an international bank.

In regards to information disclosure and transparency the management of the NcCCB was initially not transparent at all. Some of the financial data that was given to the German investors did not accurately reflect the true picture on the ground. This gave the German investors cause for concern.

4.4.2 What the German investors did to improve corporate governance

The project consultant advised that SBFIC's role was intermediary: they would ascertain from the German investors what their objectives were for the NcCCB, the changes the German investors wanted and the processes and procedures to be implemented. In turn the SBFIC would ascertain what the Chinese bank (NcCCB) wanted and the project consultant would convey the message to the German partners. The SBFIC acted as a conduit and the consultant would make two to three trips per year to NcCCB to facilitate the communication and transformational process. When at the bank, meetings were held with the CEO, the directors and senior managers to thrash out problems, issues and governance changes needed. The consultant acts a conduit relaying instructions/requests to/from both sides.

In the beginning, soon after investing, DEG sent a banking expert in 2005 to advise the NcCCB on corporate governance changes. But the directors and board members of NcCCB were not impressed with the expert's recommendations and did not implement them. The German investors later seconded a German on a permanent basis to look after their interests at the bank but the appointed person did not speak Chinese and there were difficulties in communications. Eventually the German representative quit.

As part of the Partnership Agreement the German investors agreed to help the NcCCB in the areas of information technology, risk management, human resource and new products. The German partners have delivered – an example of a new product introduced was a debit/payment card which was well received by the bank customers. Under risk management, the German partners set up new credit systems and processes for the approval and maintenance of loans. Human resource management has been improved with meritocracy, promotions and training being emphasized. The IT improvement programme was very important as the NcCCB's information system was quite old and obsolete. The German party arranged for the installation of new systems and processes.

Currently the German investors have two board seats (one each from DEG and SIDT) and they normally fly in and spend one to two weeks at the NcCCB for board meetings and other related matters. The overall standard and conduct of board meetings has improved and is much more professional now. Previously board meetings were ad hoc with scanty minutes kept and insufficient notification being given. There has been improvement in the preparation of financial accounts and annual reports as the German partners have requested more transparency and information disclosure. Previously the annual report and accounts were very sketchy but now, at German insistence, the annual accounts are more complete and informative. The NcCCB had Deloitte Touche Ross (an international firm of auditors) as their external auditors for three years but have recently changed to a local auditor as a cost-cutting measure.

On the question of independent directors, the NcCCB has four independent directors out of a total of 14, i.e. about one-third. This is unlike Europe where the norm is for independent directors to comprise 75 per cent of the total. However, the independent directors are independent as they are mostly university professors. The other directors do have some relationship with the bank or with the larger shareholders.

The Chinese directors and senior management in the bank appear to want good corporate governance. However, this is not always matched by their actions as they often still revert to their old ways. What happens is that the Chinese management profess that they will implement the changes recommended by the German investors during their periodic meetings but when the Germans leave, they continue their old ways. An example is the formation of the various management committees. Officially the bank has set up various management committees including audit, risk, human resource, new investments committees. However it is not certain if these committees are all functioning according to the precepts underlying their formation. The bank practises a mixture of old and new management practices – the new being the reconstituted board of directors, board of supervisors, various new management committees but underlying it all is the old Chinese practice of *guanxi* and *renqing*. One result of state ownership and influence is that the Nanchong city government plays a role in the key decisions of the bank and the NcCCB often ends up financing the city government's projects.

The German partners understand that training is very important for the bank to progress and they send banking experts in various fields (including corporate governance) on a regular basis (six times per year) to the NcCCB. These specialists conduct training for periods from one week to one month. Chinese staff are regularly sent for training to Shanghai (where DEG has invested in another bank there). About 40 staff per year are sent to Germany for training.

4.4.3 Summary

The German Group DEG and another German company, Sparkassen International Development Trust (SIDT) together invested US$5 million for a 13.3 per cent equity stake in the Nanchong City Commercial Bank in July 2005. The Savings Banks Foundation for International Cooperation (SBFIC) provided consultancy services and acted as a conduit between the Chinese bank (NcCCB) and the German investors.

The bank has grown significantly since the German investors became a partner. Bank assets increased 26.9 per cent in 2006, 79.8 per cent in 2007 and 55.2 per cent in 2008 (see Table 10.10). Net profits also increased 26.9 per cent in 2006, 1.9 per cent in 2007 and 104.7 per cent in 2008. As of the end of 2008 return on equity was 30.12 per cent and NPLs were low at 1.14 per cent and CAR was well maintained at 11.29 per cent. The percentage of state-owned shares was maintained at 39.3 per cent.

Corporate governance at the NcCCB was initially below industry average and, since the German investors invested, has slightly improved. However, according to the project consultant appointed to oversee the investment, it has not improved to standards desired by the German investors. This could be due to the fact that the German investors did not successfully second any permanent

Table 10.10 Nanchong City Commercial Bank financial performance

Details	*2005*	*2006*	*2007*	*2008*
Bank assets (000s, RMB)	463,848	588,784	1,057,722	1,641,846
Percentage increase		+26.9	+79.8	+55.2
Net profits (000s, RMB)	8,300	10,400	10,600	21,700
Percentage increase		+25.3	+1.9	+104.7
Return on equity (%)	23.52	19.38	20.15	30.12
Non-performing loans (%)	3.25	3.96	2.1	1.14
Capital adequacy ratio (%)	18.42	20.87	13.68	11.29
Loans to deposit ratio (%)	45.7	46.8	50.6	49.1
State-owned shares (%)	n/a	n/a	39.3	39.3
Related party loans	n/a	n/a	78,640,000	42,320,000

Source: adapted from Nanchong City Commercial Bank Annual Reports (2006–2008).

staff to the NcCCB. There have been improvements, but they have been slow. Implementation has also been slow. There have also been instances when recommendations by the German partners have been rejected at board level as being impractical.

The partnership between DEG and SIDT and the Nanchong City Commercial Bank may be considered to be moderately successful. It is not a failure as there have been improvements in corporate governance and the bank has shown marked improvements in their financial performances. This is the final arbiter of how successful a partnership has been.

5 Part 3: the Asian banks

The author interviewed two Asian banks that had invested in China's CCBs. They were the OCBC Bank from Singapore which invested in the Ningbo City Commercial Bank in May 2006 (later renamed Bank of Ningbo) and the Hong Leong Banking Group of Malaysia that invested in the Chengdu City Commercial Bank in October 2007 (later renamed Bank of Chengdu). One reason for Asian banks investing in the CCBs in China is similar to the reason why Australian and European banks invested in China: stiff competition in domestic markets and the desire for higher profits and margins overseas. Let us consider the case of the OCBC Banking Group of Singapore which invested in the Ningbo City Commercial Bank. The OCBC Banking Group is the second largest bank in Singapore[2] but Singapore is a city-state with a population of four million and limited scope for growth. Although Singapore is a financial centre for the Asia Pacific region, banks have to look overseas for expansion and long-term growth. Similarly the Hong Leong Group in Malaysia[3] is a very large diversified conglomerate in Malaysia but it has to look overseas for long-term growth and expansion. China is the biggest market in Asia and as both OCBC and Hong Leong Banking Group are owned and controlled by the overseas Chinese diaspora, they feel quite comfortable about investing in a country which shares similarities in culture, language and business practices.

5.1 The experience of the OCBC Bank

In a report prepared by KPMG in 2007, the Ningbo City Commercial Bank (NgCCB) was rated the top City Commercial Bank in China according to various measures of risk capital, earnings and liquidity (KPMG Report 2007). It was not the biggest bank by assets – that distinction went to the Bank of Beijing with RMB265 billion – the NgCCB was the eleventh largest with RMB55 billion in assets but it was probably the best managed CCB. The NgCCB was already well on its way to being listed on the stock market when the OCBC took a 12.2 per cent equity stake for US$75 million in May 2006. The bank subsequently listed on the Shenzhen Stock Exchange in July 2007.

In an interview with the Chief Investment Officer of the OCBC Group, the CIO revealed that the strength of the NgCCB and the quality of its management was one of the key issues why the OCBC decided to invest in the bank in May 2006. The strength of the bank was also reflected in good corporate governance and good corporate governance was one of the key factors for the OCBC's decision to invest in the NgCCB.

Due diligence also found that the management of the NgCCB was 'advanced in its thinking', pursued commercial objectives and the bank was run in a commercial and business-like manner. All this convinced the OCBC to proceed. Another reason was the diversified shareholding of the bank. The bank's employees including management and staff own 20 per cent of the equity and a number of diversified private shareholders/business interests hold another 50 per cent. State-owned enterprises own about 18 per cent and the OCBC owns 12.2 per cent. As a result the state influence is minimal and the private business interests play a dominant role.

An appropriate question to ask is perhaps why the NgCCB chose the OCBC as its foreign strategic partner in 2006? As the top City Commercial Bank in China, the bank was courted by many foreign international suitors but chose the Singapore based OCBC Bank. The reason may perhaps be found in the fact that the OCBC Bank of Singapore had maintained a presence in China since 1925 and also throughout the 1950s through to the 1990s. Both the NgCCB and the OCBC Bank have also had extensive business dealings and the senior management were known to each other.

5.1.1 What the OCBC Bank did to improve corporate governance

The Chief Investment Officer (CIO) stated that OCBC invested in May 2006 and thereafter worked to improve corporate governance. This was done by ensuring that the various board and management committees acted and performed in the manner they were designed for. When the OCBC first arrived, there was form but no substance – on paper initially the NgCCB had all the governance structures directed by the CBRC. However, the bank only paid lip service initially. But another event that helped improve corporate governance was the IPO of the Bank in July 2007. The OCBC Bank being a listed bank was able to assist in the preparation for the IPO as the listing process necessitated more transparency, information disclosure and the adoption of various governance procedures and mechanisms. One of the corporate governance problems that the OCBC faced initially related to the role of the state/CCP. Although the state holds a small stake in the bank and plays a small role in the management, nevertheless on certain issues it still wields influence. For example, the president/CEO of a bank in the West would be chosen by the board, but in China, the state/CCP would make the choice which will be ratified by the board.

NPLs in the NgCCB were never a problem both before and after the OCBC invested in it and the reason is because of the superior management of the bank and its pursuit of commercial objectives. The bank concentrated its lending to SMEs in China and their credit evaluation and monitoring processes were very up to date. The NgCCB has 18 directors of whom six are independent. The independent directors are nominated by the bank and are approved by the CBRC. In the CIO's opinion they are really independent directors and have shown this by both word and deed. The OCBC has one director on the board and representation on three board committees which are the risk, audit and the strategy committee. The OCBC Bank ensured that proper board procedures were followed for all board meetings, minutes and follow up actions taken.

The OCBC has seconded only one staff member to work in the treasury department of the bank and this was at the bank's request. The external auditors are Ernst & Young and the OCBC has worked with them to implement some corporate governance improvements on internal controls and accounting standards. The OCBC is normally called upon by its partner bank to help solve problems when they arise and the management of both banks work very closely together. One needs to be aware and respectful of the cultural practices in China and although *guanxi* and *renqing* are practices that exist, they are not highly relevant in the Bank of Ningbo. An instance of being respectful of local practices is that if the OCBC wants to implement certain new corporate governance changes, it does not prepare a detailed report on why it should be done. Rather, the OCBC will consult with relevant parties, explain and strive to obtain consensus so that there is unanimity in its adoption. Similarly, if the NgCCB wants to apply for a licence, for example for foreign exchange dealings, it is not sufficient to just send in the application form to the CBRC. One must visit the regulatory authorities, consult, explain and justify.

The Partnership Agreement provides for a training fund of US$5 million to be used annually for training of Chinese staff. Senior management and the board of the NgCCB have all been invited to spend one to two weeks in Singapore, visiting the OCBC headquarters and understanding banking operations. The target is to send 100 senior management of the bank to Singapore for one to three months training over five years. The OCBC also sends banking experts to conduct training for the bank staff in China. Corporate governance in Chinese banks has improved substantially over the last four to five years and a lot of the credit goes to the CBRC, which has played a prominent role. Currently the NgCCB enjoys excellent ratings and has attained best practice in many corporate governance indicators including accountability, transparency, information disclosure and protection of minority interests.

5.1.2 Summary

The OCBC Bank's investment in the NgCCB has been an outstanding success. Corporate governance at the bank was already well established when the OCBC invested in 2006 and it has grown progressively better. For a successful partnership, it is not only necessary for the Chinese management to learn about best international practice, but also for the foreign bank to learn about banking in China. This is because the banking business in China is quite different from other countries and it would be a mistake to attempt to transfer a Western model lock stock and barrel into a Chinese bank. The partnership can be described as happy and successful.

Table 10.11 Ningbo City Commercial Bank financial performance

Details	*2005*	*2006*	*2007*	*2008*
Bank assets (000s, RMB)	42,429,348	56,546,233	75,510,771	103,263,191
Percentage increase		+33.3	+33.5	+36.7
Net profits (000s, RMB)	471,115	641,444	916,339	1,352,636
Percentage increase		+36.2	+42.8	+47.6
Return on equity (%)	21.54	20.07	11.42	15.36
Non-performing loans (%)	0.61	0.33	0.36	0.92
Capital adequacy ratio (%)	10.81	11.48	21.00	16.15
Loans to deposit ratio (%)	52.26	57.79	63.95	64.49
State-owned shares (%)	n/a	22.98	19.52	17.96
Related party loans (000s)	n/a	n/a	752,949	939,000

Source: adapted from Ningbo City Commercial Bank Annual Reports (2006–2008).

The NgCCB has performed very well in the last four years (see Table 10.11). Bank assets increased by 33.3 per cent in 2006, 33.5 per cent in 2007 and 36.7 per cent in 2008. Net profits maintained an upward trend, increasing by 36.2 per cent in 2006, 42.8 per cent in 2007 and 47.6 per cent in 2008. Over the same period, NPL has also been kept low and was 0.61 per cent in 2005 and 0.92 per cent in 2008. The CAR was good, being 16.15 per cent in 2008 which exceeded the minimum 8 per cent set by the Basel Convention. The percentage of state-owned shares was reduced from 22.98 per cent in 2006 to 17.96 per cent in 2008 thus confirming the declining influence of the state. Most important of all the CBRC, being satisfied with the corporate governance at the bank and its excellent track record, approved the bank's applications for a regional licence. In 2008 the bank established new branches in Shenzhen, Suzhou and Nanjing as part of its expansion plan. This is recognition of its corporate governance improvements and the fact that its NPL and CAR were better than the relevant average ratios of the JSCBs. Corporate governance in China can be enhanced when the whole banking industry in China is further liberalized and when the influence of the state/CCP is further reduced. Both are already happening.

5.2 The experience of the Hong Leong Banking Group

The Hong Leong Banking Group (HLBG) of Malaysia was one of several financial institutions that were invited in October 2007 to bid for a 19.9 per cent equity stake in the Chengdu City Commercial Bank (later renamed Bank of Chengdu) and Hong Leong Bank's bid of RMB1.95 billion (US$240 million) was successful. In KPMG's report of October 2007 entitled 'China's City Commercial Banks – Strategic Options', the Chengdu City Commercial Bank is rated at number 19 out of China's top 20 City Commercial Banks according to measures of risk, capital, earnings and liquidity. In terms of asset size, the Chengdu City Commercial Bank only had RMB36 billion, ranking it at number 18 out of the top 20 of China's CCBs. It is however a leading CCB in western China and has an extensive branch network in Chengdu.

There are several reasons for Hong Leong's choice. By 2007, most of the CCBs in the cities along the eastern seaboard had foreign shareholders or were in negotiations with foreign bankers. Only the CCBs in the central and western parts of China were available for investment. The Hong Leong Banking Group also had some business activities in Chengdu, including property development and trading and the senior management of Hong Leong knew the chairman and the CEO of the Chengdu City Commercial Bank and some of its larger shareholders well. So when the invitation came to bid, the Hong Leong Banking Group was keen. Hong Leong had earlier also investigated other Chinese CCBs but they did not materialize because the pricing was not right and there was not a cultural fit.

Although the Chengdu City Commercial Bank was not large in terms of assets, it is located in Chengdu, the capital of Sichuan province which has a population of over 15 million and a per capita GDP of RMB30,855 (US$4,408) which is higher than the national average of RMB23,205. This made it attractive to investors who saw potential for growth and expansion. Corporate governance in the bank was an item that the HLBG also looked at and evaluated. They did due diligence and found it, while not perfect, to be fairly good.

5.2.1 What Hong Leong Banking Group did to improve corporate governance[4]

The Hong Leong Banking Group (HLBG) prides itself on proactive management and, immediately after the equity investment, the Group invested in a 'Bank-wide Business Re-engineering Program' for the Chengdu City Commercial Bank. This was a programme conducted by Deloitte – an international firm of accountants – and was a detailed analysis and evaluation of the strengths and weaknesses of the bank – a SWAT analysis with detailed recommendations for improvement. The HLBG ensured that all the recommendations made were strictly implemented.

The HLBG has also helped to dispose of NPLs. In 2005, the NPL ratio was 11.6 per cent (see Table 10.12). Since then it has been reduced progressively to 8 per cent in 2007 and, in 2008, it was 3.45 per cent. The HLBG implemented a training programme for the Chinese staff and the Partnership Agreement provides for a training fund of RMB30 million and a technical fund of

RMB20 million. The Chinese staff are sent to various countries in Asia for training in all areas of banking including finance, consumer banking, treasury, information technology, computer training, etc. Every year, 20–30 management staff from the Chengdu City Commercial Bank are sent overseas for training. The HLBG also sends in experts to conduct training in China when needed.

Since investing in the bank, the HLBG has helped the Chengdu City Commercial Bank improve their financial reporting system, management information systems and helped to centralize management. This is important as the bank management is now able to get important financial information quickly and take action to remedy problems. Previously financial information was produced quarterly but now monthly data are prepared very quickly. The bank has 15 directors of whom five are independent. The HLBG has two directors on the board and they attend all board meetings and ensure that all recommendations made by the Deloitte Report on 'Bank Re-engineering Program' are followed. The board meetings are very professional now and the two HLBG directors chair the risk and strategy committee. One of the HLBG directors also sits on the remuneration committee.

As part of the Partnership Agreement, the HLBG negotiated for the following positions to be occupied by its representatives from Malaysia: the deputy chairmanship of the bank, the chief financial officer and the chief risk officer. As the chief financial officer and the chief risk officer are both HLBG appointees, no large loan can be approved without the approval of the Malaysian investor and the HLBG has firm control on the finances of the Chengdu City Commercial Bank. The HLBG has also seconded five full-time staff to the Bank of Chengdu and they work in the risk/credit evaluation, treasury and finance departments. The staff have been seconded to teach and to implement best practice in banking operations and to ensure that the risk culture is firmly established. The HLBG wants to establish best corporate governance practices and has invested a lot of resources into this.

The Chengdu City Commercial Bank uses a local Chinese auditor but the HLBG has pressed for change to IAS (International Accounting Standards) and has retained Ernst & Young to complement the work of the local auditor and to prepare accounts to IAS standards. This has been emphasized by the HLBG as the bank intends to have an IPO soon which necessitates higher standards of corporate governance. Before HLBG invested, the four parameters of corporate governance, i.e. transparency, information disclosure, accountability and protection of minority interests, were all below industry average but are much better now.

The current shareholding structure of the Chengdu City Commercial Bank has local government companies owning about 45 per cent. As the largest shareholder, they have the biggest say but they also heed the views of the minority shareholders. For example when state shareholders wanted to approve a large loan recently, the HLBG objected because of risk concerns. The board decided not to proceed with the loan.

For the Chengdu City Commercial Bank, corporate governance has improved significantly over the last few years. However, corporate governance in the bank can be further enhanced at the lower levels if the staff can be taught to understand the needs and objectives of corporate governance. It can be said that the Chengdu City Commercial Bank has come closer as a bank to operating on a full commercial basis

5.2.2 Summary

On an overall basis, the HLBG's investment in the Chengdu City Commercial Bank has been a success. Corporate governance, which was once below industry average, has improved and is now well above average. The bank has also recently submitted an application to the Shanghai Stock Exchange for an IPO and it worked hard to ensure that measures of transparency, information disclosure and accountability met listing standards. The HLBG was a comparative latecomer, investing in China's third tier of banks in October 2007. It has, however, worked extremely hard to ensure its investment pays dividends. Establishing the highest standards of corporate governance will help ensure that.

The bank has made remarkable financial progress in the period 2007/2008 (see Table 10.12). Part of the reason appears to be due to adjustments in the basis

Table 10.12 Chengdu City Commercial Bank financial performance

Details	*2005*	*2006*	*2007*	*2008*
Bank assets (000s, RMB)	29,152,163	37,445,259	52,606,861	72,511,537
Percentage increase		+28.4	+40.5	+37.8
Net profits (000s, RMB)	44,264	12,391	443,160	915,290
Percentage increase		–72.0	+3476.5	+106.5
Return on equity (%)	3.82	0.91	29.57	13.72
Non-performing loans (%)	11.6	9.80	6.25	3.45
Capital adequacy ratio (%)	6.01	7.17	4.89	16.84
Loans to deposit ratio (%)	60.42	59.35	64.64	64.27
State-owned shares (%)	n/a	n/a	44.35	44.35
Related party loans (000s)	n/a	n/a	6,357,000	1,591,550

Source: adapted from Chengdu City Commercial Bank Annual Reports (2006–2008).

of computation of net profits over 2006 and 2007. However the new management is dynamic and is determined to raise efficiency and improve overall operating standards, including corporate governance, quickly.

6 Conclusion

The conclusion to be drawn from the above research is that all of the ten partnerships between foreign strategic partners and the CCBs have been successes. Some are more successful than others because the foreign partners invested more time, effort and money.

Corporate governance in the CCBs with foreign shareholders improved substantially following the foreign shareholding entry. In nine out of the ten CCBs investigated, governance standards was strongly believed by management to have improved substantially and this was proven by financial statistics after their entry. Only in the case of one CCB (Nanchong City Commercial Bank) have governance standards not improved as much as desired by its foreign partners. Even then, in that bank, the NPL was low at 1.14 per cent in 2008 and the CAR ratio of 11.29 per cent in 2008 still exceeded the 8 per cent minimum recommended by the Basel Banking Accords.

Most of the foreign strategic partners were reluctant to talk about the role of the state/CCP in the bank's operations except to confirm that their presence is felt but that it is a diminishing role. This position is confirmed by Alex Thursby, managing director of the ANZ Bank, Asia Pacific, who believes the CCP plays a peripheral role in the overall scheme of things and it is likely to further reduce in future.

Most of the foreign banking shareholders seconded staff to work in key areas of the Chinese banks and all of them had a 'Technical Expertise Transference Program' under which Chinese staff were sent overseas for training. All of the CCBs were initially lacking in risk and credit evaluation skills and the foreign strategic shareholders helped overcome that. Not only was credit management improved but other areas including liquidity risks, market risks, operational risks and foreign exchange risks. As a result of the technical expertise brought in by foreign strategic shareholders, operational efficiency improved substantially and profits surged while maintaining high capital adequacy ratios in accordance with the Basel Banking Accords. NPL ratios were also substantially reduced – in many cases below 2 per cent while the loan deposit ratios were kept at safe levels. Management information systems were another area of concern to foreign investors and again this was addressed to enable remedial actions to be taken speedily when problems arose.

The three main protagonists impacting on corporate governance are the board of directors, the foreign strategic shareholders and the Chinese authorities. The fact is that all three parties want better corporate governance. The model of corporate governance that China is evolving towards is one where transparency, accountability, information disclosure and protection of minority interests are all important but it will also have some special features, i.e. it will be 'a model of corporate governance with Chinese characteristics'. This model of future corporate governance is a model where the state, the CCP and the CBRC will have a continued role.

11 Corporate governance reforms made after entry of foreign partners

1 Introduction

In the previous chapter, we read of the ten CCBs with foreign shareholdings that were investigated. We remember that because the CCBs were amalgamated from UCCs originally, corporate governance was lacking initially. Corporate governance structures and mechanisms were lacking because there was little need for such standards and many of the CCBs simply operated as when they were UCCs. The CCBs were wholly owned by the state or SOEs and there were no minority, external or foreign shareholders. Hence, there was little need for transparency, accountability and information disclosure. There was no need to protect minority shareholders as there were none.

It was only after reorganization and restructuring when foreign banking partners became shareholders that the CCBs had to apply governance standards and implement corporate governance structures and mechanisms. Our investigations showed that by and large all ten of those CCBs investigated improved their standards of corporate governance. Some banks improved by a greater and others by a lesser degree. We will describe the changes made: these changes were compiled and collated by the author after interviews with the banks and also by reference to their annual reports.

Many of the early foreign investors found that the Chinese CCBs were casual in their approach to corporate governance with informal networks taking the place of governance structures. This was due to the absence of a comprehensive legal system and the lack of strong *rule of law* under the planned economy. La Porta *et al.* (2000a) found that corporate governance systems in different countries were markedly impacted by the laws and theorized that the legal approach to corporate governance laid down the best basis for the protection of both shareholders and creditors. Foreign partners therefore wisely decided that the appropriate approach was to establish corporate governance structures and placed them on a legal footing so that there can be no doubt about their necessity or importance. The Partnership Agreement was the legal document setting out the rights, duties and obligations of both parties and foreign partners ensured that it was both detailed and comprehensive.

2 Corporate governance reforms

2.1 Annual shareholder meetings

The Company's Act requires all corporate entities to hold annual shareholder meetings. And all members shall be notified of such meeting at least 15 days in advance (Article 42). Their rights are detailed clearly in Articles 37 and 38 of the Act. Before foreign shareholders invested, such meetings of shareholders were perfunctory affairs without adequate notice being given, but once foreign shareholders invested, at the request and insistence of the foreign partners, such meetings became serious and business-like. All of the foreign partners including the ANZ Bank, Commonwealth Bank of Australia, ING Banking Group, HSBC, OCBC and BNP Paribas stressed the importance of shareholder annual meetings, ensuring that proper notice was given, that all proper documentation was sent to all shareholders, that the meeting was held in accordance with the Articles of Association of the bank, that all directors were duly elected and that all issues raised were discussed and recorded.

It is at the annual shareholder meetings that shareholders have the opportunity to query directors over the management of the banks, demand answers to unsatisfactory matters and elect or reject directors. Thus, ensuring that all shareholders are given the opportunity to attend these meetings is extremely important and an indication of the transparency and information disclosure regime of the bank.

2.2 Board of directors

The board of directors is the body that wields ultimate power in the banks for it is from the board that policy decisions are made, directives are issued, and strategic goals established. Thus it is extremely important that all board meeting proceedings are accurately recorded: how meetings are called, what documents were circulated, who was present, what matters were discussed, how decisions were arrived at and what actions are to be taken. This will enable an audit trail to be established and allow future boards to ascertain how correct or incorrect decisions were made. The proper functioning of the board of directors is extremely important for effective corporate governance as is that of the annual shareholders meeting and the supervisory committee.

Previously, before foreign investors arrived, board meetings usually rubber-stamped the decisions of one or two key members of the board. Minutes were brief and merely recorded the resolutions passed. After the foreign partners invested, this situation was obviously untenable and all of the foreign partners stressed the importance of detailed minutes, records of discussions, voting results and follow-up instructions. Foreign investors insisted on regular director meetings with adequate notice being given and the circulation of minutes. All this is standard procedure in international commercial banks but they were not initially practised in the CCBs. Table 11.1 shows the many improvements made at the board level: in the way meetings are called, documents circulated, resolutions

Table 11.1 Board of directors – improvements made

	Before foreign partners invested	*After foreign partners invested*
Adequate notification of meeting	Usually ad hoc	Yes
Agenda prepared	Yes	Yes
Meeting documents prior circulated	Not always	Yes
Minutes recorded	Not detailed	Detailed minutes
Resolutions passed	Yes	Yes
Resolutions signed by all directors	Sometimes	Yes
Minutes circulated before meeting	No	Yes
Follow-up action	Usually	Always
Decisions taken	CEO/chairman	Board majority
Directors approved by CBRC	Yes	Yes

Source: author interviews with ten CCBs supplemented by their annual reports.

proposed and follow-up actions taken. All these resulted in improvements in corporate governance.

2.3 Independent directors

The importance of independent directors cannot be over-emphasized. In the UK and the United States independent directors constitute the majority in a board but in the Chinese banks they did not exist initially. It was not until 7 January 2002 that the Code of Corporate Governance (Zhengjianfa No. 1 of 2002) was promulgated by the China Securities Regulatory Commission (applies to listed companies) which stipulated that one-third of the board should comprise independent directors. The CBRC, which was established in 2003, has not come out with any such regulation although banks wishing to list on the stock exchanges do so on their own accord. A small minority of the CCBs had independent directors but these directors usually had some relationship to the bank or major shareholders.

Foreign shareholders have pushed for independent directors to be appointed to the board as this helps protect their investments. They have been helped by the CBRC, which is required to approve all directors and tries to ensure that independent directors are in fact independent. Again the numbers and status of independent directors was pushed for by the foreign partners. This certainly has helped to improve and protect minority shareholder interests and ensured that the bank is managed for the benefit of all shareholders and not for the benefit of controlling shareholders. The improvements are summarized in the Table 11.2.

2.4 Board committees

The establishment of various board and management committees is crucial to the proper and efficient functioning of a modern bank and the CCBs in China are

Table 11.2 Independent directors – improvements made

	Before foreign partners invested	*After foreign partners invested*
Presence of independent directors	None	Yes
Numbers	n/a	One third of board
Qualifications	n/a	Yes, experienced
Active participants	n/a	Active
Nominated by board committee	n/a	Yes
Chair board committees	No such committees	Yes
Elected at AGM	n/a	Yes
Approved by CBRC	n/a	Yes

Source: author interviews with ten CCBs supplemented by their annual reports.

generally lacking in this area. Before the foreign shareholders invested, most of the CCBs did not have board and management committees, or if they did have them, such committees were perfunctory and did not perform the duties and responsibilities expected of them. In part this was because the other supporting corporate governance structures were not present.

The Code of Corporate Governance (2002) specifically directs the board of directors to set up the following committees which are to have majority independent directors (Article 52):

- corporate strategy committee;
- audit committee – to be chaired by an independent director;
- nominations committee – to be chaired by an independent director;
- remuneration and appraisal committee – to be chaired by an independent director;
- any other committee as directed per shareholders' meeting.

All of the CCBs investigated have established the above board committees in accordance with the Code. This is because most of the CCBs with foreign shareholders want to be listed within the next few years and compliance with the Code of Corporate Governance issued by the CSRC is the first step. In addition, some of the more progressive CCBs, like the Bank of Shanghai, have also established other committees like the 'Related Party Transactions Committee'.

Although the CBRC has directed all banks to set up various board committees, some of these board committees were inactive and that was why all the foreign partners took steps to ensure that the principles and *raison d'être* for such committees were practised. Foreign partners were also careful to ensure that the more important board committees were chaired by independent directors and that their own representative directors were also represented on the important board committees. Table 11.3 summarizes the position of board committees before and after foreign partners invested.

Table 11.3 Board committees – improvements made

	Before foreign partners invested	*After foreign partners invested*
Board committees	No	Yes
Properly functioning	No	Yes
Chaired by independent director	n/a	Yes
Majority independent directors	n/a	Yes
Audit committee	No	Yes
Nominations committee	No	Yes
Remuneration committee	No	Yes
Strategy committee	No	Yes

Source: author interviews with ten CCBs supplemented by their annual reports.

2.5 Management committees

It is the duty of the bank management to set up various management committees to ensure the efficient operations of the bank. These include the credit review committee, the asset and liabilities management committee, risk management committee, internal control committee and may include other committees. Normally these management committees will report not to the board but to the CEO who will of course report to the board. Different CCBs may have different priorities and thus have different management committees. For example, the Bank of Hangzhou in addition to the four management committees mentioned in the paragraph above also has an information technology management committee while the Bank of Shanghai has a marketing management committee

Many of the foreign partners found that the management committees suffered from the same weaknesses as the board committees mentioned in the paragraph above and they took immediate steps to remedy the shortcomings. Again as in the board committees foreign partners ensured that they had their own seconded personnel sitting on some of these management committees to monitor decisions made. Table 11.4 summarizes the position of management committees before and after foreign partners.

Table 11.4 Management committees – improvements made

	Before foreign partners invested	*After foreign partners invested*
Management committees	Ad hoc	Yes
Properly functioning	No	Yes
Credit review committee	No	Yes
Assets and liabilities committee	No	Yes
Risk management committee	No	Yes
Internal control committee	No	Yes

Source: author interviews with ten CCBs supplemented by their annual reports.

2.6 Strengthening credit and risk evaluation

Chinese scholars investigating corporate governance in CCBs realize the importance of credit and risk evaluation and both Liu (2004) and Hu and Feng (2009) wrote about its importance. Indeed, risk management is the single most important basis for ensuring that the bank operates on a commercial basis. In commercial banking, attention is paid to three main areas of risk: credit risk (CBRC 2004b), market risk (CBRC 2004a) and operational risk. Credit risks relate to the viability and the profitability of the project for which the loan is disbursed. The primary concern here will be – how viable is the project for which the loan is applied for? Is the loan likely to be repaid and if not what are the likely consequences? Are the securities lodged to secure the loan sufficient? Is there any corporate guarantor that can act as an additional safeguard? In assessing the credit risk, the financial performance of the borrowing company is analysed – over the past and into the future. The earnings record of the borrower is studied and its future repayment capacity assessed.

Market risk is the possibility of the client defaulting on its loans because of events in the marketplace. These events will include changes in the economic environment either locally or globally. An example is the steep decline of the US dollar globally – what is the likely impact on the borrower – is the borrower an exporter? If so how will its export earnings be impacted and what is the impact on its repayment capacity? Another example is the recent Global Financial Crisis which has impacted heavily on the American and European economies. These are all risks that bank lenders should consider when evaluating a loan. Yet another important market risk concerns the funding requirements of the bank. Are the bank's deposits sufficient to meet the demand for loans? If not how should the shortfall be met? Should the bank borrow from the inter-bank money market or should it increase interest rates on term deposits to attract more deposits? An early warning system should be set up to warn the senior management of such market risks and crucial to this ability is the establishment of an economic research department.

Operational risk is the risk of the bank suffering financial loss due to inadequacies of or failed internal processes, people and systems. To overcome this risk, the bank must implement strict and regular training programmes for all levels of staff: from junior clerical levels all the way up to senior management and directors. Bank manuals and procedures for staff to learn about their duties and responsibilities are absolutely imperative. The bank must also have plans in place to meet emergencies caused by the following:

1 computer failure;
2 terrorist threats;
3 fire/loss/destruction of records;
4 massive and unexpected deposits withdrawals;
5 other potential threats.

Most if not all of the CCBs initially did not have a full and adequate risk culture. They had been in existence for a limited time as commercial banks, most of them for less than ten years. As mentioned before, in the early years many loans were disbursed on instructions from the CEO or the chairman of the board and the authority often consisted of no more than a piece of paper with a request that the loan be approved and disbursed. Obviously this practice could not continue with foreign shareholders on the share registry and that was why the risk culture had to be implemented. What this change meant was that risk techniques had to be applied across ALL aspects of banking including personal banking, business banking and foreign exchange. The new foreign partners ensured that risk programmes were implemented in all areas of personal banking including mortgages, personal loans; in all areas of business banking including corporate loans, trade financing and property development and finally foreign exchange and credit cards. The implementation of a risk culture meant not only the initial evaluation but also the annual review of loan facilities granted.

The implementation of a strong risk culture is very important and all of the foreign partners were able to assist the CCB in these areas. Some of the foreign partners have even gone further and insisted on regular stress testing to ensure that the systems established are in order and can meet contingencies. Many of the foreign partners seconded senior staff to head up the risk department so that they could monitor all large credit applications coming into the bank. In addition, this is to ensure that no loan gets approved without the knowledge of the foreign partners. There have been cases where the foreign partners objected to various loan applications and the board eventually agreed to reject the loan. Table 11.5 shows the position of risk and credit control in many of the CCBs before and after foreign partners invested.

2.7 Internal controls

Internal controls help to safeguard an organization's assets, prevent irregularity and fraud while promoting operational efficiency. Hence it is extremely important

Table 11.5 Strengthening of credit and risk evaluation – improvements made

	Before foreign partners invested	*After foreign partners invested*
State of risk culture	Poor	Strong
Were all loans properly evaluated?	Only some	Yes
Were there annual reviews?	Not usually	Yes
Was foreign exchange risk managed?	No	Yes
All personal banking risks evaluated	No	Yes
All business banking risks evaluated	No	Yes
Security in place before loan disbursement	Not always	Definitely yes
Was there a head of risk at bank	No	Yes
'Risk guaranteed bonds' for staff	Yes, some	Yes, some

Source: author interviews with ten CCBs supplemented by their annual reports.

Table 11.6 Internal controls – improvements made

	Before foreign partners invested	*After foreign partners invested*
State of internal controls	Poor	Strong
Annual review of internal controls	No	Yes
Understand need for internal controls	No	Yes
Internal control committee established	No	Yes
Principle of audit trail maintenance	No	Yes

Source: author interviews with ten CCBs supplemented by their annual reports.

that adequate internal controls be established in a bank as it deals with cash and the opportunities for fraud and malfeasance are many. Basically a system of internal control requires the bank to establish limits for approval of loan facilities, expenditure and purchases. Above approved limits, two or more officers have to sign off and for substantial amounts approval must come from the board. Along the way there must be a proper audit trail indicating who the approving officers were. The study and examination of the internal controls established in a bank is part of the auditing process and is an area that the external auditors look into very carefully. Normally the external auditors are also auditors for other banks and they can see clearly from their audit which banks have strong internal controls and which don't. This is where international audit firms have an advantage over local audit firms as the international auditors can call on their vast overseas experience. The CBRC has also issued guidelines on internal controls and conducted on-site examinations to see how banks have progressed in this area. Credit should be given to the CBRC for their work here and the strengthening of internal controls has resulted in a reduction of fraud and misdemeanours. All of the foreign banks are very supportive of the CBRC's reform efforts in this area. Table 11.6 shows the position of internal controls at the CCBs before and after the foreign partners invested.

2.8 Management information systems

Management information systems (MIS) are an important tool to help senior management manage a bank efficiently and the system should prepare management reports expeditiously. This enables senior management to take remedial action quickly. For this to happen, financial accounts, overdue loan instalments, loans disbursements, maturing term deposits, immediate and contingent liabilities – all these reports must be timely and accurate. It is no use if these reports are available six months after the event, they have to be timely and accurate. For this to happen, the management information system must be up to date. Usually this is only possible when the system is fully computerized and adequate banking software installed to facilitate the process. Almost all of the CCBs prior to reorganization did not have modern and up-to-date MIS. All of the foreign partners stressed the installation of an up-to-date MIS immediately on becoming a

Table 11.7 Management information systems (MIS) – improvements made

	Before foreign partners invested	*After foreign partners invested*
State of MIS	Poor	Strong
Preparation of accounts	Quarterly	Monthly
Profitability of different banking sections	Not available	Accurate
Preparation of loan repayments schedule	Generally late	Up to date
NPL schedule	Ad hoc	Half yearly
Delinquent loans schedule	Not prepared	Regular
Computerization of systems	Obsolete	Up to date

Source: author interviews with ten CCBs supplemented by their annual reports.

partner. This is because they want to know how their investment is doing and this is only possible through timely and accurate financial accounts, budgets and performance reports. Table 11.7 shows the state of MIS in the CCBs before and after foreign partners invested.

2.9 Accounting standards

Transparency is a corporate governance standard that all banks must have and one of the most important measures of transparency is the way that the bank's financial accounts are prepared. Most of China's banks have their accounts prepared according to China's ASBE (Accounting Standards for Business Enterprises). The ASBE cover almost all of the major topics found in the International Financial Reporting Standards (IFRS) and taken as a whole are in line with the IFRS. The new ASBE rules have been applicable to all listed Chinese companies since 2007 and the Ministry of Finance has strongly encouraged all companies that are not listed to adopt the ASBE standards. China's convergence to the IFRS is well documented by Luo Ping (Luo 2008).

As a corollary to the adoption of international accounting standards, most foreign shareholders have also pushed for the appointment of international firms of accountants and auditors. This is because the foreign partners are often able to better communicate with the international firms of accountants who prepare and audit the accounts and who can explain the accounts in terminology that they can understand. Currently out of the ten CCBs investigated only three of them have international accounting firms as external auditors. One of the main reasons is cost and the Bank of Nanjing has switched from an international to a local firm of auditors. Another reason is that the Chinese accounting standards are becoming more international and hence the urgency for international firms of auditors who may cost three times more than local auditors is somewhat reduced. Local auditors are also raising their standards and this is giving foreign investors more confidence in the financial statements prepared.

Table 11.8 International accounting standards – improvements made

	Before foreign partners invested	*After foreign partners invested*
Transparency of financial accounts	Not detailed enough	Transparent – good
Accounts prepared to IFRS	No	Yes
External auditors/accountants	Mostly local	Some international
Accounting standards	Fair	Good

Source: author interviews with ten CCBs supplemented by their annual reports.

The CBRC has played a role in promoting good governance by implementing a programme in 2004 whereby 32 CCBs were selected for a pilot programme on information disclosure requiring them to disclose information about their business activities in accordance with the 'Rules on Information Disclosure by Commercial Banks' and the 'Notice on Standardizing Annual Reports of Joint Stock Commercial Banks'. Results showed that the 2003 annual reports of all 32 banks was basically complete and in accordance with the guidelines. The Bank of Shanghai's information disclosure was singled out for special mention as being of a high standard. Table 11.8 shows the state of accounting standards in the CCBs before and after foreign partners invested.

2.10 Bank objectives

One of the main indicators of a transition from planned to market economy is the changeover from social political objectives to commercial objectives. Whereas under the centrally planned economy the business enterprise operated as an appendage of the state and adhered to state planning policies; under a market based economy, the business enterprise must be operated as a commercial enterprise and earn a return for the shareholders of the company, in other words, earn profits for the shareholders.

In the case of the CCBs, there has been a profound change in the mindset of the management. Bearing in mind that these CCBs were originally credit cooperatives where the profit motive was absent, the management had to quickly

Table 11.9 Bank objectives – improvements made

	Before foreign partners invested	*After foreign partners invested*
Commercial objectives	No	Yes
Social, political objectives	Yes	No
Profit maximization	No	Yes
Open tendering system used	Hardly	Always
Guanxi, renqing	Strong	Reduced influence

Source: author interviews with ten CCBs supplemented by their annual reports.

learn commercial principles of profit and loss management and apply them to every aspect of their business. The process was of course expedited by the foreign shareholders who were only too happy to ensure that the bank followed commercial principles and objectives. An example is the calling of tenders which is now an accepted form of business procurement. Previously, many contracts were awarded on the basis of *renqing* and *guanxi* but after the entry of foreign partners, the practice has stopped. Table 11.9 summarizes the bank objectives before and after foreign partners invested.

2.11 Transparency and accountability

Transparency and accountability are crucial to good corporate governance in CCBs (Han and Wei 2006). Both measures improved substantially in the CCBs with foreign partners because the foreign shareholders insisted on it and did whatever was necessary. What the foreign shareholders did was to ensure that there was transparency and accountability at the highest levels – at the annual general meeting of the shareholders, at the board of director level and working its way down to the managers and the employees. Along the way approval limits were established for all executive staff who were thus made accountable for their actions. Transparency is greatest in those banks listed on the stock exchanges and those preparing for an IPO. This is because of the stringent information disclosure requirements of the Shanghai and Shenzhen stock exchanges. Nevertheless, in all of the CCBs with foreign shareholders, transparency and accountability have improved and will continue to do so in the years ahead.

Accountability is another vital aspect of corporate governance. The CEO must be accountable for decisions made and senior managers must be accountable for their actions taken. Under the old system, directors usually held themselves accountable not to all shareholders, but only to the state who appointed them and similarly management did the same. The result was somewhat chaotic as there appeared to be little or no accountability and NPLs loomed large as a result. All this changed with the arrival of foreign shareholders. All of the foreign partners acknowledged that both transparency and accountability were initially weak but have since improved substantially. This is because transparency helped minority shareholder investors understand what is happening in the

Table 11.10 Transparency and accountability – improvements made

	Before foreign partners invested	*After foreign partners invested*
Transparency	Veiled	Transparent
Information disclosure	Poor	Much better
Accountability	Only to state	To all shareholders
Annual report posted on website	Not usually	Yes

Source: author interviews with ten CCBs supplemented by their annual reports.

bank they invested in and accountability helps ensure that all levels of management are held responsible for their actions. Table 11.10 summarizes the transparency and accountability position in CCBs before and after foreign partners invested.

2.12 Minority shareholder rights

The protection of minority shareholders is integral to the practice of good corporate governance and companies must ensure that all minority shareholders are protected (HanYan 2002). This is done by ensuring that minority shareholders are not deprived of their rights as can happen when controlling shareholders coerce the company to enter into non-arm's-length transactions.

In the case of joint venture CCBs, the foreign partner will have one or two board seats. After an IPO, the bank will of course have many more minority shareholders. That is why boards have been reconstituted to have a third of their members as independent directors so that minority interests are protected. The protection of minority shareholders and their rights to legal action are enshrined in the Revised Company Law (Article 153, 2005) and in the Code of Corporate Governance. Nevertheless minority shareholders depend to some extent on independent directors to protect their interests and independent directors must be aware of this responsibility. The laws for protection of minority shareholders are there but legal actions are costly and time consuming and minority shareholders may fear to proceed with them. Table 11.11 summarizes the position of minority shareholders before and after foreign partners invested.

3 Governance scores

We come back to our research objective – what was corporate governance like in the CCBs before the foreign strategic shareholders invested in them? Remembering that the CCBs started life as UCCs which were amalgamated into CCBs from the mid 1990s, it is not surprising that governance standards were initially low. Some CCBs were reorganized earlier, others later and the process continues to this day. The first foreign institution to invest in a CCB was the IFC (International

Table 11.11 Minority shareholder rights – improvements made

	Before foreign partners invested	*After foreign partners invested*
Minority rights protected	No	Yes
Right of legal action	Ambiguous	Yes (since 2005)*

Source: author interviews with ten CCBs supplemented by their annual reports.

Note

* Article 153 of the Revised Company Law 2005 gives shareholders the right to take legal action against director or senior manager for damages to their interest.

Finance Corporation) which invested in the Bank of Shanghai in 1999. Thereafter, it was followed by HSBC Bank and then later on the ANZ Bank, the Commonwealth Bank of Australia and BNP Paribas and ING and so on. The Asian interest came from OCBC Bank of Singapore, which was one of the earlier investors while the Hong Leong Banking Group of Malaysia was a latecomer investing only in October 2007. Most of the early foreign strategic investors chose to invest in CCBs along the eastern seaboard and later foreign partners had to choose banks to the centre and south-west because the choice ones had already been taken.

Table 11.12 shows the governance standards in the ten CCBs researched by the author, before foreign bankers invested in them. Out of a maximum score of ten, with ten being best practice, five is the pass mark. Six out of the ten CCBs researched had corporate governance scores that indicated their standards passed the governance test while four out of ten failed the strict test of governance. What the scores indicated was that those six banks had the basic framework of corporate governance. For those four banks that failed the tests, i.e. their scores were four or lower, this indicates that their basic corporate governance structures were either missing or, if present, were perfunctorily organized and were not practised according to established principles.

Table 11.13 shows the latest corporate governance status in the ten CCBs after the foreign banks invested. Most of the foreign strategic partners invested around 2004/2005. Except for one bank, the results for the other nine are very encouraging. Seven of the ten banks have scored eight or nine out of ten for all measures of corporate governance and another three banks scored seven out of ten on those measures of governance. The maximum score is ten, which represents best standards and practice. Scores of between seven and nine indicate efficient corporate governance structures were in place and functioning according to accepted practices. A score of six indicates that basic corporate governance structures were in place.

4 Conclusion

CCBs emerged during the mid to late 1990s when UCCs were amalgamated into CCBs under the guiding hand of the state. These CCBs initially suffered from poor corporate governance practices and exhibited the same symptoms as the entire Chinese banking system: high NPLs and low CARs. They were encouraged to seek foreign strategic shareholders who would not only inject much needed capital into the banks but also introduce modern techniques, systems and best practice.

The author conducted research in ten CCBs with foreign equity partners and found substantial improvements after the entry of the foreign shareholders. These improvements were found in every aspect of management of the banks. Some of the changes made were major and necessitated a change of mindset of the directors of the bank. An example of this was the reorientation of the bank towards commercial goals and the pursuit of the profit objective. Other changes were procedural but equally important. An example of this relates to the

Table 11.12 Corporate governance status at CCBs *before* foreign shareholders invested

Details	*Ningbo*	*Beijing*	*Hangzhou*	*Shanghai*	*SRCB**	*Nanjing*	*Jinan*	*Tianjin*	*Chengdu*	*Nanchong*
AGMs	6	6	5	5	5	6	4	4	4	4
Directors' meetings	6	6	5	5	5	6	4	4	4	4
Independent directors	6	6	5	5	5	6	4	4	4	4
Board committees	6	6	5	5	5	6	4	4	4	4
Management committees	6	6	5	5	5	6	4	4	4	4
Credit and risk culture	6	6	5	5	5	6	4	4	4	4
Internal controls	6	5	5	5	5	5	4	4	4	4
Management information systems	6	5	5	5	5	5	4	4	4	4
International firm of auditors	No	No	No	No	No	No	No	No	No	No
Commercial objectives	Yes	No	No	No	No	No	No	No	No	No
Transparency/accountability	6	6	5	5	5	6	4	4	4	4
Information disclosure	6	6	5	5	5	6	4	4	4	4
Minority shareholder rights	6	5	5	5	5	5	4	4	4	4

Source: author interviews with ten CCBs supplemented by their annual reports.

Notes
Maximum score is 10 which represents best international standards. Score of 5–6 indicates basic corporate governance structures were in place. Score of 4 or lower indicates that basic corporate governance structures were either missing or not practised according to established principles.
* Shanghai Rural Commercial Bank.

Table 11.13 Corporate governance status at CCBs *after* foreign shareholders invested

Details	*Ningbo*	*Beijing*	*Hangzhou*	*Shanghai*	*SRCB**	*Nanjing*	*Jinan*	*Tianjin*	*Chengdu*	*Nanchong*
AGMs	9	9	8	8	8	9	7	7	8	7
Directors' meetings	9	9	8	8	8	9	7	7	8	7
Independent directors	9	9	8	8	8	9	7	7	8	7
Board committees	9	9	8	8	8	9	7	7	8	7
Management committees	9	9	8	8	8	9	7	7	8	7
Credit and risk culture	9	9	8	8	8	9	7	7	8	7
Internal controls	9	9	8	8	8	9	7	7	8	7
Management information systems	9	9	8	8	8	9	7	7	8	7
International firm of auditors	Yes	Yes	Yes	Yes	No+	No#	No	Yes	No	No#
Commercial objectives	Yes	Yes	Yes	Yes	Yes	Yes	Yes	Yes	Yes	Yes
Transparency/ accountability	9	9	9	9	8	9	7	7	7	6
Information disclosure	9	9	9	9	8	9	7	7	7	6
Minority shareholder rights	9	9	9	9	8	9	7	7	8	6
Implemented Basel Committee's 'Corporate Governance Guidelines'	Yes	Yes	Yes	Yes	Yes	Yes	Yes	Yes	Yes	Yes

Source: author interviews with ten CCBs supplemented by their annual reports.

Notes

Maximum score is 10 which represent best international standards. Scores of 7–9 indicate efficient corporate governance structures are in place and functioning according to accepted practices. Score of 6 indicates basic corporate governance structures are in place.

* Shanghai Rural Commercial Bank.

Switched from international to local auditor.

+ Intend to appoint international auditor for IPO.

procedure for notification of board meetings and the complete and accurate recording of board minutes.

Most if not all of those reforms were made at the request of the foreign partners and there were many reasons. The first reason was that improvements in corporate governance led to operational efficiency in those CCBs. The second reason was that it ensured the correct allocation of the bank's limited financial resources. The third reason was that it prevented mistakes, misdemeanours and fraud through a system of strong internal controls and the fourth reason was that strong corporate governance meant it could raise capital funds relatively easily and cheaply. The final and the most important reason was because all the foreign partners wanted to protect their investment in the banks they invested in and the best way to achieve that was by ensuring a strict regime of corporate governance.

12 The Global Financial Crisis and its implications

1 Introduction

The Global Financial Crisis (GFC) started in the United States in the second half of 2008 and spread throughout the world in 2009 causing massive unemployment and recession in the whole Western Hemisphere. The crisis spread to developing countries and Russia plunged into recession even as China embarked on a huge fiscal stimulus package to rescue its economy from contraction.

The GFC started as a sub-prime mortgage crisis in the United States which had its origin in the years following the collapse of the dotcom boom and the 9/11 terrorist attacks when interest rates were kept at near zero for about five years. Cheap money and unrestricted lending to sub-prime borrowers resulted in a property bubble (Bianco 2008) and when interest rates rose in 2006/2007 the bubble burst as sub-prime borrowers defaulted on mortgages they could ill afford. During the intervening years, American financial institutions had embarked on a dangerous course – they repackaged these sub-prime mortgages as 'Collateralised Debt Obligations' (CDO) and 'Mortgage Backed Securities' (MBS) and arranged for reputable ratings agencies (Standard & Poor's & Moody's) to categorize them as investment grade bonds which enabled them to be sold all over the world (Nanto 2009).

The world had experienced and overcome the Russian Currency Crisis, the LTCM Hedge Fund Crisis and the Asian Financial Crisis – all of them in the late 1990s. What was different about this event? There are several reasons for its ferocity. The first is that many of these CDOs and MBOs were sold all over the world and especially to Europe whose banks were only too happy to invest in what appeared to be investment grade bonds offering returns higher than US government bonds and securities. Another reason is that world financial markets are so inextricably linked now that what happens in one financial centre will inevitably impact on other centres. But the third and most important reason is that the American financial markets are still the dominant force in world financial markets and following the collapse of Lehman Brothers in October 2008, other American financial icons like Citigroup, Bank of America, AIG, Wells Fargo Bank, Merrill Lynch and Goldman Sachs all teetered on the verge of bankruptcy. The world financial markets shuddered to a halt as they faced the worst disaster since the Great Depression of 1929–1932.

2 What are sub-prime mortgages?

A sub-prime mortgage is one where the borrower does not meet the lending institution's usual standards: most of the sub-prime borrowers have no credit history or do not have repayment capacity. Many sub-prime institutions did not even bother to check the applicant's data on income and repayment capacity and apparently much of the data supplied by sub-prime borrowers was false (Bianco 2008).

Sub-prime mortgages are part and parcel of the American mortgage market. In 1995 sub-prime mortgages constituted 5 per cent of total mortgages but by 2006 the sub-prime mortgage market accounted for 20 per cent and amounted to over US$600 billion (Demyanyk and Van Hemert 2008). Current estimates in 2008 put the total sub-prime loans outstanding at over US$1.3 trillion (Bianco 2008). In order to create liquidity in the secondary mortgage market, mortgages were securitized, i.e. bundled together and repackaged as MBOs and CDOs and sold to investors. The fact that these bonds had been assigned 'Investment Grade' status by reputable ratings agencies like Standard & Poor's and Moody's convinced investors to buy them. Initially they were sold in the US market but later on they were sold all over the world. Once the property bubble burst, many sub-prime borrowers merely handed the house keys back to the banks and mortgage originators, defaulted and walked away from it all. When 20 per cent of the mortgage market comprises sub-prime borrowers, many of whom walk away from their mortgages, the results can be calamitous for the whole system.

3 What did world economies do to overcome the Global Financial Crisis?

As the American economy went into a tailspin in late 2008, the government realized that a massive government fiscal stimulus was necessary and announced a US$787 billion spending package on infrastructure, education, technology, tax cuts, unemployment benefits, health and nutrition on 17 February 2009. It also announced a US$700 billion Troubled Assets Relief Program (TARP) under which it invested in dozens of banks and others like General Motors, Chrysler and the insurer AIG to prevent further contagion.

China, anxious to keep economic growth at above 8 per cent, announced a US$586 billion package on 10 November 2008 and pledged to do its part to keep the world economy afloat. The European Union announced spending of US$256 billion while Japan announced a package of US$396 billion. In addition to the fiscal packages, all major economies slashed their borrowing and interest rates to near zero in the United States and Europe and by more than half in China and Australia. The immediate impact of these massive spending packages was that a simultaneous, deep worldwide recession was averted. An unforeseen danger then was that these massive spending packages would exacerbate the debt situation in many countries. Greece had to be bailed out by the IMF while Spain and Italy have encountered unsustainably high interest rates in refinancing their long-term national debt.

4 Impact on China

The Global Financial Crisis has had a limited impact on China. First of all China's financial system is relatively insulated from the rest of the world through its controls on capital and currency movements. Individuals are not allowed to invest outside of China and foreign investments are done mainly by Chinese government agencies and majority-owned Chinese state-controlled banks. They have been conservative in their investments and the losses from the crisis have been limited. The Chinese government's investments in Fannie Mae and Freddie Mac were substantial (about US$450 billion) but after they were placed under conservatorship of the US government in September 2008, those Chinese investments were safe. China's foreign currency reserves held in US government securities at the end of December 2008 amounted to US$1.4 trillion (Nanto 2009).

Nevertheless, China felt the after effects of the GFC as exports plummeted and foreign direct investments nosedived. China's exports fell for seven consecutive months from November 2008 to May 2009 with exports in May 2009 down 26.4 per cent on a year to year basis. Foreign direct investments also fell eight months in a row from October 2008 to May 2009 (Nanto 2009). The Shanghai stock index fell to below 1750 in October 2008 and with 20 million Chinese entering the workforce every year the situation was grim. That was why the Chinese government was at pains to declare that it would strive to maintain economic growth in 2009 to at least 8 per cent. Premier Wen Jiabao also announced the fiscal package of US$586 billion in November 2008 to shore up the economy.

Table 12.1 China's fiscal package

Details	*Chinese RMB billions*	*US$ billions*	*% total stimulus package*	*% of China's 2008 GDP*
Transport and infrastructure	1,500	220	37.5	5.0
Earthquake reconstruction	1,000	146	25.0	3.3
Public housing	400	59	10.0	1.3
Rural infrastructure	370	54	9.3	1.2
R&D	370	54	9.3	1.2
Environmental development	210	31	3.8	0.7
Health care and education	150	22	3.8	0.5
TOTAL	4,000	586	100.0	13.3

Source: adapted from Nanto (2009).

5 What the United States is doing to prevent a recurrence

One of the main causes of the GFC and its ensuing contagion is that there was no supervision of financial products in the United States that are sophisticated and highly technical. These products are mostly financial derivatives of one form or another which are all highly complex and are not easily comprehensible. Investment banks create these products and hedge funds use the power of money and geometric leverage to invest in these products. The MBOs and CDOs are part of this toxic cocktail and these were never supervised or regulated by the SEC, the Federal Reserve Bank or any agency. When questioned subsequently, Alan Greenspan, the then Chairman of the Federal Reserve Bank during those crucial years, stated that he thought that it was best left to 'free market forces to self regulate'. With the benefit of hindsight we can see how erroneous this approach was.

The American Congress has proposed a whole host of new rules and regulations to prevent a recurrence (Nanto 2009):

1 a new Financial Services Oversight Council to identify systemic risks;
2 new powers for the Federal Reserve Bank to supervise all firms;
3 stronger capital and other prudential standards;
4 a new National Bank Supervisor;
5 registration of advisers of hedge funds;
6 enhanced regulation of securitization markets;
7 regulation of all derivatives;
8 a new Consumer Financial Protection Agency;
9 stronger regulation to improve transparency, fairness.

The United States has taken the lead in pressing for reform of financial markets but wants financial centres in different countries to follow suit. Otherwise it will not work as institutions will merely relocate. This is a problem that global leaders must find a solution for otherwise the chances of a recurrence are real.

6 Implications for the rest of the world

The US model of corporate governance has until recently been widely accepted as a model worthy of emulation. However, recent events have called it into question. The first was the Enron and WorldCom corporate failures in 2001/2002, which highlighted the failure of directors, accountants and auditors to perform their duties professionally. The second and more calamitous event was the subprime mortgage crisis in the United States which led to the GFC.

Does the GFC signal the demise of capitalism and the end of the 'free market'? No, it does not. But it has taken a battering and the shine has come off it. The American economy, which was once touted as 'an advanced and innovative financial system that buttressed an economy that created half the world's wealth' was brought to its knees and had to be rescued by the American government printing trillions of dollars to salvage iconic financial institutions on the verge of bankruptcy. The Citibank Group, American International Group and Bank of America all had to be rescued from bankruptcy.

The GFC was not due to a failure of corporate governance. It was due to the unwavering American belief in free enterprise, the conviction that the free market forces could sort out all problems and that the financial markets could 'self-regulate'. The fallacy that the financial markets could self-regulate led to the belief that the private sector should be left alone to its devices and that government should be kept as small as possible. Above all it was due to a lack of supervision and regulation of key segments of the financial markets that plunged the world financial markets into chaos. In the end, of course, almost all of the major private sector American financial institutions had to be bailed out by the government.

China has emerged relatively unscathed and is poised to play a greater role in financial affairs on the world stage. The Chinese model of governance may have some applicability too and developing and transitional countries are having a second look at it. The conclusion that the world can draw from the GFC is that free markets cannot be left to regulate themselves and there is a definite need for government regulatory bodies and mechanisms to ensure that private sector greed and excesses do not overwhelm the financial sector of the economy.

7 Whither corporate governance in China after the Global Financial Crisis?

The GFC has dealt a blow to global confidence in the American theory of corporate governance as encased in the Shareholder Value model. It has been shown to be somewhat lacking and free market forces can never be a substitute for some measures of government supervision and enforcement. The Chinese model of corporate governance, where the state plays a more active role, is now seen to be worthy of attention.

The Chinese model of corporate governance is converging towards an international model of corporate governance but 'with Chinese characteristics'. What are these characteristics? The characteristics can be summarized as follows:

1 The state has a role in determining the outcome of important decisions. What is considered important is something that will vary over time and change according to circumstances.
2 The CCP has a role to play in determining the outcome of important decisions. Again as in the case of the state, what is considered important will vary over time and depend on circumstance.
3 Government regulators like the CBRC and CSRC will continue to play an important role in defining, improving and enforcing corporate governance
4 Cultural traditions and practices like *guanxi* and *renqing*, together with informal networks, will continue to play a role in business practices in China, although it may be a diminishing role.

5 Currently the CEO and the chairman of all Chinese banks are appointed by the state and approved by the CCP. This practice is likely to continue.
6 Chinese banks currently invite CBRC representatives to sit in on board of director meetings. This practice is likely to continue.
7 China's model of corporate governance is currently more prescriptive and directive. This is likely to continue. Unlike in the UK and United States, good corporate governance practices are not pervasive and yet to reach all strata of society.

Having made the above points, it is emphasized that the Chinese model of corporate governance is based on the United States and UK model. The key parameters of transparency, information disclosure, accountability and protection of minority shareholder interests are all enshrined in legislation and codes of conduct. The role of the state and the CCP are the key differences but, in some ways, the latest developments in the United States have shown clearly that there is a role for the state to play in the overall scheme of things. This finding is echoed by Malin and Xie (1998) who conclude in their paper that 'any model of corporate governance which develops in China is likely to embody the special role of the State and certain idiosyncratic cultural aspects of China while taking on certain characteristics of the UK/USA model of corporate governance'.

How soon will corporate governance standards in Chinese CCBs reach international standards? Bearing in mind that there were 136 CCBs in China at the end of 2008 and that only 13 of them had foreign strategic partners, it will take many years. It is also clear that those CCBs with foreign shareholders have improved their corporate governance standards substantially. The implementation of corporate governance practices is not like instant noodles, it will take time to adjust, adopt and implement. However all the key players in the corporate governance equation want it – the Chinese banks, the foreign partners and the government regulatory bodies. This augurs well for the future of corporate governance in China.

13 Conclusion

1 Introduction

Chapter 1 mentions that both Naughton and Lardy researched China's financial system: the former making the point that reform of the banking system was crucial to the well-being of the economy (Naughton 1998) and the latter (Lardy 1998) stressing that the NPL issue had to be addressed urgently. Although both writers did not mention it as such, the implementation of sound corporate governance in the banking system was a crucial issue central to the attainment of both objectives.

We also made the point early on that the CCBs play an important role in the economic activity in China. First of all they are growing rapidly: more rapidly than the rest of the banking industry: increasing total assets between 2005 and 2008 by 103 per cent, from RMB20,367 million to RMB41,320 million, whereas the banking industry as a whole only increased its total assets by 66 per cent, from RMB374,697 million to RMB 623,876 million (see Appendix 2). The rapid growth of the CCB sector is partly due to the introduction of good corporate governance practices instigated by both foreign partners and the CBRC.

Statistics from the CBRC indicate that CCBs lend the vast majority of their loans to SMEs. As of the end of 2008, a total of 71.16 per cent of the total loan portfolio of all CCBs went to SMEs (CBRC Annual Report 2008). Huang (2009) writes that China's economic growth has largely stemmed from property rights improvements and entrepreneurship in the SME sector. Hence we can make the assertion that CCBs play an important role in fostering economic growth in China.

2 Corporate governance and banking in China

In Chapter 2 we noted that the UK and the United States practise the Shareholder Value model whereas France, Germany and Japan have adopted the Stakeholder model of corporate governance. Through the passage of the Company Law in 1994 (amended in 2005) and the Securities Law in 1998, it was clear that Chinese authorities had chosen a model of corporate governance closer to the UK/US model than the European model. Scholars have questioned the appropriateness of such a model (Tam 2000a, 2000b) while others argue that China's model of corporate governance can be described as being a transitional model (Hu and Hu 2002; Lu 2004). Another view is that China practises a control model (Chen and Strange 2004) as the state retains majority control even after listing. My view is that China has adopted a hybrid model of corporate governance but with Chinese characteristics.

The problems of corporate governance in transitional economies are discussed in Chapter 3 and we find that China and CEEFSU (Central and Eastern Europe and the Former Soviet Union) adopted radically different economic models for their transition from planned to market economies. China adopted a gradual incremental approach (Lin *et al.* 1996b; Naughton 1998; Qian 2000) while the CEEFSU countries followed the Washington Consensus (Williamson 1993) and largely adopted the Big Bang approach (Lipton *et al.* 1990). The former model has been seen by economists as being more successful than the latter; nevertheless both models have largely succeeded in their objective of converting large parts of their formerly planned economies into free market economies. We also see that the problems of corporate governance faced are largely similar in these transitional economies: they still suffer from a lack of strong institutions, lack of transparency, accountability and independent judiciary.

Problems of corporate governance in China can be analysed from both a macro and micro level. At the micro level we study the relationships between and among the various parties that bind a business enterprise together and at the macro level we look at institutions like voice and accountability, control of corruption and rule of law. We also consider external determinants of corporate governance and in this context we study how government agencies like the CBRC and the CSRC have impacted on corporate governance. The role of the state and the CCP is also studied and Chinese traditions of *guanxi* and *renqing* are also evaluated. The above are explained in Section 5 of Chapter 6.

Chapters 7 and 8 deal with local banking in China and the origins of the CCBs can be traced to the UCCs in cities all over China which were amalgamated into CCBs from the mid 1990s onwards. This was done at the prodding of the CBRC who saw foreign equity partners as not only injecting fresh capital into the CCBs, but more importantly, as introducing modern banking techniques and expertise. We also study the theoretical foundations of banking and look at economic development from both a bank based and free market based system. Examples of bank based economies are France, Germany and Japan while the UK and the United States with their highly developed capital markets exemplify the free market based economies. China has a relatively underdeveloped capital market compared to the UK and the United States and as such should be considered a bank based economy although Chinese capital and securities markets have made developed remarkably in recent years. China is also extremely concerned over the income and wealth disparity between the rich and the poor and has promulgated policies to promote economic development in the poorer regions. Examples of these policies are the Opening of the West [西方大开发] and A Harmonious Society [和谐社会]. In this regard, the reorganization of the CCBs is part of this policy and CCBs have been encouraged to extend their loans to SMEs and open up in the remote west.

The latter chapters of this book study corporate governance reforms in the CCBs with foreign shareholders. My research into the CCBs with foreign shareholders indicated that the impact of foreign partners on corporate governance has been substantial and positive. This is because the foreign equity partners take an active management role in the CCBs they invest in and, furthermore, they look to embed good corporate governance practices as a means of protecting their investment.

3 Financial performance

In Chapter 10 we read that foreign banks invested in China because they had reason to believe they would do well and that their presence would improve financial performance (Berger *et al.* 2009) and (Garcia-Herrero and Santabarbara 2008). We next compare the financial performance of the ten CCBs with foreign shareholders, first with the CCB sector and second against the whole banking industry. We are able to make the necessary comparisons because we have the statistics. From the CBRC annual reports we extracted statistics for the whole banking industry as well as for the CCB sector, while for the ten CCBs, the author obtained the annual reports for 2007/2008. This enabled Table 13.1 to be compiled and comparisons made.

In the case of the ten CCBs whose data were collated, their banking assets increased by 179 per cent over the period 2005 to 2008 whereas the CCB sector only increased by 103 per cent. This is an outperformance of 76 per cent (179 per cent minus 103 per cent) by the ten CCBs over the whole of the CCB sector (see Table 13.1). If we compare the performance of the ten CCBs with the whole banking industry, then the outperformance was even more – by 113 per cent (179 per cent minus 66 per cent). Of course one can say that this was due to the expansion of the Chinese economy and that these CCBs were the '*crème de la crème*'. I prefer to draw the conclusion, however, that there is a positive correlation between the presence of foreign shareholders and substantial increases in bank assets.

The next financial statistic to compare is that of net profits. From the 2008 Annual Report of the CBRC we gather that the whole banking industry had total net profits growth of 130 per cent between 2005 and 2008, whereas the net profits growth for the whole of the CCB sector was an incredible 238 per cent. We collated the total net profits growth from the annual reports of the ten CCBs and found only a net profits growth of 175 per cent between 2005 and 2008 (see Table 13.1)

While this may appear disappointing initially, there are reasons for this statistical aberration. The reason for the high net profits growth of the whole CCB sector is because of the continuing amalgamation of existing UCCs into CCBs, i.e. the number of CCBs is increasing every year. For example, in 2006 there were 113 CCBs. This number increased to 124 in 2007 and then increased to

Table 13.1 Bank data: comparison of percentage changes in period 2005–2008

Details	*Whole banking industry (%)*	*Average of all 136 CCBs (%)*	*Average of 10 CCBs researched (%)*	*Average of 12 JSCBs (%)*
Bank assets	+66	+103	+179	+179
Net profits	+130	+238	+175	+191
NPLs as at 31 December 2008	2.4	2.3	1.72	1.3
Capital adequacy ratio (CAR)	11.8	13.00	14.50	10.5
	(as at 30 September 2009)*	(as at 31 December 2008)#	(31 December 2008)@	(31 December 2008)+

Source: adapted from annual reports of the ten CCBs and China Banking Regulatory Commission Annual Reports 2006–2008.

Notes

* Xinhua News dated 16 December 2009: www.xinhuanet.com/english.

\# Xinhua News dated 28 October 2009: www.xinhuanet.com/english.

\+ Asia Info Services dated 19 March 2009.

@ Data from annual reports of the ten CCBs.

136 in 2008. Hence, a net profits increase of 238 per cent for the whole CCB sector cannot be used as a comparison and instead we use the average of the banking industry over the period 2005–2008. The relevant profit increase over the period was 130 per cent for the whole banking sector while the profit increase for the ten CCBs was 175 per cent. Again the ten CCBs outperformed the banking industry by 45 per cent (175 per cent minus 130 per cent).

The third financial parameter we consider is that of NPLs. Every bank survives and prospers on its ability to control and manage its NPLs and this is a statistic that CCBs with foreign partners have done particularly well on. According to the 2008 CBRC Annual Report, as at the end of 2008, the whole banking industry had a NPL ratio of 2.4 per cent, while the whole CCB sector had a NPL ratio of 2.3 per cent (Table 13.1). These are very low numbers and while I do not wish to cast doubt on the numbers, it is possible that the fast growing economy may mask some otherwise delinquent loans.

However, the important fact to stress is that the ten CCBs investigated had an even lower NPL ratio of 1.72 per cent (see Table 13.1, column 4). These figures confirm that the foreign strategic partners have implemented a strong risk regime which is reflected in the low NPL figures. The difference between the group of ten CCBs and the whole banking industry was 0.68 per cent (2.4 per cent minus 1.72 per cent) which is quite substantial when applied to the loan base. Again a conclusion can be drawn that foreign shareholders have helped to reduce NPLs in the CCBs they invested in.

The last financial statistic we investigate is the Capital Adequacy Ratio. The CAR is an amount of money which a bank has to maintain in the form of shareholders' capital, shown as a percentage of its assets. The CBRC has designated that the minimum CAR ratio should be kept at 8 per cent in accordance with the Basel Accords. Again the CAR for the group of ten CCBs was 14.50 per cent which was well above the industry average of 11.8 per cent and the CCB sector's CAR average of 13.0 per cent. Again the presence of the foreign partners has helped raise CARs above minimum requirements. As mentioned in earlier chapters, the foreign partners have made CAR management a part of their overall risk management strategy.

Although the arrival of the foreign partners has clearly strengthened corporate governance in the CCBs they invested in and this was reflected in their financial performances, it does not mean that the checks and balances and system of internal controls put in place are perfect. This was shown to be the case when a case of alleged fraud occurred at the Bank of Qilu at the end of 2011 and the financial institution is believed to have accepted forged commercial bank bills to the value of around RMB1.5 billion (US$240 million). The case is under investigation and highlights the problems and challenges that foreign partners have to be aware of.

4 How does this research contribute to new knowledge?

Earlier on we posed various questions relating to the role corporate governance played in the reform of the CCB sector in China and more specifically what role foreign shareholders played in the CCBs they invested in. We now give the answers.

Corporate governance has played a crucial role in the reform of the CCB sector. In this regard, the CSRC and the CBRC were pioneers. The CSRC was established in 1992 to regulate listed entities and it promulgated many regulations on good corporate governance practices. Although these rules were meant for listed companies, many banks also followed them as they wanted to get listed on the stock exchanges too. The CSRC introduced the QFII scheme in 2003 (see Chapter 6, Section 3.4) as a first step towards opening the capital markets and also expected that problems of corporate governance faced by the listed companies would be ameliorated. However, it was found that the impact of the QFII scheme on improving corporate governance was limited (Tan 2009b). It was limited because none of the foreign investors played any role in the management of the companies they invested in.

Banks were initially supervised by the PBOC. However the regulatory functions were spun off to the CBRC in 2003. The supervisory role played by the CBRC was three-fold – first in promulgating the rules and regulations of sound corporate governance, second in promoting these practices and mechanisms and finally in their enforcement. However, the CBRC concentrated initially on the SOCBs and as the QFII had only a limited impact on improving corporate governance in listed entities, encouraged the newly reorganized CCBs to seek foreign partners as a means of improving their governance standards. CCBs were initially a motley lot of UCCs that were reorganized into commercial banks. The fact that many of them have evolved into well managed commercial banks with a number of them in the world's top 500 banks[1] is an indication of how far and how fast they have progressed in terms of corporate governance. This rapid progress has been helped by the foreign partners who invested in 13 CCBs in China. Chapter 11 details the corporate governance changes brought about by the foreign partners. In many cases, corporate governance standards have been brought close to international standards.

The reforms in corporate governance have also resulted in financial performance improvements. Table 13.1 shows that not only did those ten CCB outperform the whole banking industry, they also outperformed the entire CCB sector on many counts including growth in assets, lower NPL and higher CAR. All these statistics show the important role of foreign partners in improving corporate governance and its flow-on effects on the overall operational efficiency of the banks.

5 Were the research objectives met?

We posed in Chapter 1, Section 3 some research objectives. We can state that these research objectives have been met.

- What was corporate governance in the CCBs like before the foreign partner invested? We see in Table 11.12 that corporate governance in all the CCBs was initially poor with six CCBs just above average and four CCBs below average. However, after partnering foreign investors, corporate governance has improved with nine CCBs scoring eights and nines out of a maximum of ten and only one CCB scoring seven out of ten (see Table 11.13).

- What was NPL like before and after foreign investors invested? In all cases the NPL ratio was reduced significantly as Table 13.2 shows. The Chengdu CCB had high NPL ratio of 11.6 per cent in 2005 but it was brought under control and reduced to 3.45 per cent in 2008. At the Tianjin CCB, the NPL was reduced from 6.92 per cent in 2005 to 1.55 per cent in 2008 while at the Jinan CCB the NPL was reduced from 6.66 per cent to 2.55 per cent over the same period. Both the Hangzhou and the Ningbo CCBs had low NPL ratios for a long time, being well managed commercially focused banks.
- The reasons for high initial NPLs were simple: the lack of a credit culture, loose internal controls, ill-defined approval limits and low accountability. The NPL ratio was reduced substantially because of the insistence by foreign partners that all credit applications undergo rigorous examination before approval and the implementation of a framework for the approval and disbursement of loans.
- What is the current shareholding structure of the banks? Initially, in the majority of cases, the state or SOEs were the majority shareholder. However, over time, the state shareholding in the CCBs with foreign partners has been reduced. The presence of the state on the shareholding registry, however, has not resulted in the majority of loans being made to SOEs as CBRC statistics indicate that 71.16 per cent of all CCB loans outstanding at the end of 2008 were to SMEs.
- What, if any, is the relationship between bank expansion and corporate governance? The CBRC announced in 2004 that CCBs with sound corporate

Table 13.2 NPLs of the CCBs investigated: before and after foreign partners invested

Name of CCB	*NPL in 2005 (%) before*	*NPL in 2008 (%) after*
Bank of Chengdu	11.6	3.45
Bank of Tianjin	6.92	1.55
Qilu Bank	6.66	2.55
Bank of Beijing	4.38	1.55
Shanghai Rural Commercial Bank	4.07	2.29
Bank of Shanghai	3.92	2.23
Nanchong City Commercial Bank	3.25	1.14
Bank of Nanjing	2.47 (2006)	1.64
Bank of Hangzhou	2.03	0.84
Bank of Ningbo	0.61	0.92

Source: adapted from annual reports of above ten CCBs 2006, 2007 and 2008.

Note
Table 13.2 incorporates latest name changes of the city commercial banks.

governance and excellent track records can expect to have regional licences granted. In particular their CAR and NPL ratios must be superior to the average of similar statistics for JSCBs. In this regard many of the large CCBs had aspirations to expand beyond their provincial boundaries and they worked assiduously to improve their standards of corporate governance. The Bank of Shanghai, Bank of Beijing, Bank of Hangzhou, Bank of Ningbo and Bank of Nanjing have made the grade and been granted regional licences by the CBRC. Thus the implementation of good corporate governance has helped these local banks expand nationwide.

- What is the influence of the state and the CCP on the management of CCBs? All the CCBs agree that the state and the CCP are playing a diminishing role in the management of the banks. This is because the banks are becoming more commercially oriented in their operations and this is with the concurrence of the state, the Chinese shareholders and the foreign partners.
- To what extent have the CCBs with foreign partners implemented the Basel Committee on Banking Supervision's guidelines on 'Enhancing Corporate Governance for Banking Organisations'? The answer to that question is that all ten banks have, to a large degree, implemented it.

6 Findings

The findings enable us to draw the following conclusions.

Conclusion 1: corporate governance has helped in the reform of the CCBs in China. From being a group of poorly managed UCCs, they have blossomed into thriving commercial banks forming the third tier in China's banking system providing finance to the SME sector. The model of corporate governance that is emerging in China is a hybrid model that exhibits distinct Chinese characteristics.

Conclusion 2: the presence of foreign shareholders has enormously improved corporate governance in CCBs. In fact, we can go further and state that the foreign partners played a pivotal role in establishing sound corporate governance practices. These practices included the implementation of a strong credit culture, internal controls and adherence to the Basel Committee on Banking Supervision Guidelines on 'Enhancing Corporate Governance for Banking Organisations'. Foreign investors were keen to implement good corporate governance practices because they wanted to ensure that their investment would be profitable in the long term and embedding sound corporate governance practices was the best way of ensuring that. One notable result of high standards of corporate governance established is that it facilitated the regional expansion of some CCBs, as the CBRC allowed them to establish branches in other provinces.

Conclusion 3: the presence of foreign strategic shareholders has resulted in improved financial performance of CCBs. Many foreign partners shrewdly clothed their proposed corporate governance changes as improvements to operational profits and efficiency which allayed Chinese fears and expedited their acceptance. And it did eventuate – the financial performances in the foreign invested CCBs improved with the implementation of corporate governance practices and these were superior to the average for the CCB sector as a whole.

Conclusion 4: the research findings on CCBs in this book are positive and augur well for future partnerships between similar banks and foreign equity partners.

Appendices

Appendix 1

The Chinese banking system: Central Bank – People's Bank of China

Three policy banks

China Development Bank
Export Import Bank of China
Agricultural Development Bank of China

Five state-owned commercial banks – tier one

Industrial & Commercial Bank of China
China Construction Bank
Bank of China
Agricultural Bank of China
Bank of Communications

12 joint stock commercial banks – tier two

China Merchants Bank
China Minsheng Bank
China CITIC Bank
Industrial Bank
Shanghai Pudong Development Bank
China Everbright Bank
Guangdong Development Bank
Shenzhen Development Bank
Hua Xia Bank
Bank of Jiangsu
China Zheshang Bank
Bohai Bank

136 city commercial banks – tier three

22 rural commercial banks

163 rural cooperative banks

One postal savings bank

32 foreign banks

Source: adapted from China Banking Regulatory Commission: Annual Report (2008).

Appendix 2

Total assets of banking institutions (31 December 2005 to 31 December 2008)

Table A2 Total assets of banking institutions (31 December 2005 to 31 December 2008) (unit RMB 100 million)

Type of bank	*2005*	*2006*	*2007*	*2008*	*2008 (%)*
Policy banks	29,283	34,732	42,781	56,454	9.05
State-Owned Commercial Banks	210,050	242,363	280,070	318,358	51.03
Joint Stock Commercial Banks	44,655	54,445	72,494	88,091	14.12
City Commercial Banks	20,367	25,937	33,404	41,320	6.62
Rural Commercial Banks	3,029	5,038	6,096	9,290	1.49
Rural Cooperative Banks	2,750	4,653	6,459	10,033	1.65
Urban Credit Cooperatives	2,033	1,830	1,311	804	0.12
Rural Credit Cooperatives	31,427	34,502	43,434	52,113	8.35
Non Bank Financial Institutions	10,162	10,594	9,717	11,802	1.88
Postal Savings Bank	13,787	16,122	17,687	22,163	3.54
Foreign Banks	7,155	9,278	12,524	13,448	2.15
Grand total	374,697	439,500	525,982	623,876	100

Sources: adapted from CBRC Annual Report (2008); Assets of City Commercial Banks 2005–2008.

Note
CCBs outperformed the overall industry, increasing total assets between 2005 and 2008 by 103 per cent (from 20,367 million to 41,320 million) whereas the banking industry as a whole only increased its total assets by 66 per cent (from 374,697 million to 623,876 million)

Appendix 3

Total owner's equity of banking institutions (31 December 2005 to 31 December 2008)

Table A3 Total owner's equity of banking institutions (31 December 2005 to 31 December 2008) (unit RMB 100 million)

Type of bank	*2005*	*2006*	*2007*	*2008*
Policy Banks	1,523	1,726	3,578	3,806
State-Owned Commercial Banks	9,597	13,540	15,741	19,574
Joint Stock Commercial Banks	1,335	1,904	3,387	4,408
City Commercial Banks	827	1,215	1,883	2,669
Rural Commercial Banks	156	249	330	534
Rural Cooperative Banks	177	295	410	652
Urban Credit Cooperatives	32	50	64	47
Rural Credit Cooperatives	1,320	1,497	1,867	2,220
Non Bank Financial Institutions	1,036	1,170	1,756	2,311
Postal Savings Bank	Not in existence	Not in existence	120	220
Foreign Banks	625	747	1,172	1,420
Grand total	16,627	22,394	30,307	37,861

Source: adapted from CBRC Annual Report (2008).

Note

The rate of change of the total owner's equity is an indication of how rapid the sector of the banking industry is undergoing reorganization and, in the case of the CCBs, owner's equity increased by a very substantial amount between 2005 and 2008 by 223 per cent (from 827 million to 2,669 million) whereas the banking industry as a whole only increased its total owner's equity by 128 per cent (from 16,627 million to 37,861 million).

This statistic confirms the fact that the city commercial banks underwent substantial and rapid reorganization during this period which resulted in substantial increases of equity. The whole banking industry also underwent substantial reorganization as evidenced by the fact that overall owner's equity in the industry also increased by a substantial percentage.

Appendix 4

Profit after tax of banking institutions (31 December 2005 to 31 December 2008)

Table A4 Profit after tax of banking institutions (31 December 2005 to 31 December 2008) (RMB 100 million)

Institutions	*2005*	*2006*	*2007*	*2008*
Policy Banks	274.1	311.0	489.3	229.8
State-Owned Commercial Banks	1,560.7	1,974.9	2,466.0	3,543.2
Joint Stock Commercial banks	289.0	434.2	564.4	841.4
City Commercial Banks	120.7	180.9	248.1	407.9
Rural Commercial Banks	29.4	40.9	42.8	73.2
Rural Cooperative Banks	30.1	53.7	54.5	103.6
Urban Credit Cooperatives	9.2	10.2	7.7	6.2
Rural Credit Cooperatives	120.3	186.2	193.4	219.1
Non Bank Financial Institutions	62.6	129.5	333.8	284.5
Postal Savings Bank	–	–	6.5	6.5
Foreign Banks	36.6	57.7	60.8	119.2
Total	2,532.6	3,379.2	4,467.3	5,833.6

Source: adapted from CBRC Annual Reports (2006, 2008).

Note

CCBs outperformed the overall industry, increasing net profits after tax between 2005 and 2008 by 237.9 per cent (from 120.7 million to 407.9 million) whereas the banking industry as a whole only increased its net after tax profits by 130.3 per cent (from 2,532.6 million to 5,833.6 million).

Appendix 5

Number of entities of the various banking institutions (31 December 2008)

Table A5 Number of entities of the various banking institutions, 31 December 2008

Institution	*Number*
Policy Banks	3
State-Owned Commercial Banks	5
Joint Stock Commercial banks	12
City Commercial Banks	136
Urban Credit Cooperatives	22
Rural Credit Cooperatives	4,965
Rural Commercial Banks	22
Rural Cooperative Banks	163
Village and Township Banks	91
Lending Companies	6
Mutual Credit Companies	10
Finance Cooperatives of Enterprise Groups	84
Trust Companies	54
Financial Leasing Companies	12
Auto Finance Companies	9
Money Brokerage Firms	3
Postal Savings Bank	1
Financial Asset Management Companies	4
Foreign Financial Institutions	32
Total	5,634

Source: adapted from CBRC Annual Report (2008).

Appendix 6

Top 20 CCBs by asset value (31 December 2006)

Table A6 Top 20 CCBs by asset value, 31 December 2006

	Bank	*Asset size (RMB billions)*	*Overall ranking*[a]
1	Bank of Beijing	265	5
2	Bank of Shanghai	262	9
3	Bank of Dalian	96	10
4	Shenzhen City Commercial Bank	82	14
5	Tianjin City Commercial Bank	81	11
6	Guangzhou City Commercial Bank	77	20
7	Huisheng Bank	70	13
8	Shenyang City Commercial Bank	59	12
9	Hangzhou City Commercial Bank	57	2
10	Nanjing City Commercial Bank	56	3
11	Ningbo City Commercial Bank	55	1
12	Dongguan City Commercial Bank	50	15
13	Wuxi City Commercial Bank	43	8
14	Harbin City Commercial bank	43	16
15	Baotou City Commercial Bank	39	4
16	Xian City Commercial Bank	38	18
17	Wuhan City Commercial Bank	37	17
18	Chengdu City Commercial Bank	36	19
19	Changsha City Commercial Bank	33	7
20	Chongqing City Commercial Bank	33	6

Source: adapted from KPMG Report (2007).

Note

a Rated according to risk, capital adequacy, earnings and liquidity.

Appendix 7

Impact of corporate governance on local banking in China

Questionnaire

This questionnaire studies the relationship between corporate governance and the emergence of local banking in China and is in four parts. Investigations will be made into the relationship between corporate governance and the emergence of local banking.

Background of the bank
Emergence of the bank
Corporate governance measures adopted by the bank
General questions

1 **Background of the bank**
   - 1.1 Please give a brief history of the bank
   - 1.2 Does the bank have a mission statement that states clearly the bank's goals and objectives?
   - 1.3 Does the mission statement incorporate good corporate governance as an objective?
   - 1.4 What was corporate governance like in the bank before the foreign partner invested?
   - 1.5 Is profit maximization the objective of the bank?
   - 1.6 Was the local government involved in the bank formation? What percentage do they hold of the bank's shareholdings?
   - 1.7 How many directors sit on the board of the bank?

2 **Emergence of the bank**

   Has the bank applied to open new branches since inception and has the CBRC approved? Is the bank aware that branch expansion is dependent on the bank meeting various terms and conditions set by the CBRC?
   - 2.1 New branches
     - 2.1.1 What are some important successes the bank has had since formation?
     - 2.1.2 Has the bank opened new branches? Name them.
   - 2.2 Financial statistics
     - 2.2.1 Has the bank been increasing annual profits since inception?
     - 2.2.2 Has the bank been increasing total bank loans since inception?
     - 2.2.3 Do you report to the CBRC the bank's CAR ratio over the years?
     - 2.2.4 Has better corporate governance improved financial performance?
   - 2.3 New services
     - 2.3.1 Has the bank increased its range of services over the years? Give details.

3 Corporate governance measures adopted by the bank

Explain briefly the corporate governance measures adopted by the bank and what the foreign partner did to improve corporate governance.

3.1 Annual general meetings
- 3.1.1 Are the AGMs publicized in newspapers/Internet?
- 3.1.2 Do large shareholders usually attend the AGMs?
- 3.1.3 Do many small shareholders usually attend the AGMs?
- 3.1.4 Does the bank allow postal votes?
- 3.1.5 Does the bank allow proxy votes?
- 3.1.6 Are votes for independent directors allowed to be cumulative?
- 3.1.7 Does the bank have special voting shares or shares with no votes?

3.2 Board of directors
- 3.2.1 Who appoints the members of the board of directors?
- 3.2.2 Does the board of directors hire and fire senior management?
- 3.2.3 Is the board in charge of overall risk management of the bank?
- 3.2.4 Are directors given advance notice and minutes of meetings?
- 3.2.5 Do directors meet regularly?
- 3.2.6 Are directors elected at shareholders' AGMs?

3.3 Accountability
- 3.3.1 Accountability is important for good corporate governance. This means that the board of directors and senior management must be held accountable for their actions.
- 3.3.2 Is this principle being practised in your bank?

3.4 Transparency
- 3.4.1 Transparency means that the bank should be open in all of its dealings and transactions. There should be no secret transactions to favour large shareholders or senior managers.
- 3.4.2 Is this principle being practised in your bank?

3.5 Independent directors
- 3.5.1 Does the bank have any independent directors?
- 3.5.2 When were the independent directors first appointed?
- 3.5.3 How are independent directors appointed?
- 3.5.4 Do independent directors need to have special qualifications/experience?
- 3.5.5 Do the independent directors perform a useful role in the bank?

3.6 Supervisory board
- 3.6.1 How many members sit on the supervisory board?
- 3.6.2 What does the board of supervisors actually do?
- 3.6.3 How often does the board of supervisors meet?

3.7 Management committees
- 3.7.1 Does the bank have an 'audit committee'?

3.7.2 What are its duties and responsibilities?
3.7.3 Who does it report to?

3.8 Does the bank have a 'related transactions committee'?
3.8.1 What are its duties and responsibilities?
3.8.2 Who does it report to?

3.9 Does the bank have an 'investments committee'?
3.9.1 What are its duties and responsibilities?
3.9.2 Who does it report to?

3.10 Does the bank have a 'remunerations committee'?
3.10.1 What are its duties and responsibilities?
3.10.2 Who does it report to?

3.11 Does the bank have a 'risk management committee'?
3.11.1 What are its duties and responsibilities?
3.11.2 Who does it report to?
3.11.3 When was it established?

3.12 Risk management

What is the bank's approach to risk management in the past and how does it compare to the present? In regards to NPLs in the bank how did they arise and how were they dealt with?

3.12.1 Risks faced by a bank are market risk, credit risk and operational risk.
3.12.2 Market risk is the risk of financial loss due to changes in the marketplace and includes strategic risk.
3.12.3 Does the bank fix strategic allocations for exposure of the total loan portfolio to various industries? e.g. a bank may decide that no more than 20 per cent of its total loan portfolio be exposed to the construction and building industry or no more than 15 per cent of the total loan portfolio be lent to food processing.
3.12.4 When was this type of strategic allocation constraint first implemented?
3.12.5 Does the bank have an early warning system in place to warn it of possible losses if certain events occur? For example the current sub-prime mortgage market losses in the United States have resulted in losses by US banks because of substandard home loans given when interest rates were very low.
3.12.6 Does the bank have a system in place to monitor funding requirements and the risk of insufficient funds from the inter-bank money market?
3.12.7 Does the bank have a research department to investigate the impact of various risks and their impact on the operations and profitability of the bank?
3.12.8 Does the research department produce periodic economic reports?

3.13 Credit risk is the risk of the borrower not repaying the loan borrowed.

3.13.1 Does the bank have a credit or loan evaluation department?

3.13.2 When was it set up?

3.13.3 Does the loan evaluation include the ability of the borrower to repay loans if the interest rate increases by substantial amounts?

3.13.4 Does the loan evaluation include the ability of the borrower to repay loans if the costs of production including commodity prices increase by a substantial amount?

3.13.5 If the borrower sells its production overseas, does the loan evaluation include the ability of the borrower to repay loans if the currency fluctuates by substantial amounts?

3.13.6 Are these loan evaluations fully documented?

3.13.7 Does the bank have 'chit loans'?

3.13.8 Does the bank approve 'bundle loans'?

3.13.9 How are special loans authorized by the bank?

3.13.10 What percentage of total loan applications are rejected?

3.13.11 Do the shareholders have any impact on the lending policies and decisions made by the bank?

3.13.12 What are the current percentages of the bank's current loan portfolio:

a Government related loans

b Private sector loans

c SOE loans

d Other loans

3.13.13 Does the bank have an annual loan review system in place?

3.13.14 Are large loans recommended by the credit department reviewed by the chief risk officer before disbursement of loan?

3.13.15 Are there credit-checking facilities available to allow the bank to check the credit standing of the applicant before loans are approved?

3.13.16 When are loans considered non-performing?

3.13.17 When they are in arrears by … months

3.13.18 When are loans recalled by the bank?

3.13.19 The CBRC has five categories for the classification of loans. Does the bank follow these loan categorizations?

3.13.20 If not the above, what categorizations does the bank follow?

3.13.21 Please advise the current percentages of these categories.

3.13.22 Is there a special department to collect non-performing loans?

3.14 Operational risk is the risk of financial loss due to inadequacies of or failed internal processes, people and systems.

3.14.1 Are the bank staff being internally trained on the bank's working procedures and updated regularly?

3.14.2 Are the bank staff being externally trained and updated on the banking industry's modern and updated procedures?
3.14.3 Are there bank manuals and procedures for staff to learn about their duties and responsibilities?
3.14.4 Are there internal control measures in place to ensure that work is being checked for accuracy and completeness for cash transactions and cash related transactions?
3.14.5 Is there a system in place where important transactions are always checked before completion?
3.14.6 When was this system set up?
3.14.7 Are loans to any borrower limited to say 5 per cent of the Bank's total loan portfolio?
3.14.8 Does the definition of borrower in the above include related companies?
3.14.9 Does the bank have fraud policies and controls in place?
3.14.10 Does the bank have a plan to meet emergencies caused by the following:
i computer failure
ii terrorist threats
iii fire/loss/destruction of records
iv massive and unexpected deposits withdrawals
iv other potential threats.

3.15 Computerization
3.15.1 Has the bank installed new computer banking software?
3.15.2 When?
3.15.3 Has the bank installed new computer monitors/terminals?
3.15.3 When?
3.15.4 In your opinion are they effective?
3.15.5 Has the bank fully computerized its services?
3.15.6 Please advise which services are computerized
3.15.7 State which services are not computerized
3.15.8 Does the bank have a plan to fully computerize all of its services?

3.16 Human resources
3.16.1 How does the bank measure the performance of employees?
3.16.2 For senior managers?
3.16.3 For supervisory staff?
3.16.4 For clerical staff?
3.16.5 What kinds of key performance indicators does the bank use?
3.16.6 What kinds of incentives schemes does the bank have for staff?

3.17 Management and staff training
3.17.1 Does the bank pay important attention to staff training?
3.17.2 Do all of the bank staff attend some kind of staff training?

- 3.17.3 Does the bank have online electronic staff training courses?
- 3.17.4 Do senior managers also complete online electronic training courses?
- 3.17.5 Have any staff been sent to attend courses on corporate governance?

3.18 Internal audit department

- 3.18.1 Does the bank have an internal audit department?
- 3.18.2 When was it introduced?
- 3.18.3 Who does the internal audit department report to?
- 3.18.4 Are all of internal audit department's recommendations implemented?
- 3.18.5 If the answer is No, what percentage are implemented?
- 3.18.6 What accounting standards does the bank adopt?
- 3.18.7 EAS (Enterprise Accounting Standards)
- 3.18.8 IAS (International Accounting Standards)

3.19 External auditors

- 3.19.1 Who is the Bank's external auditor?
- 3.19.2 Has there been any change?
- 3.19.3 Are all the external auditor's recommendations implemented?

4 General questions

- 4.1 What is the future of City Commercial Banks in China?
- 4.2 How important is corporate governance in China?
- 4.3 In your opinion has the implementation of corporate governance measures helped the bank? How?
- 4.4 Has the foreign partner contributed to better corporate governance? What was corporate governance like in the bank after the foreign partner invested?
- 4.5 What can be done to ensure better corporate governance in banks in China.
- 4.6 What role does the CCP play in the management of the bank? Is there any interference from the state?

Notes

1 Introduction

1 Dongfang, Cinda, Hurong & Great Wall Asset Management Companies.

2 Models of corporate governance

1 Junk bonds are high-yield speculative bonds rated as 'below investment' grade below BBB by Moody's and below Baa by Standard & Poor's.

4 The Chinese perspective on corporate governance

1 According to 2004 CSRC Annual Report, 95 per cent of investors were individuals who held the shares for less than six months.

5 Chinese corporate governance problems encountered

1 The complaint is that there are too many departments who each have a hand in approving projects. Bureaus like the Environmental Bureau, Public Security Bureau and the Civil Defence Bureau all come into play for approving property development projects in Shanghai.
2 The Shanghai Stock Exchange started operations started in 1990 and the first delisted company was PT Narcissus in April 2000. In spite of the many fraudulent activities there were only six companies under temporary suspension as of the end of December 2004 (CSRC Annual Report 2004).
3 The author worked in Shanghai from 1997/1998 on a large property project belonging to DBS Land (Singapore).

7 Financial systems and economic growth

1 Nobel prize winner for Economics Sciences in 1993.

10 Foreign partners in China's City Commercial Banks

1 Bank of Tianjin, Shanghai Rural Commercial Bank, Qilu Bank, Bank of Hangzhou, Bank of Shanghai, Bank of Beijing, Bank of Nanjing, Bank of Ningbo, Bank of Chengdu and Nanchong City Commercial Bank.
2

> One of Asia's leading financial services groups and one of the largest financial institutions in the combined Singapore-Malaysia market with total assets of S$188 billion, a network of over 490 branches and representative offices in 15 countries

and territories including Singapore, Malaysia, Indonesia, Thailand, Vietnam, China, Hong Kong SAR, Taiwan, Brunei, Myanmar, Japan, Korea, Australia, UK and USA. OCBC is Singapore's longest established local bank.

(www.ocbc.com.sg)

3 Founded in 1963 the Hong Leong Group has 14 listed companies on the Malaysian stock exchange and is a diversified conglomerate encompassing financial services, manufacturing, property development, semiconductors, newsprint, building materials and hotels (www.hongleong.com.group).

4 Author interviewed the assistant general manager in Hong Leong Banking Group in charge of the investment in Chengdu City Commercial Bank on 24 July 2009.

13 Conclusion

1 Bank of Shanghai was ranked 288th in Global Top 1000 Banks in terms of Tier 1 Capital by the *Banker Magazine* for 2008 (Bank of Shanghai Annual Report 2008: 32). The Bank of Beijing was similarly ranked 178th (Bank of Beijing Annual Report 2008: 29).

Bibliography

Adeoye, A. (2009) 'Macro-Level Corporate Governance and FDI in Emerging Economies: Is there a Close Relationship?', *Journal of Political Finance* 1 (2): 30–43.

Alchian, A. and Demsetz, H. (1972) 'Production, Information Costs & Economic Organization', *American Economic Review* 62: 777–95.

Allen, F. and Gale, D. (1999) *Comparing Financial Systems*, Cambridge, MA: MIT Press.

Allen, F., Qian, J. and Qian, M.J. (2003) 'Comparing China's Financial System', *China Journal of Finance* 1: 1–28.

Allens Arthur Robinson Report (2007) *Focus China Property Rights Law*. Available at: www.aar.com.au.

ANZ Bank Report (2005) *Investment in Tianjin City Commercial Bank 6th Dec 2005*.

ANZ Press Release (2006) *Shanghai Rural Commercial Bank and ANZ Bank*, 21 November. Available at: www.anz.com.

ASTD (American Society for Training & Development) International Comparison Report (2000) *ASTD's Annual Accounting of Worldwide Patterns of Employer Provided Training*. Available at: www.ilo.org/public/english/employment/skills.

Bagehot, W. (1920) *Lombard Street: A Description of the Money Market*, New York: EP Dutton & Company.

Bai, C.E., Hsieh, C.T. and Qian, Y.Y. (2006) 'The Return to Capital in China', *Brookings Papers on Economic Activity* 2: 61–102.

Bai, C.E., Liu, Q., Lu, J., Zhou, S., Frank, M. and Zhang, J.J. (2004) 'Corporate Governance and Firm Valuations in China', *Journal of Comparative Economics* 32: 599–616.

Bank for International Settlements (2002) 'Supervisory Guidance on Dealing with Weak Banks', Basel Committee on Banking Supervision.

Bank for International Settlements (2003) 'Sound Practices for Management & Supervision of Operational Risk', Basel Committee on Banking Supervision.

Bank for International Settlements (2005) 'Enhancing Corporate Governance for Banking Organization', Basel Committee on Banking Supervision.

Bank of Beijing Annual Report (2007, 2008).

Bank of Shanghai Annual Report (2007, 2008).

Banker magazine (April 2006) 'Best Banks to Buy in China'.

Basel Committee on Banking Supervision (2006) 'Core Principles for Effective Banking Supervision', BIS.

BBC News (30 December 2001) 'HSBC Buys into China Mainland Bank'.

Beck, T. and Levine, R. (2000) 'New Firm Formation & Industry Growth: Does Having a Market Based or a Bank Based System Matter?', World Bank Policy Research Working Paper.

Beck, T., Demirguc-Kunt, A., Levine, R. and Maksimovic, V. (2000) 'Financial Structure & Economic Development: Firm, Industry & Country Evidence', World Bank Policy Research Working Paper, no. 2423.

Belka, M., Krajewska, A. and Krajewski, S. (1999) 'Corporate Governance & Economic Performance in Poland', *Journal of Eastern European Economics* 37 (1): 5–38.

Benjamin, D. and Brandt, L. (2002) 'Property Rights, Labour Markets, and Efficiency in a Transition Economy: The Case of Rural China', *Canadian Journal of Economics* 35 (4): 689–716.

Benjamin, D., Brandt, L. and Giles, J. (2005) 'The Evolution of Income Inequality in Rural China', *Economic Development and Cultural Change* 53 (4): 769–824.

Berger, A. and Udell, G.F. (2001) 'Small Business Credit Availability and Relationship Lending: The Importance of Bank Organizational Structure', FEDS Working Paper, no. 2001–36.

Berger, A., Hasan, I. and Klapper, L.F. (2004) 'Further Evidence on the Link Between Finance & Growth: An International Analysis of Community Banking & Economic Performance', *Journal of Financial Services* 25 (2): 169–202.

Berger, A., Hasan, I. and Zhou, M.M. (2009) 'Bank Ownership & Efficiency in China', *Journal of Banking & Finance* 33 (1): 113–30.

Berle, A. and Means, G. (1932) *The Modern Corporation & Private Property*, New York: Macmillan.

Bhattasali, D. (2002) 'Accelerating Financial Market Restructuring in China', World Bank.

Bianco, K. (2008) 'The Sub Prime Lending Crises: Causes & Effects of Mortgage Meltdown', CCH Federal Banking Law Report, Wolters Kluwer Law and Business, CCH, Chicago, pp. 1–21.

Binder, S., Ngai, J. and Wang, Y. (2007) 'Asset Management Opportunities in China', *McKinsey Quarterly Report.*

Black, B., Kraakman, R. and Tarasova, A. (2000) 'Russian Privatization: What Went Wrong', *Stanford Law Review* 52: 1731–808.

Blair, M. (1995) *Ownership & Control: Rethinking Corporate Governance in the 21st Century*, Washington, DC: The Brookings Institution.

Blanchard, O., Dornbusch, R., Krugman, P., Layard, R. and Summers, L. (1993) *Reform in Eastern Europe*, Cambridge, MA: MIT Press.

Blasi, J. and Schleifer, A. (1996) 'Corporate Governance in Russia – An Initial Look', in R. Frydman, C.W. Gray and A. Rapazynski (eds) *Corporate Governance in Central Europe & Russia*, Vol. 2, Budapest, London and New York: Central European University Press, pp. 78–108.

Bloomberg (5 July 2010) 'Former Chief Economist of the IMF, Kenneth Rogoff Predicts Collapse of Property Prices in China'.

Boeva, B. and Prohaska, M. (2002) 'Disclosure of Information & Corporate Governance of Bulgarian Public Companies', 2nd OECD Roundtable Conference.

Bonin, J.P., Hasan, I. and Wachtel, P. (2004) 'Bank Performance, Efficiency and Ownership in Transition Countries', Bank of Finland Institute for Economics in Transition. Discussion Paper No. 7.

Bottelier, P. (2006) 'China & The World Bank: How a Partnership was Built', Stanford Center for International Development, Stanford, California, Working Paper, no. 77, pp. 1–29.

Boudriga, A., Boulila, N. and Jellouli, S. (2009) 'Does Bank Supervision Impact on Non Performing Loans: Cross Country Determinants', MPRA.

Brada, J.C. and King, A. (1992) 'Is there a J Curve for the Economic Transition from Socialism to Capitalism?', *Economics of Planning Journal* 25 (1): 37–53.

Brada, J.C., Fleisher, B.M., Rozelle, S. and Swinnen, J. (2009) 'Economic Consequences of Urbanisation & Urbanisation Policy in China – Symposium Introduction', *Journal of Comparative Economic Studies* 51 (3): 281–3.

Brandt, L. and Rawski, T. (eds) (2008) *China's Great Economic Transformation*, New York: Cambridge University Press.

Brandt, L. and Zhu, X.D. (2000) 'Redistribution in a Decentralized Economy: Growth and Inflation in Reform China', *Journal of Political Economy* 108: 422–39.

Brandt, L. and Zhu, X.D. (2007) 'China's Banking Sector & Economic Growth', in Charles Colamaris (ed.) *Chinese Finance at the Cross Roads*, New York: Columbia University, pp. 86–136.

Brandt, L., Li, H.B. and Roberts, J.K. (2005) 'Banks and Enterprise Privatization in China', *Journal of Law, Economics and Organization* 21 (2): 524–46.

Brenner, R. (1998) 'The Causes of Economic Growth', Cato Policy Report.

Business Week (20 April 1998) 'Executive Pay Increases'.

Business Week (4 February 2002) 'Former Chief Executive Officer Wang Xuebing of Bank of China (HK) Detained in Connection with US$480 mln Disappearance'.

Business Week (4 November 2009) 'The World Bank Estimates China's GDP Growth for 2009 at 8.4%'.

Bystrom, H. (2007) 'Structured Micro-Finance in China', Lund University, Department of Economics Working Paper.

Cameron, A. (2002) 'Effective Enforcement – the Australian Experience', paper presented at the 2nd International Roundtable Conference on Securities Markets in China, Shanghai.

Chandler, A.D. (2004) 'The Managerial Revolution in American Business', in T. Clarke (ed.) *Theories of Corporate Governance*, Oxford: Routledge, pp. 34–44.

Chang, E. and Wong, S.M.L. (2004) 'Political Control and Performance in China's Listed Firms', *Journal of Comparative Economics* 32 (4): 617–36.

Chen, C.T. (2004) 'State Shareholders Should Push for Implementation of Corporate Governance Quickly', OECD Corporate Governance Conference in Shanghai.

Chen, R. and Chen, C. (2005) 'Chinese Professional Managers and Issues of Ethical Behaviour', *Ivey Business Journal Online* 69 (5): 1–5.

Chen, J. and Strange, R. (2004) 'Evolution of Corporate Governance in China', Research Paper 25, Kings College London.

Chen, Z.W. (2003) 'Capital Markets and Legal Development: The China Case', Yale School of Management paper.

Cheng, X.Q. and Degryse, H. (2007) 'Impact of Bank and Non Bank Financial Institutions on Local Economic Growth in China', Katholic Universitie, Dept of Economics Naamsestraat, Bank of Finland, Institute for Economies in Transition.

Chengdu City Commercial Bank Annual Report (2007, 2008).

China Banking Regulatory Commission (CBRC) (2004a) 'Further Strengthening the Market Risk Management of Commercial Banks'.

China Banking Regulatory Commission (CBRC) (2004b) 'Guidelines on Due Diligence of Commercial Banks in Lending Activities'.

China Banking Regulatory Commission (CBRC) (2006) 'On Further Prevention of the Related Risks in the Transactions Between Banking Financial Institutions and Securities Companies'.

China Banking Regulatory Commission (CBRC) Annual Reports (2006, 2007, 2008).

China Corporate Governance Survey (2007) CFA – Centre for Financial Market Integrity Survey August 2006.

China Daily (19 December 2008) 'Report that Siemens had Agreed to Pay Total Fines and Penalties of US$1.4 Billion in Germany and the USA for Bribing Officials in Several Countries including China between 2001 and 2007'.

China Securities Regulatory Commission (CSRC) Annual Reports (2004/2007/2008).

Chow, G. (1993) 'How and Why China Succeeded in Economic Reforms', *China Economic Review Journal* 4 (2): 117–28.

Clarke, D. (2003) 'An Overview of Corporate Governance in China', *China Economic Review* 14: 494–507.

Clarke, D. (2006) 'The Independent Director in Chinese Corporate Governance', *Delaware Journal of Corporate Law* 31: 125–228.

Clarke, D. (2008) 'The Ecology of Corporate Governance in China', SSRN George Washington University Legal Studies Research Paper, no. 433.

Clarke, T. (2004) *Theories of Corporate Governance*, London: Routledge.

Classens, S., Djankov, S. and Pohl, G. (1997) 'Ownership & Corporate Governance-Evidence from the Czech Republic', World Bank Working Paper.

Clegg, S.K., Wang, K. and Berrell, M. (eds) (2007) *Business Networks and Strategic Alliances in China*, Cheltenham: Edward Elgar.

Code of Corporate Governance 2002 (China) Issued by the CSRC (Zhengjianfa No. 1 of 2002).

Coffee, J. Jnr (2004) 'What Caused Enron's Failure?', *Cornell Law Review* 89.

Cohen, J.A. (2010) 'Politics, "*Guanxi*" and the Rule of Law', *South China Morning Post*, 4 March.

Cole, G.A. (2004) *Management Theory & Practice*, London: Geraldine Lyons.

Commonwealth Bank of Australia Press Release (2005) 'CBA Paid US$78 Millions for a 19.9 Per Cent Stake in the Hangzhou City Commercial Bank'.

Constitution of the CCP. Available at: www.chinability.com/ccp (see Chapter 5, Article 31 Section 7).

Cooper, M. (2002) 'The Regional Distribution of Company Listing in China', paper presented at the Annual Meeting of the American Political Science Association of Boston, Marriott, Copley Place, Boston, Massachusetts.

Crystal, J.S., Dages, G. and Goldberg, L.S. (2002) 'Has Foreign Bank Entry led to sounder banks in Latin America?' *Economics & Finance 8*, Federal Reserve Bank of New York.

CSRC (2004) 'China's Securities and Futures Markets'.

CSRC directive (2001) 'The Role of the Independent of Independent Director in Listed Companies'.

Cui, R.P. (2004) *Corporate Governance: System and Performance*, Beijing: Chinese Academy of Social Sciences.

Da Costa, M.M.N. and Carroll, W. (2001) 'Township & Village Enterprises, Openness & Regional Economic Growth in China', *Journal of Post Communist Economies* 13 (2): 229–41.

Dallago, B. and Iwasaki, I. (2007) *Corporate Restructuring and Governance in Transition Economies*, Basingstoke: Palgrave Macmillan.

Da Silva, L.C., Goergen, M. and Renneboog, K. (2004) '*Dividend Policy & Corporate Governance*' Oxford University Press.

Davis, J.H., Schoorman, D. and Donaldson, L. (1997) 'Towards a Stewardship Theory of Management', *Academy of Management Review* 22 (1): 20–47.

Dean, R.N. (2004) 'Corporate Governance: Is there a Village behind the Façade?', in D.J. McCarthy, S.M. Puffer and S.V. Shekshnia (eds) *Corporate Governance in Russia*, Cheltenham: Edward Elgar, pp. 376–93.

DeCosta, M.M.N. and Foo, J.P.N. (2002) 'China's Financial System: Two Decades of Reforms', *Journal of Managerial Finance* 28 (10): 3–18.

Demirguc-Kunt, A. and Huizinga, H. (1999) 'Determinants of Commercial Bank Interest Margins & Profitability: Some International Evidence', *World Bank Review* 13: 379–408.

Demirguc-Kunt, A. and Levine, R. (2001) *Finance Structure & Growth: A Cross Country Comparison of Banks, Markets and Development*, Cambridge, MA: MIT Press.

Demirguc-Kunt, A. and Maksimovic, V. 'Law, Finance & Firm Growth', *Journal of Finance* 53 (6): 2107–37.

Demyanyk, Y.S. and Van Hemert, O. (2008) 'Understanding the Subprime Mortgage Crisis'. Available at: http://ssrn.com/abstract=1020396.

DEG, www.deginvest.de/En_home.

Djatej, A., Sarikas, R. and Senteney, D. (2008) 'Corporate Governance in Russia: Consideration of Different Perspectives', Robert McGee (ed.), *Corporate Governance in Transitional Economies*, New York: Springer, pp. 243–50.

Djankov, S., Qian, Y., Roland, G. and Zhuravskaya, E. (2006) 'Who Are China's Entrepreneurs?', *American Economic Journal* 95 (2): 348–52.

Donaldson, L. and Davis, J.H. (1991) 'Agency Theory or Stewardship Theory', *Australian Journal of Management* 16: 49–64.

Dornbusch, R. and Reynoso, A. (1989) 'Financial Factors in Economic Development', Working Paper, no. 2889, National Bureau of Economic Research, Cambridge, MA.

Dyck, A., Volchkova, N. and Zingales, L. (2007) 'The Corporate Governance Role of the Media – Evidence from Russia', ECGI Working Paper, no. 15/4/2007.

Fama, E. and Jensen, M. (1983a) 'Separation of Ownership & Control', *Journal of Law & Economics* 26 (2): 301–25.

Fama, E. and Jensen, M. (1983b) 'Agency Problems & Residual Claims', *Journal of Law & Economics* 26: 327–49.

Fan, J., Wong, T.J. and Zhang, T. (2005) 'The Emergence of Corporate Pyramids in China', Chinese University of Hong Kong.

Fan, J., Morck, R., Xu, C. and Yeung, B. (2007) 'Institutions & Foreign Direct Investments – China vs Rest of the World', World Bank Working Paper.

Feng, C.Y. (2008) 'Democrats within the CCP since 1989', *Journal of Contemporary China* 17 (57).

Feng, C.Y. (2009) 'The Rights Defence Movement, Rights Defence Lawyers & Prospects for Constitutional Democracy in China', *Cosmopolitan Civil Societies Journal* 1 (3): 150–69.

Ferguson, M. and McGuinness, P. (2004) 'Chinese Securities Reform: The Role of QFII in the Corporate Governance Process', *Business Horizons* March/April: 53–61.

Finckenauer, J.O. and Voronin, Y.A. (2001) 'The Threat of Russian Organized Crime', *Issues in International Crime*, US Department of Justice, pp. 1–30.

Fox, M. and Heller, M. (1999) 'Lessons from Fiascos in Russian Corporate Governance', William Davidson Institute Working Paper, no. 282.

Freeman, R.E. and Reed, D.L. (1983) 'Stockholders and Stakeholders: A New Perspective on Corporate Governance', *California Management Review* XXV (3): 88–106.

Garcia-Herrero, A. and Santabarbara, D. (2004) 'Where is the Chinese Banking System Going with the Ongoing Reform?', Banco de Espana, Madrid.

Garcia-Herrero, A. and Santabarbara, D. (2008) 'Does the Chinese Banking System Benefit from Foreign Investors', Bank of Finland Discussion Papers.

Giradin, E. and Xie, P. (1997) 'Urban Credit Cooperatives in China', OECD Paper.

Goldsmith, R. (1969) *Financial Structure and Development*, New Haven: Yale University Press.

Gompers, P. and Ishii, J. (2003) 'Corporate Governance & Equity Prices', *Quarterly Journal of Economics* 118 (1): 107–55.

Green, S. (2005) 'Making Monetary Policy Work in China', Stanford Center for International Development, Working Paper, no. 245.

Guillen, M. (2004) 'Corporate Governance & Globalization: Is there Convergence across Countries?', in Thomas Clarke (ed.),*Theories of Corporate Governance*, London: Routledge, pp. 223–40.

Guo, N.N. (2007) 'Causes & Solutions of Non Performing Loans in Chinese Commercial Banks', *Chinese Business Review* 6 (6): 13–19.

Guo, Y.J. (2004) *Cultural Nationalism in Contemporary China: The Search for National Identity Under Reform*, London: Routledge.

Guo,Y.J. (2005) 'China's New Nationalism: Pride, Politics & Diplomacy', Book Review, *The China Journal* 53: 235–8.

Guo, Y.J. (2008) 'Domestic Openness in Post WTO: Central & Local Perspectives', *Journal of Contemporary China* 17 (55): 339–59.

Guriev, S. and Rachinsky, A. (2005) 'The Role of Oligarchs in Russian Capitalism', *Journal of Economic Perspective* 19 (1): 131–50.

Hangzhou City Commercial Bank Annual Report (2007, 2008).

Hawes, C. (2007) 'Interpreting the PRC Company Law through the Lens of Chinese Political and Corporate Culture', *The UNSW Law Journal* 30 (3): 813–23.

Hawes, C. and Chiu, T. (2006) 'Flogging a Dead Horse: Why Western Style Corporate Governance Reform Will Fail in China and What Should be Done Instead', *Australian Journal of Corporate Law* 20 (1): 25–54.

Hawes, C. and Chiu, T. (2007) 'Foreign Strategic Investors in the Chinese Banking Market: Cultural Shift or Business as Usual?', *Banking and Finance Law Review* 22 (2): 203–37.

Hay, J., Schleifer, A. and Vishny, R. (1996) 'Towards a Theory of Legal Reform', *Journal of European Economic Review* 40 (3–5): 550–67.

He, J.C. (2004) *Corporate Governance: Structure, Mechanisms and Efficiency: A Comparison of International Case Studies*, Beijing: Economics and Science Publishers.

Heilmann, S. (2002) 'The Chinese Stock Market – Pitfalls of a Policy Driven Market', Centre for East Asian & Pacific Studies, Trier University, Germany, China Analysis Paper 15.

Hendrischke, H. (2003) 'The Role of Social Capital, Networks, & Property Rights in China's Privatisation Process', in B. Krug (ed.), *China's Rational Entrepreneurs: The Development of the New Private Business Sector*, New York and London: Routledge, pp. 97–118.

Hendrischke, H. and Feng, C.Y. (2001) *The Political Economy of China's Provinces: Comparative & Competitive Advantage*, London: Taylor & Francis.

Hong Leong Group, www.hongleonggroup.com.

Huang, R. and Orr, G. (2007) 'China's State Owned Enterprises: Board Governance & the Communist Party', *The McKinsey Quarterly* 1: 108–11.

Huang, X. (2009) 'Shareholder Revolt? The Statutory Derivative Action in China', CLPE Research Paper 49/2009 Vol. 05, no. 09.

Huang, Y.S. (1996) 'Central-Local Relations in China During the Reform Era: The Economic & Institutional Dimensions', *Journal of World Economy Development* 24 (4): 652–72.

Huang, Y.S. (2001) 'Economic Fragmentation & FDI in China', William Davidson Institute Working Paper Series 374.

Huang, Y.S. (2003) 'One Country, Two Systems: Foreign-Invested Enterprises and Domestic Firms in China', *China Economic Review* 14 (4): 404–16.

Huang, Y.S. (2004) 'A Tale of Two Provinces: The Institutional Environment & Foreign Ownership in China', MIT Sloan School of Management Working Paper 4482–04.

Huang, Y.S. (2008a) *Capitalism with Chinese Characteristics: Entrepreneurship & the State*, Cambridge: Cambridge University Press.

Huang, Y.S. (2008b) 'Just How Capitalist is China?', MIT Sloan Research Paper, no. 4699–08.

Huang, Y.S. (2009) 'Private Ownership: The Real Source of China's Economic Miracle', *McKinsey Quarterly* 1: 148–65.

Hu, A.G. and Hu, G. (2002) 'Corporate Governance in China in the Transitional Era', Working Paper, Center of Chinese Studies, Tsinghua University.

Hu, A.G. and Hu, G. (2004) *Corporate Governance in China & Overseas: A Comparison*, Beijing: Xinhua.

Hu, F. (2005a) 'Capital Flows, Overheating & the Nominal Exchange Regime in China', *Cato Journal* 25 (2): 357–66.

Hu, R.Y. (2005b) 'Corporate Governance of the State Controlled Listed Companies in China: Problems Progress & Prospects', paper presented at Conference on Corporate Governance in Beijing.

Hu, Z.L. and Khan, M.S. (1997) 'Why Is China Growing So Fast?', IMF Working Paper 96/75 IMF's Research Department.

Hulpke, J. and Lau, C. (2008) 'Business Ethics in China – A Human Resource Management Issue?', *Journal of Chinese Economy* 41 (3): 58–67.

Hwa, E.C. (2008) 'Progress in Reforming China's Banks', paper presented to Conference on China's Policy Reforms 22–24, Stanford Center for International Development.

IFC Publication World Bank (2005) 'Step by Step Corporate Governance Models for China'.

IMF Fact sheet (January 1999) www.imf.org.external.

ING Group, www.ing.com/group/index.

ING Press Release (25 March 2005) 'ING to Acquire up to 19.9 Per Cent of Bank of Beijing'. Available at www.ing.com/group.

Jacobson, T. (2010) 'Speech & Harmony: An Experiment'. Available at: http//blogs.worldbank.org/publicsphere.

Jefferson, G., Rawski, T. and Zheng, Y. (1992) 'Growth, Efficiency & Convergence in China's State & Collective Industry', *Journal of Economic Development & Cultural Change* 40 (2): 239–66.

Jensen, M. and Meckling, W. (2004) 'Theory of the Firm: Managerial Behaviour, Agency Costs & Ownership Structure', in T. Clarke (ed.), *Theories of Corporate Governance*, London and New York: Routledge, pp. 58–63.

Jiang, Z.M. (2002) Report to the 16th Chinese Communist Party Congress, 17 November. Available at: www.china.org.cn/english/features/49007.htm.

Jinan City Commercial Bank Annual Report (2007, 2008).

Jing, L.H., Zhou, W.Q. and Tse, Y.C. (2007) 'Corporate Governance in China – Ethical & Legal Problems', City University, Hong Kong.

Johnson, P.M. (2005) 'Growth Theory: A Glossary of Political Economy Terms', Department of Political Science, Auburn University, Alabama, USA.

Johnson, S., La Porta, R., Lopez de Silanes, F. and Shleifer, A. (2000) 'Tunnelling', *American Economic Review Papers & Proceedings* 90 (2): 22–7.

Kaufmann, D., Kraay, A. and Mastruzzi, M. (2008) *Governance Matters IV: Governance Indicators for 2003–2007*, World Bank Survey.

Kenyon, T. (2005) 'When do Controlling Shareholders Support Corporate Governance Reform and Why?', paper presented at Annual Meeting of the Midwest Political Science Association.

Kim, Y.B., Ho, I. and Giles, M. (2003) 'Developing Institutional Investors in the PRC', World Bank Country Study Paper.

King, R. and Levine, R. (1993) 'Finance & Growth: Schumpeter Might be Right', *Quarterly Journal of Economics* 108: 717–38.

Knack, S. (2002) 'Governance & Growth: Discussion', paper 02/05, IRIS Discussion Paper on Institutions & Development, Washington, DC.

Kornai, J. (1986) 'The Soft Budget Constraint', *Kyklos International Review for Social Sciences* 39 (1): 3–30.

Kornai, J. (1998) 'The Place of the Soft Budget Constraint in Economic Theory', *Journal of Comparative Economics* 26 (1): 11–17.

Kornai, J., Maskin, E. and Roland, G. (2002) 'Understanding the Soft Budget Constraint', Institute for Advanced Study, School of Social Science, Economics Working Paper no. 0019 Available at: www.sss.isc/publications.

Kosmala, K. and Sucher, P. (2006) 'On the (Im) Possibility of Auditor Independence: Insights from Central & Eastern Europe', in *Advances in Public Interest Accounting*, Emerald Group Publishing, pp. 133–48.

KPMG Report (2006) 'China's City Commercial Banks – Opportunity Knocks'.

KPMG Report (2007) 'China's City Commercial Banks – Strategic Options'.

'Knowledge at Wharton'; May 2006 Edition http://knowledge.wharton.upenn.edu/article.

Lai, P.Y. (2002) 'Foreign Direct Investment in China-Recent Patterns & Trends', *Journal of China & World Economy* 2: 25–32.

Lambstaff, J.G. (2007) Transparency International. 'Corruption Perception Index'.

Lannes, B., Stratton, O. and Turner, G. (220207) 'Tapping China's Booming Retail Banking Market', FEER Vol 170 Issue 2.

La Porta, R., Lopez-de-Silanes, F., Schleifer, A. and Vishny, R. (1997) 'Legal Determinants of External Finance', *Journal of Finance* 52: 1131–50.

La Porta, R., Lopez-de-Silanes, F., Schleifer, A. and Vishny, R. (1998) 'Law and Finance', *Journal of Finance* 106: 1113–55.

La Porta, R., Lopez-de-Silanes, F., Schleifer, A. and Vishny, R (2000a) 'Investor Protection and Corporate Governance', *Journal of Financial Economics* 58 (1–2): 3–27.

La Porta, R., Lopez-de-Silanes, F., Schleifer, A. and Vishny, R (2000b) 'Agency Problems and Dividend Policy around the World', *Journal of Finance* 55: 1–33.

Lardy, N.R. (1995) 'The Role of Foreign Trade and Investment in China's Economic Transformation', *The China Quarterly* 144: 1065–82.

Lardy, N.R. (1998) *China's Unfinished Economic Revolution*, Washington, DC: Brookings Institution Press.

Lardy, N.R. (2002) 'Integrating China into the Global Economy', Brookings Institution Press.

Lardy, N.R. (2006) 'China's Rise: Challenges and Opportunities': The Balance Sheet Public Affairs.

Laurenceson, J. and Qin, F.M. (2008) 'Has Minority Foreign Investment in China's Banks Improved their Cost Efficiency?', *China & World Economy Journal* 16 (3): 57–74.

Lazareva, O., Rachinsky, A. and Stepanov, S. (2008) 'A Survey of Corporate Governance in Russia', in Robert McGee (ed.) *Corporate Governance in Transitional Economies*, Springer, p. 324.

Lazonick, W. and O'Sullivan, M. (2004) 'Maximising Shareholder Value: A New Ideology for Corporate Governance', in T. Clarke (ed.) *Theories of Corporate Governance*, Routledge.

Lee, K.Y. (2000) *From Third World to First – Story of Modern Singapore*, Straits Times Press.

Leigh, L. and Podpiera, R. (2006) 'The Rise of Foreign Investments in China's Banks – Taking Stock', IMF Working Paper WP 06/292.

Leng, J. (2009) *Corporate Governance & Financial Reform in China's Transitional Economy*, Hong Kong University Press.

Lensink, R. and Naaborg, I. (2007) 'Does Foreign Ownership Foster Bank Performance?', *Journal of Applied Financial Economics* 17 (11): 881–5.

Leung, E., Liu, L., Lu, S., Tasback, K. and Wang, L. (2002) 'Financial Reform & Corporate Governance in China', MIT Sloan School of Management 50th Anniversary Proceedings.

Levine, R. (1996) 'Financial Development & Economic Growth', Policy Paper 1678 The World Bank.

Levine, R. (1998) 'The Legal Environment, Banks & Long Run Economic Growth', *Journal of Monetary Credit & Banking* 30: 596–613.

Levine, R. and Zervos, S. (1998) 'Stock Markets & Economic Growth', *American Economic Review* 88: 537–58.

Levine, R., Loayza, N. and Beck, T. (2000a) 'Financial Intermediation & Growth: Causality & Causes', paper provided by The World Bank in its Policy Research Working Paper Series, no. 2059.

Levine, R., Loayza, N. and Beck, T. (2000b) 'Finance & Sources of Growth', paper provided by The World Bank in its Policy Research Working Paper Series, no. 2057.

Lewis, W.A. (1950) *The Principles of Economic Planning*, London: G. Allen & Unwin.

Li, W.A. (2008) *Corporate Governance in China: Research & Evaluation*, John Wiley & Sons Pty Ltd.

Lin, J.Y., Cai, F. and Li, Z. (1996a) *The China Miracle: Development Strategy and Economic Reform*, Hong Kong Chinese University Press.

Lin, J.Y., Cai, F. and Li, Z. (1996b) 'Lessons of China's Transition to Market Economy', *Cato Journal* 16 (2): 201–31.

Lin, C., Shum, C.C.Y. and Wong, S.M.L. (2009) 'The Emergence of Shareholder Protection in China', in *China's Emerging Financial Markets*, Springer USA.

Linton, K.C. (2006) 'Access to Capital in China: Competitive Conditions for Foreign & Domestic Firms', United States International Trade Commission.

Lipton, D., Sachs, J., Fischer, S. and Kornai, J. (1990) 'Creating a Market Economy in Eastern Europe – Case of Poland', Brookings Paper on Economic Activity. Issue 1.

Liu, M.K. (2003) Chairman of CBRC Address to 16th Plenary Session of CCP on Establishment of China Banking Regulatory Commission.

Liu, Q. and Lu, Z. (2007) 'Corporate Governance & Earnings Management in the Chinese Listed Companies: A Tunnelling Perspective', *Journal of Comparative Finance* 13: 881–906.

Los, C.A. and Yu, B. (2008) 'Persistent Characteristics of the China Stock Markets', *International Review of Financial Analysis* 17 (1): 64–82.

Lower, M.L. (2009) 'Employee Participation in Corporate Governance: An Ethical Analysis'. Available at: http://ssrn.com/abstract=1408360. Company Law of China (2005) Section 4, Article 118.

Lu, D., Thangavelu, S.M. and Hu, Q. (2005) 'Biased Lending & Non Performing Loans in China's Banking Sector', *Journal of Development Studies* 41: 1071–91.

Lu, T. (2004) *Corporate Governance Reform – International Experience & China's Practice*, Beijing Press.

Lu, X.H. (1997) 'Business Ethics in China', *Journal of Business Ethics* 16 (14): 1509–18.

Luo, P. (2003) 'Challenges for China's Banking Sector and Policy Responses', paper presented at Banking Conference at New Delhi.

Luo, P. (2008) 'China's Convergence to IFRS with Particular Respect to its Banking Industry', *Financial Market, Institutions & Instruments* 17 (1): 43–9.

Ma, G.N. (2006) 'Sharing China's Bank Restructuring Bill', *China & World Economy* 14 (3): 19–37.

Ma, G.N. (2007) 'Who Pays China's Restructuring Bill?', *Asian Economic Papers* 6 (1): 47–73.

McCarthy, D., Puffer, S and Shekshnia, S. (2004) *Corporate Governance in Russia*, Cheltenham: Edward Elgar.

McGee, R. (2008) *Corporate Governance in Transition Economies*, New York: Springer.

McKinnon, R. (1973) *Money and Capital in Economic Development*, Washington, DC: Brookings Institution.

McMillan, J. and Naughton, B. (1992) 'How to Reform a Planned Economy: Lessons from China', *Journal of Oxford Review of Economic Policy* 8 (1): 130–43.

McNally, C., Guo, H. and Hu, G.W. (2007) 'Entrepreneurship & Political Guanxi Networks in China's Private Sector', East West Centre Working Paper, no. 19.

Maher, M. and Andersson, T. (1999) 'Convergence and Diversity in Corporate Governance Regimes and Capital Markets', paper presented at the Law and Economics Conference on 'Convergence and Diversity in Corporate Governance Regimes and Capital Markets', Eindhoven, the Netherlands.

Malin, C. and Xie, R. (1998) 'The Development of Corporate Governance in China', *Journal of Contemporary China* 7 (17): 33–42.

Marx, K. (1843) 'A Contribution to the Critique of Hegel's Philosophy of Right'.

Mayer, C. (1998) 'Financial Systems and Corporate Governance: A Review of the International Evidence', *Journal of Institutional and Theoretical Economics (JITE)* 154 (1): 144–65.

Moneyhon, M.D. (2003) 'China's Great Western Development Project in Xinjiang: Economic Palliative or Political Trojan Horse?', *Denver Journal of International Law & Policy* 1–29 .

Morck, R. and Nakamura, M. (1999) 'Banks & Corporate Control in Japan', *Journal of Finance* 54 (1): 319–39.

Morck, R., Wolfenzon, D. and Yeung, B. (2005) 'Corporate Governance, Economic Entrenchment, and Growth', *Journal of Economic Literature* 43: 655–720.

Muriel, P. and Wang, Y.J. (1993) 'When Privatization Should be Delayed: The Effect of Communist Legacies on Organizational & Institutional Reforms', *Journal of Comparative Economics* 17 (2): 385–406.

Murrell, P. (1993) 'What is Shock Therapy: What it did for Poland & Russia', *Journal of Post Soviet Affairs* 9 (2): 111–40.

Naalborg, I., Scholtens, B., de Haan, J., Bol, H. and deHaas, R. (2004) 'How Important are Foreign Banks in the Financial Development of European Transition Countries', *Journal of Emerging Market Finance* 3 (2): 99–123.

Nanchong City Commercial Bank Annual Report (2007, 2008).

Nanjing City Commercial Bank Annual Report (2007, 2008).

Nanto, D. (2009) 'The Global Financial Crises: Analysis & Policy Implications', Congressional Research Service.

Naughton, B. (1995) *Growing out of the Plan: Chinese Economic Reform 1978–1993*, Cambridge: Cambridge University Press.

Naughton, B. (1998) 'China's Financial Reform: Achievements & Challenges', BRIE Working Paper, no. 112.

Naughton, B. (2007) *The Chinese Economy: Transition & Growth*, Cambridge, MA: MIT Press.

Naughton, B., Keidel, A. and Woo, W. (2009) 'Reframing China Policy', The Carnegie Debate.

Nee, V., Opper, S. and Wong, S. (2007) 'Developmental State & Corporate Governance in China', *Management and Organization Review* 3 (1): 19–53.

The New York Times (29 March 2005) 'China Focuses on Bank Corruption'. Available at: www.nytimes/2005/03/28/business.

Ningbo City Commercial Bank Annual Report (2007, 2008).

Nolan, M. (2003) 'Religion, Culture & Economic Development', Peterson Institute Working Paper Series, no. WP03–8.

Nolan, P. (1993) 'China's Post Mao Political Economy: A Puzzle', *Journal of Contributions to Political Economy* 12: 71–87.

Nolan, P. (1994) 'The China Puzzle: Touching Stones to Cross the River', *Challenge Journal* January/February: 25–31.

OCBC Bank, www.ocbc.com.sg.

OECD (2004a) 'Rural Finance & Credit Infrastructure in China'.

OECD (2004b) Preamble 'Principles of Corporate Governance', OECD Publication.

OECD (2006) 'Policy Brief on Corporate Governance of Banks in Asia', Asia Round Table on Corporate Governance.

OECD Survey on China (2005) 'Reforming the Financial System to Support the Market Economy'.

Ong, L. (2006) 'The Political Economy of Township Government Debt, Township Enterprises and Rural Financial Institutions in China', *The China Quarterly* 186: 377–400.

Opper, S., Wong, S. and Hu, R.Y. (2002) 'Party Power, Market & Private Power: CCP Persistence in China's Listed Companies', in Kevin Leicht (ed.) *The Future of Market Transition, Research in Social Stratification & Mobility*, North Holland: Elsevier, pp. 103–36.

Opper, S., Wong, S. and Hu, R.Y. (2004) 'Shareholding Structure, Depolitization & Firm Performance', *Economics of Transition Journal* 12: 29–66.

Paredes, T. (2005) 'Corporate Governance & Economic Development', Washington University School of Law Working Paper, no. 05–04–04 Regulation, Vol. 28, No. 1.

Pedersen, M. (2006) 'Business Integrity in China', *The China Business Review* 33 (1): 32–6.

Peerenboom, R. (2002) *China's Long March toward Rule of Law*, Cambridge: Cambridge University Press.

Pei, M.X. (2006) 'The Tide of Corruption Threatening China's Prosperity', *Financial Times*, 27 September.

Pierre-Gauillaume, M. and Weill, L. (2005) 'Does Better Governance Foster Efficiency: An Aggregate Frontier Analysis', *Economics of Governance* 6 (1): 75–90.

Pistor, K., Raiser, M. and Gelfer, S. (2000) 'Law & Finance in Transition Economies', European Bank for Reconstruction & Development Working Paper, no. 48.

Podpiera, R. (2006) 'Progress in China's Banking Sector: Has Bank Behaviour Changes?', IMF Working Paper WP/06/71.

Puffer, S. and McCarthy, D. (2003a) 'The Emergence of Corporate Governance in Russia', *Journal of World Business* 38 (4): 284–98.

Puffer, S. and McCarthy, D. (2003b) 'Corporate Governance for Russia: A Framework for Analysis', *Journal of World Business* 38 (4): 397–415.

Qian, Y.Y. (1999) 'The Institutional Foundations of China's Market Transition', Annual World Bank Conference on Development Economics.

Qian, Y.Y. (2000) 'The Process of China's Market Transition (1978–1998): The Evolutionary, Historical & Comparative Perspectives', *Journal of Institutional & Theoretical Economics* 156 (1): 151–71.

Qian, Y.Y. (2002) 'How Reform Worked in China', CEPR Discussion Paper no. 3447, London, Centre for Economic Policy Research. Available at: www.cepr.org/pubs/dps/DP3447.asp.

Qian, Y.Y. and Wu, J.L. (2003) 'China's Transition to a Market Economy: How to Cross the River?', Center for Research on Economic Development and Policy Reform, Working Paper, no. 69, pp. 1–38.

Qian, Y.Y. and Xu, C.G. (1993) 'Why China's Economic Reforms Differ: The M Form Hierarchy & Entry/Expansion of the Non-State Sector', *The Economics of Transition* 2: 135–70.

Rajan, R. and Zingales, L. (1998) 'Financial Dependence and Growth', *American Economic Review* 88: 559–86.

Rarick, C. (2008) 'Historical Antecedents of Chinese Business Ethics'. Available at: http://ssrn.com/abstract=1127667.

Reardon, J. (2004) 'The Perilous Road to the Market: The Political Economy of Reform in Russia, China and India', *Journal of Economic Issues* 38 (3): 873–5.

Sachs, J.D. and Woo, W.T. (1994) 'Structural Factors in the Economic Reform of China, Eastern Europe and the former Soviet Union', *Journal of Economic Policy* 9: 101–31.

Sachs, J.D. and Woo, W.T. (1997) 'Understanding China's Economic Performance', National Bureau of Economic Research Working Paper 5935.

Schipani, A. and Liu, J.H. (2002) 'Corporate Governance in China: Then & Now', *Columbia Business Law Review* l: 1–69.

Schleifer, A. and Vishny, R. (1997) 'A Survey of Corporate Governance', *Journal of Finance* 52 (2).

Schumpeter, J.A. (1911) *The Theory of Economic Development*, Cambridge, MA: Harvard University Press.

Shanghai Rural Commercial Bank Annual Report (2007, 2008).

Shanghai Stock Exchange: Rules of Listing, www.sse.com.cn.

Shekshnia, S., Puffer, S.M. and McCarthy, D. (2004) 'Corporate Governance in a Cultural Context', in D.J. McCarthy, S.M. Puffer and S.V. Shekshnia (eds) *Corporate Governance in Russia*, Cheltenham: Edward Elgar, pp. 110–36.

Shi, S. and Weisert, D. (2002) 'Corporate Governance with Chinese Characteristics', *China Business Review* 29 (5): 40–4.

Sprenger, C. (2002) 'Ownership & Corporate Governance in Russian Industry: A Survey', EBRD.

Standard & Poor's (2005) 'Transparency & Disclosure by Russian Banks 2005'.

Standard & Poor's (2007a) 'Corporate Governance: Russia's Slow March to Global Corporate Governance Standards'.

Standard & Poor's (2007b) 'Transparency Index for Russia'.

Standard & Poor's (2007c) 'Transparency & Disclosure by Russian Companies'.

Standard & Poor's Report (2008) 'How Does Corporate Governance in Russia Stack up Against the BRIC Countries?'.

The Star Newspaper (26 October 2007) 'HLB Buying into China's Chengdu Bank', www.the star.com.my.

Stulz, R. (2000) 'Financial Structure, Corporate Finance & Economic Growth', Ohio State University mimeo.

Sturm, J.E. and Williams, B. (2004) 'Foreign Bank Entry, Deregulation & Bank Efficiency in Australia', *Journal of Banking & Finance* 7: 175–9.

Summers, R. and Heston, A. (1991) 'The Penn World Tables: An Expanded Set of International Comparisons 1950–1988', *Quarterly Journal of Economics* 106 (2): 327–68.

Sun, L.X. (2001) 'Economics of China's Joint Stock Cooperatives', Discussion Paper 2001/24, UN University.

Sydney Morning Herald (7 May 2010) 'ANZ Bank Opens Branch in Chongqing, China'.

Tam, O.K. (2000a) 'Models of Corporate Governance for Chinese Companies' BL Direct Blackwell Publishers 8 (1): 52–64.

Tam, O.K. (2000b) 'Corporate Governance & the Future of China's Corporate Development', paper presented for EAMSA 2000 Conference at INSEAD's Asian Campus in Singapore.

Tam, O.K. (2002) 'Ethical Issues in the Evolution of Corporate Governance in China', *Journal of Business Ethics* 37 (3): 303–20.

Tan, M. (2009a) 'Foreign Investments in China's Local Banking Sector: The Australian Experience', *China Economic Journal* 2 (2): 209–17.

Tan, M. (2009b) 'Has the QFII Strengthened Corporate Governance in China?', *China – An International Journal* 7 (2): 353–69.

Tang, X. (2008) 'Protecting Minority Shareholders in China: A Task for Both Legislation & Enforcement', in C. Milhaupt (ed.) *Transforming Corporate Governance in East Asia*, Oxford: Routledge, pp. 141–68.

Taylor, P. (2007) 'Reforming the Governance of China's Banks', draft paper.

Tenev, S. and Zhang, C. (2002) 'Corporate Governance and Enterprise Reform in China', World Bank Publication.

Thursby A: CEO of ANZ Bank Asia & Pacific – video conference interview with author in Sydney on 6 March 2008.

Tian, J.J. and Lau, C.M. (2001) 'Board Composition, Leadership Structure & Performance in Chinese Shareholding Companies', *Asia Pacific Journal of Management* 245: 256–60.

Tianjin City Commercial Bank Annual Report (2007, 2008).

Todeva, E. (2007) 'Business Networks in China: Legacies & Practice', in S. Clegg, K. Wang and M. Berrell (eds), *Business Networks and Strategic Alliances in China*, Cheltenham: Edward Elgar, pp. 252–72.

Trumpbour, J. (2007) 'China: Banking Reform & Economic Development Revisited', Harvard Law School Labour and Worklife Program.

Tsai, K. (2001) 'Beyond Banks: The Local Logic of Informal Finance & Private Sector Developments in China', paper presented at Conference on Financial Sector Reform in China.

Tsai, K. (2002) *Back Alley Banking – Private Entrepreneurs in China*, Ithaca: Cornell University Press.

Tsang, S.K. (1996) 'Against the Big Bang in Economic Transition: Normative & Positive Arguments', *Cambridge Journal of Economics* 20: 256–60.

Votaw, D. (1965) *Modern Corporations*, Englewood Cliffs: Prentice Hall Press.

Wall Street Journal (4 July 2009) 'Siemens AG has been Banned by the World Bank from Bidding for its Projects for 2 Years because of Fraud and Bribery in its Projects in Russia, China, Argentina & Israel'.

Wang, C.B., Wong, S.L. and Sun, W.B. (2006) 'Haigui: A New Area in China's Policy towards the Chinese Diaspora', *Journal of Chinese Overseas* 21 (2): 294–309.

Wang, T.X. (2005) 'Corporate Governance and the Role of Independent Directors', Wuhan University.

Wang, X.Z., Xu, L.X. and Zhu, T. (2004) 'State-owned Enterprises Going Public', *Journal Economics of Transition* 12 (3): 467–87.

Wang, Y.Z. (2006) 'Introduction of China's Banking Sector & Postal Financial Services', China Banking Regulatory Commission.

Ward, R. (2002) CEO of UBS Warburg, www.en.chinabroadcast.cn, 'Foreign Investors embrace QFII', 23 November.

Weinstein, D. and Yafeh, Y. (1998) 'On the Costs of Bank Centered Financial System: Evidence from the Changing Main Bank Relations in Japan', *Journal of Finance* 32 (2): 635–72.

Williamson, J. (1993) 'Democracy & the Washington Consensus', *Journal of World Development* 21 (8): 1329–36.

Wong, S. and Wong, S. (2001) 'Competition in China's Domestic Banking Industry', *Cato Journal* 21: 19–41.

Wong, S., Opper, S. and Hu, R. (2004) 'Shareholding Structure, Depolitization and Firm Performance', *Journal of Economics of Transition* 12: 29–66.

World Bank (2005) 'Corporate Governance Models in China: The Experience of the International Finance Corporation'.

Xinhua (7 January 2007) Report by Chinese Academy of Social Sciences (CASS), 'China's Worrisome Income Gap Shows No Signs of Narrowing Despite Government Efforts'.

Xu, C., Zhu, T. and Lin, Y.M. (2005) 'Politician Control, Agency Problems & Ownership Reforms: Evidence from China', *Economics of Transition* 13 (1): 1–24.

Yang, J.Z. (2007) 'Shareholder Meetings & Voting Rights in China: Some Empirical Evidence', *International Company & Commercial Law Review* 15 (1): 4–16.

Yao, S.J. and Han, Z.W. (2007) 'Ownership Reform, Foreign Competition & Efficiency of Chinese Commercial Banks: A Non Parametric Approach', Discussion Paper no. 14, China Policy Institute, Nottingham University.

Yeo, S. (2003) 'The PRC Qualified Foreign Institutional Investors Market', *China Economic Review* 14: 443–50.

Yeung, A. and DeWoskin, K. (2001) 'Transformation at Haier', in D.R. Denison (ed.) *Managing Organizational Change in Transitional Economies*, London: Taylor & Francis.

Yu, R. and McMahon, D. (22 December 2006) 'Deals & Deal Makers', *Wall Street Journal*.

Yun, M. (2003) 'Understanding Russian Organised Crime: Causes, Present Situation & Significance', Research Paper.

Zhang, J. (2002) 'China's Corporate Governance: A Steep Learning Curve', UBS Warburg, Hong Kong.

Zhang, J., Mohaputra, S. Boucher, S. and Rozelle, R. (2009) 'Regulation of Local Government & Enterprise Formation in Rural China', *Journal of Chinese Economics & Business Studies* 7 (3): 321–39.

Zhang, L.X. (2007) 'Benchmarking to Basel II', presentation given to Conference in Melbourne.

Zheng, Y.N. and Tok, S.K. (2007) 'Harmonious Society and Harmonious World: China's Policy Discourse under Hu Jintao', Nottingham University, China Policy Institute.

Zhou, X.C. (2005) Governor of the People's Bank of China, speech at BOAO, Hainan, China, 26 April.

Zhuplev, A. and Shein, V. (2004) 'Corporate Governance in a Cultural Context', in D.J. McCarthy, S.M. Puffer and S.V. Shekshnia (eds) *Corporate Governance in Russia*, Cheltenham: Edward Elgar Limited, pp. 110–36.

Zuo, X.J. (2001) 'The Development of Credit Unions in China: Past Experiences & Lessons for Future', Shanghai Academy of Sciences.

Index

Page numbers in *italics* denote tables.